DOMESTIC SPACE

DOMESTIC SPACE

Reading the nineteenth-century interior

edited by

Inga Bryden & Janet Floyd

Manchester University Press

MANCHESTER & NEW YORK

distributed exclusively in the USA by St. Martin's Press

Published by Manchester University Press
Oxford Road, Manchester M13 9NR, UK
and Room 400, 175 Fifth Avenue, New York, NY 10010, USA
http://www.man.ac.uk/mup

Distributed exclusively in the USA by
St. Martin's Press, Inc., 175 Fifth Avenue, New York, NY 10010, USA.

Distributed exclusively in Canada by
UBC Press, University of British Columbia, 6344 Memorial Road, Vancouver, BC, Canada V6T 1Z2

British Library Cataloguing-in-Publication Data
A catalogue record for this book is available from the British Library

Library of Congress Cataloging-in-Publication Data applied for

ISBN 0 7190 5450 8 *hardback*

First published 1999

06 05 04 03 02 01 00 99   10 9 8 7 6 5 4 3 2 1

Typeset in Simoncini Garamond
by Northern Phototypesetting Co Ltd, Bolton
Printed in Great Britain
by Bookcraft (Bath) Ltd, Midsomer Norton

Contents

List of illustrations *page* vii
List of contributors ix
Acknowledgements xi

Introduction 1
Inga Bryden & Janet Floyd

What a rag rug means 18
Carolyn Steedman

Bodies and mirrors: the childhood interiors of Ruskin, Pater and Stevenson 40
Ann C. Colley

Political pincushions: decorating the abolitionist interior 1787–1865 58
Lynne Walker & Vron Ware

Refracting the gaselier: understanding Victorian responses to domestic gas lighting 84
Sarah Milan

Tranquil havens? Critiquing the idea of home as the middle-class sanctuary 103
Moira Donald

District visiting and the constitution of domestic space in the mid-nineteenth century 121
Martin Hewitt

Gendered space: housing, privacy and domesticity in the nineteenth-century United States 142
S. J. Kleinberg

Theatre and the private sphere in the fiction of Louisa May Alcott 162
Alan Louis Ackerman, Jr

The architecture of manners: Henry James, Edith Wharton and The Mount 186
Sarah Luria

Index 211

List of illustrations

1 'Tomitude', Uncle Tom and Little Eva, earthenware figure group, *c*. 1855. (Royal Pavilion, Libraries and Museums, Brighton and Hove. Reproduced with kind permission.) 61

2 Charlotte Bosanquet, 'Drawing Room, Hollington House', East Woodhay, Hants, watercolour, 1843. (Ashmolean Museum, Oxford. Reproduced with kind permission.) 63

3 Plan of lower deck of slave ship, engraving after the 'Brooks' of Liverpool, detail, 1788, with seal of the London Committee for the Abolition of the Slave Trade, distributed free by Plymouth committee. (Bristol Record Office 17562/1/. Reproduced with kind permission.) 67

4 Chair seat cover (originally), canvas-work panel of a kneeling slave and verse with floral border, n.d. (Wilberforce House, Kingston Upon Hull City Museums and Art Galleries. Reproduced with kind permission.) 68

5 China plate with abolitionist motifs and mottoes, early nineteenth century (1830?). (The Board of Trustees of National Museums and Galleries on Merseyside (Liverpool Museum). Reproduced with kind permission.) 68

6 Slave medallion, black on yellow jasper, impressed 'Wedgwood', late eighteenth/early nineteenth century. (By Courtesy of the Trustees of the Wedgwood Museum, Barlaston, Stoke-on-Trent Staffordshire, England.) 69

7 Antislavery 'workbag' and pamphlets, in the form of a silk purse with abolitionist image and poem (verso) printed in black, produced and sold by the Birmingham Female Society for the Relief of Negro Slaves, 1827–28. Photograph: Lynne Walker. (Victoria and Albert Museum. Reproduced with kind permission.) 72

8 Sugar bowl, inscribed in gilt lettering 'EAST INDIA SUGAR not made by SLAVES', brown glazed stoneware, *c.* 1822–34. (The Board of Trustees of National Museums and Galleries on Merseyside (Liverpool Museum). Reproduced with kind permission.) 75

9 F. & C. Osler, advertisement for crystal gaseliers and table glass, 1855. (Birmingham Museums and Art Gallery. Reproduced with kind permission.) 86

10 Plan, 41, Old Tiverton Road, Exeter, 1893. (Moira Donald. Reproduced with kind permission.) 108

11 Hablot K. Browne, 'The Visit to the Brickmaker's', in Charles Dickens, *Bleak House* [1852–53] (1948). (Oxford Illustrated Dickens. Reproduced with kind permission.) 128

12 The Mount today, terrace side/east elevation. Photograph: Steve Ziglar. (Courtesy of Edith Wharton Restoration at the Mount.) 188

13 The Mount, First (Main) Floor Plan, John G. Waites Associates Architects, *The Mount: Home of Edith Wharton* (Edith Wharton Restoration, 1997). (Courtesy of Edith Wharton Restoration at the Mount.) 196

14 The Mount, Second (Bedroom) Floor Plan, John G. Waites Associates Architects, *The Mount: Home of Edith Wharton*. (Courtesy of Edith Wharton Restoration at the Mount.) 198

15 Library, The Mount, *c.* 1905. Yale Collection of American Literature, Beinecke Rare Book and Manuscript Library, Yale University. (Reproduced with kind permission.) 200

16 The Mount today, courtyard side/west elevation. (Courtesy of Edith Wharton Restoration at the Mount.) 204

17 The Mount today, terrace side/west elevation, service wing on right. (Courtesy of Edith Wharton Restoration at the Mount.) 204

18 The Mount early 1980s, terrace side/east elevation, service wing on left. (Courtesy of Edith Wharton Restoration at the Mount.) 205

List of contributors

Alan Louis Ackerman, Jr. is Assistant Professor in the English department at the University of Toronto and at the University College Drama Programme. He is also the author of *The Portable Theatre: American Literature and the Nineteenth-Century Stage* (Johns Hopkins University Press, forthcoming).

Inga Bryden is Senior Lecturer in English in the School of Cultural Studies, King Alfred's, Winchester. She has written on Victorian culture for *The Year's Work in English Studies* and her publications include the four-volume *The Pre-Raphaelites: Writings and Sources* (Routledge, 1998). She is currently completing *Reinventing King Arthur: The Arthur-ian Legends in Victorian Culture* (Ashgate, forthcoming).

Ann C. Colley is Professor of English at the State University College of New York, Buffalo. Her publications include *Tennyson and Madness* (University of Georgia Press, 1983), *The Search for Synthesis in Literature and Art: The Paradox of Space* (University of Georgia Press, 1990), *Edward Lear and the Critics* (Camden House, 1993), and most recently *Nostalgia and Recollection in Victorian Culture* (Macmillan and St. Martin's Press, 1998). She is currently working on a project about Robert Louis Stevenson as anthropologist in the South Seas. For the academic year 1995–96, Professor Colley was a Senior Fulbright Fellow at the Institute of English Studies, University of Warsaw, Poland.

Moira Donald is Senior Lecturer in History at the University of Exeter. She is the co-editor, with Linda Hurcombe, of a three-volume series, *Gender and Material Culture* (Macmillan, 1999). She has also published on households in nineteenth-century Exeter, the European socialist movement and women in the Russian Revolution.

Janet Floyd is Senior Lecturer in American Studies in the School of Cultural Studies, King Alfred's, Winchester. Her research interests are in American domesticity and the West. She is finishing a book on the writing of housework in emigrant autobiography, and is currently working on late nineteenth-century mining fictions.

Martin Hewitt is Principal Lecturer in History at Trinity and All Saints, Leeds, and Director of the Leeds Centre for Victorian Studies. His recent work, in addition to focusing on domestic visiting, has included co- editing, with Robert Poole, *The Diaries of Samuel Bamford* (Sutton Press, forthcoming). He is also editor of the *Journal of Victorian Culture*.

S. J. Kleinberg is Professor and Head of the Department of American Studies and History at Brunel University. Her publications include *The Shadow of the Mills: Working Class Families in Pittsburgh* (University of Pittsburgh Press, 1989), *Women in American Society* (Keele University Press, 1990) and *Women in the United States, 1830–1945* (Macmillan, forthcoming). She is completing a study of widows and welfare, *Widows and Orphans First: The Family Economy and Social Welfare Policy in the United States, 1865–1939*, and is currently researching the extended family and household composition in the late nineteenth and early twentieth centuries. Professor Kleinberg is also the Associate Editor of the *Journal of American Studies*.

Sarah Luria is an Assistant Professor of American Literature at Holy Cross College in Worcester, Massachusetts. She is currently at work on a study of the architectural strategies of four political reformers, entitled '"City of Conversation": The Literary Construction of Nineteenth-Century Washington, D.C.'.

Sarah Milan has an MA in the History of Design from the Royal College of Art/Victoria and Albert Museum. She is currently completing a Ph.D., at Birkbeck College, London, in the development of advertising and its relationship to English culture in the nineteenth century.

Carolyn Steedman is Professor in the History Department at the University of Warwick, and Director of its Centre for Social History. She is currently working on eighteenth-century servants and the service relationship in the making of modern identity.

Lynne Walker was formerly Senior Lecturer in the History of Architecture and Design at the University of Northumbria and is currently writing a history of British women and architecture with the help of an RIBA Research Award. Her most recent publications include 'Home and Away': The Feminist Remapping of Public and Private Space in Victorian London', *New Frontiers of Space, Bodies and Gender*, ed. R. Ainley (Routledge, 1998) and *Drawing on Diversity: Women, Architecture and Practice* (RIBA Heinz Gallery, 1997), the catalogue of an exhibition which she curated.

Vron Ware is based at the School of Humanities, University of Greenwich, having previously worked at the Women's Design Service researching various aspects of gender and environmental design. *Beyond the Pale: White Women, Racism and History* was published by Verso in 1992. She is currently co-writing *Dark Thoughts on Whiteness* (University of Chicago Press) with Les Back, Goldsmiths' College.

Acknowledgements

This volume of essays grew out of an interdisciplinary, international conference – 'Reading the Nineteenth-Century Domestic Space' – which was held at King Alfred's College, Winchester, in April 1996. The conference addressed the question of how twentieth-century cultural critics might interpret 'domestic space' as it was constructed, negotiated and represented in nineteenth-century Britain and America. Sessions at the conference were organised around a number of themes, which included class and constructions of domestic space, material culture, fiction and domestic space and defining 'interiors'.

We are grateful to the School of Cultural Studies at King Alfred's and the British Academy for financial assistance towards organising the conference. Thanks are due to our colleagues in the School for their interest and support. We are especially grateful to our co-organiser, Laurel Forster.

Completion of the book project was facilitated by financial assistance from American Studies and English Studies within the School. We would like to thank Lynn Wharton for her help with copy-editing. Thanks are due also to Jill Barnes and to Phil Cardew for their patience and generous help with technological matters.

We would like to thank Matthew Frost and Stephanie Sloan of Manchester University Press for being so positive about the project and for seeing it through to completion.

An earlier version of Sarah Luria's 'The Architecture of Manners: Henry James, Edith Wharton and The Mount' appeared in *American Quarterly,* 49:2 (June 1997), 298–327 and a version of Carolyn Steedman's 'What a Rag Rug Means' appeared in *Journal of Material Culture*, 3:3 (November 1998), 259–81.

Finally, we would like to thank our contributors who have given us the opportunity to bring together their expertise in different areas of research.

Acknowledgements

Introduction

Inga Bryden & Janet Floyd

The photograph (taken in May 1882) of the interior of the northeast bedroom at Cherry Hill, Albany, New York, depicts a domestic space 'feminised' by the presence of an embroidered motto, a quilt on the bed, a dressing table and its trinkets, children's toys and a rocking chair (Ames, 1992: 114–5). Yet any sense in which this is a 'private' or enclosed space is questioned by the play of light and shade, by the 'blank' window spaces and by the adorned dressing-table mirror, which reflects a partial view of the room, what the viewer *cannot* see. At the same time this photograph of a private recess as shrine suggests that the nineteenth-century domestic space *was* continually on view and that it referenced more places; other spaces. In this context we are the 'uninvited guests', the 'world whose gaze most Victorians were so anxious to shut out' (Logan, 1995: 230). As viewers, we are reminded of the interior's liminal status and complex significations: the relationship between supposedly 'private' space and the outside world; between hidden recesses within a room and the body which inhabits, or is absent from, that room; between a psychologised space and objects which themselves bear a multiplicity of meanings. These, then, are the 'interior architectures' uncovered by the essays in this interdisciplinary volume. The contributors – from the interrelated perspectives of literary history and theory, social and cultural history, cultural materialism and gender studies – develop the critical debate surrounding domestic space and its relation to other 'spheres' of activity in nineteenth-century Britain and America.[1] Some of the essays directly address the issues of working-class experience of middle-class domestic space, middle-class constructions of working-class domestic space and the working-classes' sense of privacy. And the debate is shifted into consideration of cultural materialism and the interpretative difficulties involved in dealing with the status of a domestic material culture which is inevitably part of cultural-historical memory.

The home was imagined, in nineteenth-century domestic discourse, to provide a powerfully influential space for the development of character and identity. This 'domestic environmentalism', to use Katherine Grier's term, depended on a conception of the domestic space as separate and on practices that were identified as profoundly different from those of the world 'outside' (1988: 6–9). At the same time, the values and behaviour inculcated in the home were considered crucial to the formation and maintenance of national identity, a necessary protection against less predictable social and economic changes. This is the 'cult' of domesticity that became, in the scholarship of the 1970s, a site for the discussion of feminine conformity and the imprisoning oppression visited on women in the nineteenth century. It is a 'cult' that has also been identified as a code of beliefs and, for some scholars, practices, that can be linked to the development of a quiescent mass culture exemplified in the popular 'domestic' fiction and the instructional and didactic texts that 'relieved [the masses] from the burden of thinking' (Romero, 1997: 19). The nineteenth-century bourgeois home still appears as a confined, enclosed space in studies of nineteenth-century domesticity, even, at times, as the scene of neurosis and punishment (Brown, 1990; Mertes, 1992). This is despite what is now a tradition of close to twenty years of qualifying arguments that question the accuracy, not to say the likelihood, of the existence of so rigidly determined a space in British and American societies simultaneously imagined as characterised by extremes of turmoil and social stress.[2]

There is no question that the exhortations to create a separate feminised domestic sphere were pervasive in British and American culture, permeating upper-class and working-class sectors of society (Girouard, 1979: 5–8; Wilson, 1977: 2–26, 43–7). The importance and interest of domesticity and the nineteenth-century domestic space lies, after all, in the multiplicity of possibilities for the use of domestic ideology within populations more or less able to fulfil the serene ideal at the heart of domesticity's 'cult'. For most people in nineteenth-century Britain and America, only 'would-be boundaries' could exist within an 'imaginary geography' of private and public (Higonnet and Templeton, 1994: 4–5), while, in an era of huge migrations, the concept of home could scarcely maintain the stable meaning that domestic discourse attributed to it (Brah, 1996: 180).

This, then, is the domestic space with which this volume is concerned: a space designed, represented and experienced in the nineteenth century in various and disparate forms, and understood against competing readings of domestic discourse between the late eighteenth century and the early twentieth century. This range is the subject of S. J. Kleinberg's essay, 'Gendered space: housing, privacy and domesticity in the nineteenth-century United States', which begins by surveying some of the paradigms for the disposition of domestic space in the United States, using a period of time sufficient to suggest the variability in the assimilation of middle-class urban domestic norms across class, race and region. The impulse towards regulation of domestic space according to middle-class norms expressed in the interventions of institutions and groups has, since the 1980s, often been contextualised against the nineteenth-century city and middle-class anxieties around public life (Smith-Rosenberg, 1971; Wolff, 1990). Kleinberg describes some of the manifestations of that impulse, but her reading of its repercussions within the legal sphere is, at the same time, framed by a comparative perspective that draws our attention to the different uses of and demands upon domestic space, as well as to the charged encounters between classes and races in the crowded spaces of the nineteenth-century city.

This attention to the organisation of space reflects a major interest of this collection. As nineteenth-century domestic discourse prescribed what should happen in the home and, in particular, what the housewife and mother should do within it, so some late twentieth-century scholars of the nineteenth century have responded by evoking a highly structured domestic geography, citing middle-class homes in particular as designed to 'reinforce a hierarchy and to assert power' (Spain, 1992: 8). The study of space in general over the last decade, however, has tended to generate arguments that affirm that the design of the home may be read as a text 'suggesting and justifying social categories, values and relations' (Wright, 1980: 1), but that also assert that 'social actors clearly have the reflective ability to use a cultural text' such as the domestic space 'to produce a specific orientation towards a given ideology' (Moore, 1986: 8). Indeed, the meaning of a spatial text, it is argued, is to be found in the study of the way in which its users develop rules for operating within it (Bourdieu, 1977; Moore, 1986). The assumption that domestic space 'inside' is merely shaped by forces and forms imposed from 'outside' produces, as Dorothy O. Helly and Susan Reverby argue, a private/public dichotomy that leaves an 'emptiness' and lack of specificity in the delineation of both categories (1992: 6) It also produces, in its representation of the domestic, a 'typically flat and unilluminating picture' not only, as Moore argues, of women (1986: 409), but also of men, children, relatives, lodgers and all the other figures within the elaborate structure of domestic service – the cooks, maids, nannies and so on – in the middle-class home. The nineteenth-century middle-class home read as a bounded space has had the advantage, as Ruth Salvaggio points out, of being 'accessible to study' (1988: 266), but, as we have indicated, our focus on domestic space in this collection reflects our interest not only in the geography of the nineteenth-century home and indeed in the 'blind-spots, the space-off … not visible in the frame' of domestic discourse (de Lauretis, 1987: 26, cited in Salvaggio, 1988: 275), but also in its symbiotic relationships with public spaces still routinely construed as separate.[3]

Nineteenth-century apologists for domesticity were wont, of course, to encourage their female audiences to abandon 'the world' in favour of domestic seclusion, portraying in unflattering terms those who could not or would not abandon paid work or activity conducted outside the home. Yet those who took it upon themselves to judge as wanting the homes of those who lacked or did not aspire to the spatial organisation appropriate to middle-class practices and ideals were, of course, women choosing to construe 'Woman's mission' as necessitating the sacrifice of their own domestic seclusion (Berg, 1978; Vicinus, 1977). A substantial proportion of the work produced in feminist history and women's studies since the late 1970s has been devoted to recovering the history of a participation in public life seen, in various ways, to be at odds with prescribed behaviour in the nineteenth century. We have read, particularly, of women moving 'out', 'beyond' and 'up from' the constraining boundaries of the domestic space into more ambiguous and emancipatory social spaces of 'pleasures and dangers' (Wilson, 1991: 11): sometimes into the paid work through which, arguably, women might achieve greater satisfaction and power within the domestic as well as the work context; into the philanthropic work of moral reform, through the extension of their domestic mission; and into activity involving the domestication of 'foreigners' and 'natives' through the inculcation of an ethic of separation and privacy (Kerber, 1988: 28–37; Hall, 1992: 13–18).

Work on women's involvement in the world 'outside' is suggestive of the limitations of the term 'sphere' and the categories of private and public for describing the position of the domestic in the nineteenth century. Yet often these studies of women in work and in public life recreate the middle-class domestic space in particular not only as the constraining and unhealthy source of bigotry and anti-intellectualism, but also as marginal to the major political agendas of nineteenth-century

Britain and America. By contrast, the investigation of the interventions of white women across classes in the processes of colonial and imperial 'expansion' in the nineteenth century, and the uses to which domestic space was put in that context, has generated another paradigm of domestic/public relations. In this context, the domestic is accorded a much more active role in the enforcement of the authority of the dominant powers than the complicity at the periphery formerly attributed to it in studies of feminism, philanthropy and urban reform (Callan and Ardener, 1984; McClintock, 1995; Pascoe, 1990). When colonised space is constructed as marginal, domestic space can be accorded a position at the centre. Chandra Talpede Mohanty's argument that 'it is not the centre that determines the periphery, but the periphery that, in its boundedness, determines the centre' is suggestive of the political role available to a domestic sphere represented as separate, secluded and unworldly (1988: 81).

Mohanty's point, however, is made in relation to her assertion of the powerful presence of black women and their experience in white women's lives, and of their importance in determining the formation of white women's subjectivities (a point that needs also to be made in relation to the presence of working-class women in the middle-class home). Arguments about the presence of the domestic in the 'public sphere' and of black women within the middle-class home, provide us with a context against which to position Lynne Walker and Vron Ware's essay on domesticity, domestic space and abolitionism in Britain. 'Political pincushions: decorating the abolitionist interior, 1787–1865' opens up arguments about middle-class women's interest in philanthropy, their political quiescence and their understanding of difference, in a reading of abolitionist activity taking place inside and outside the home during successive phases of its life. By foregrounding the production and exchange of domestic objects generated by and catering to women's abolitionist activity, Walker and Ware show how the spaces of the home were decorated with carefully placed objects signifying the many calibrations of political activism. The discussion of activism pursued in the home by middle-class women not only politicises the domestic space, it also raises questions about the representation of women as occupying an uncomplicated or predictable position in relation to dominant ideologies of race.

Where the study of middle-class women's 'public' activity has often tended to confirm a reading of nineteenth-century domestic practices and domesticity as locked into unvarying convention, research on the range of work undertaken within the household has prompted reformulations of understandings of domestic life and of the socio-political function of the discourse of domesticity itself (Davidoff and Hall, 1987; Ryan, 1981). Since the 1980s in particular, the work performed in the nineteenth-century home has been paralleled with the organisational patterns of industrial capitalism, and understood as involved in the elaboration of those practices and their identification with the middle class. For some late twentieth-century scholars the form of household organisation adopted by the middle class in the nineteenth century is judged to be a set of repressive social practices played out in a peculiarly impoverished form; developed while 'isolated from the realms of power and economic production', yet fundamental to the task of shoring up the social and political status quo (Langland, 1995: 8). Few studies have begun to reconsider the 'density of meaning in the concept of keeping house' (Dickerson, 1995: xxi) and the particular ambiguities in the position of women – house-'keepers' and 'kept' women – in the middle-class domestic space (Colomina, 1992: 82).

The parallel with the management of labour in industrial capitalism may allow us to reformulate the relation between housewife and servant, but where worker–manager relations in the late nineteenth-century factory and office appear to have become ever more predictable and more susceptible to 'scientific engineering', for example in the adoption of Taylorism in the United States, we may question whether the overlapping tasks of servants and their employers in the small and convoluted spaces of the middle-class household may not have produced work relations of a more complex type. The anxieties, resentments and fantasies located in middle-class representations of servants have a critical and historical literature of their own. But, in this volume, Moira Donald's essay foregrounds the detailed examination of work undertaken in a range of homes, from those of the wealthy middle class to those whose incomes allowed minimal employment of servants. 'Tranquil havens? Critiquing the idea of home as the middle-class sanctuary' reflects on the domestic space as workplace with its own complex taxonomies of invisible and often unrecognised work, and its labour that is uncompensated for the 'manager'. Perhaps the major project in history and gender studies since the late 1980s has been to access the experience and recover the work of women other than those who were white and middle class. Donald's essay is suggestive of the way in which all women working in the middle-class household may be argued to inhabit the same abject constituency. But of particular interest here is the examination of the middle-class home as a working-class workplace; a reading that opens up the possibility of studying a complex social geometry of the domestic space that cannot be described merely as a reflection of structures enacted 'outside'.

The Victorian middle class, of course, aspired to a performance of housework invisible to those of the highest status within the house or to those entering it (Brown, 1990: 65–77; Halttunen, 1982). In the same vein, any association between the home and the industrialised world of mass production, especially in the form of machines and the tasks associated with them, could be considered to degrade a domestic space idealised as a shrine to the moral and emotional nurture of the family and the pursuit of a virtuous leisure (Forty, 1995: 99–104). However, the study of the first appearance, in the nineteenth century, of particular technologies in the domestic space opens up to further investigation the relations, real and imaginary, between 'inside' and 'outside'. Paradoxically, of course, labour-saving machines could make the disassociation between home and 'work' all the more secure. But, as Ruth Schwartz Cowan argues in *More Work for Mother* (1989), the acquisition of household technologies could have different implications in terms of labour and labour-saving for different inhabitants of the home. Plainly, the meanings of any object in the home are difficult to summarise when that object is open to use in multiple ways, with different purposes and with different levels of success (Silverstone, Hirsch and Morley, 1992).

The Victorian middle class's consumption of mass-produced objects in general, and their decoration of the 'public' rooms in their homes – the parlour, the dining-room – have become a *locus classicus* of the articulation of an unrestrained, irrational and unsatisfying addiction to accumulating 'things'. The desire for goods still appears as a domestic displacement activity pursued in the context of a decadent mass culture: as the expression of slightly pathetic longings for symbolic representations of 'hopes and ideals' (McCracken, 1988), as signifying the 'displacement of libidinal energy onto material things'(Logan, 1995: 217), or, indeed, as producing a 'stuffed interior' to comfort guests 'so that human hands did not have to do so' (Bronner, 1989: 52). Recently, work on the acquisition of goods has produced a less passive image of the consumers of mass-produced items, and the study of consumption now foregrounds the ways in which mass-produced household objects involve their owners in a complicated task of creating identity and of appropriation into individual domestic circumstances, while also linking themselves with a communal context. As Falk and Campbell point out, this emphasis enables us to reconceptualise relations between private and public, individual and social (1997: 3).

Sarah Milan's essay, 'Refracting the gaselier: understanding Victorian responses to domestic gas lighting', narrates the history of a particular object and the activities and meanings attached to it over a period of time. Milan moves on from explanations of the middle-class acquisition of gaseliers as a mark of aspiration and status, into an examination of the implications of their actual use within the domestic space. It is now commonplace to understand the way in which objects in the home, and perhaps especially those which use new technologies, delineate sharply the power relations and social behaviours played out in the home. Forty, for example, has discussed the way in which domestic sewing machines were designed and marketed to match social prescriptions around work for women of different classes (1995: 94–9). Milan's argument takes a different direction, looking at how the meanings of the gaselier change in the domestic space, not as a result of changing social relations within the home, but because of the use of the same object in quite other social spaces.

The subject of the ways in which bourgeois domestic space might be experienced in comparison with other interiors is also discussed by Alan Ackerman in 'Theatre and the private sphere in the fiction of Louisa May Alcott'. Whereas Milan charts the changing meanings of a particular object across domestic and other social spaces, Ackerman is interested in how the meanings and experience of the domestic space itself shift in relation to experience of 'quite other' social spaces, in this case theatre. The theatricality of middle-class familial structures, as revealed in Ackerman's essay, is more sharply brought into focus if we consider that, for nineteenth-century inhabitants and observers of domestic space, the domestic interior was increasingly understood as the private citizen's universe. It could be both a haven from which to observe antics on the world stage and a 'theatre' for the performance of intimate feelings and family dramas. If the domestic space became a 'theatre', the boundaries between fantasy and reality, performance and 'natural' behaviour were blurred, and the 'separation' of private and public problematised. Ackerman discusses the representation of the home as literally converted into the theatrical space of Alcott's fiction. These fictional representations of 'meta-private-theatricals', investigated in the context of the middle-class vogue for private theatricals in 1850s–1870s America and Europe, produce, Ackerman argues, 'unsentimental glimpses of domestic life'. Particularly, the importation of notions of 'theatricality' into the domestic space threatened social expectations of appropriate behaviour for women, given the moral anxiety surrounding 'actresses'.

Thus the domestic space could be defamiliarised in terms of social interaction and the way in which private familial roles were performed, which had a direct relation to internal design, rearrangement of furniture and use of space. If the parlour or drawing-room was designed as a stage, the potential for surprise entrances and exits was heightened and what occurred 'off-stage' could be concealed within the topography of 'secret' spaces. Passages and stairways, emblematic of the potential for encounter, meant that space could always surprise in terms of human contact, which might be across class, gender or racial 'divides'.

Where the middle-class Victorian house was concerned, design and internal organisation lent themselves to the revealing (and concealing) of interior space, allowing the display of interiors within interiors Chinese-box style: 'by opening sliding doors, whose virtue was that they disappeared into the walls; by throwing back the heavy portières hung in doorless doorways; or simply by removing the folding screens placed in or near doorways' (Halttunen, 1989: 166). Indeed, the door or its substitute both represents and transcends the separation of inner and outer: 'life flows forth out of the door from the limitation of isolated separate existence into the limitlessness of all possible directions' (Simmel, 1997: 68). Doors, as they invite entry, also protect privacy by controlling access to the house's interior. And at the heart of this unfolding space, writing could take place.

The extent to which the physical conditions of domestic architecture and design affected both social relations and the writing of literature is discussed by Sarah Luria in 'The architecture of manners: Henry James, Edith Wharton and The Mount'. In their architectural criticism, their novels and in the design of The Mount, James and Wharton subscribe to a domestic plan which hinges on the creation of an innermost space for reflection and writing. The sense of privacy as intimately connected to the production of texts – a process itself mediated by the existence (or not) of domestic or private space – was established in the nineteenth century. Indeed, the essays in this collection discuss the representation of interiors *in* texts and also interiors *as* texts. Critics have cited the first historical, truly 'private' space as the (man's) study; an intellectual space and a space of writing (and reading) (Wigley, 1992: 347–50). This gendered model has been challenged – of course we think of Virginia Woolf's plea for women to have a measure of economic independence and a 'room of one's own' – a manifesto which in turn has been criticised for its blindspots concerning the specific socio-economic status and ethnic identities of women (Marcus, 1994). Luria's essay is concerned with, in a sense, how the interior can be narrated from within. Yet, it is not only that writing was produced within a private space – that the design of the space allowed it to come into being – but that it also produced the very ideology of privacy. 'The new forms of writing both depend on, and assist in, the cultural construction of those spaces. They are literally part of the spaces' (Wigley, 1992: 350). This interdependence between literature and architecture, specifically domestic space, is part of the *ars memoria* tradition – both writing and the domestic space have a memorial function (Frank, 1979).[4]

As far as the middle classes were concerned, then, the interior of the house presented itself as a practical problem and as 'a figurative representation of newly discovered personal and social boundaries' (Agnew, 1989: 138). In other words, the practical organisation of the interior mapped social interaction in microcosmic form. Yet the domestic interior was also a sphere of self-expression, of emotional and psychological states: 'neither [only] an external object nor an inner experience' (Heidegger, 1997: 106). As an entity comprising different spaces (each with their own objects) it had its own personalities and it also, crucially, participated in the formation of the psychical lives of those who inhabited it. Recently, cultural critics have chosen to emphasise this psychological dimension in their discussion of the nineteenth-century domestic arena, in doing so retracing and reinventing the shift in the nineteenth century towards seeing the domestic space as the externalisation of multiple personalities (Sidlauskas, 1996; Halttunen, 1989).

Nineteenth-century commentators had, for example, theorised the relationship between individual perception and objects within the interior, gauging the extent to which domestic space was an invention of the mind. Walter Pater, in the conclusion to *The Renaissance: Studies in Art and Poetry* (1873, 1893), suggested that 'when reflexion begins to play upon those objects they are dissipated under its influence … the whole scope of observation is dwarfed into the narrow chamber of the individual mind' (1998: 151). In a moment of mental reflection (and reflexion between individual and object) the external (domestic) world is miniaturised and the household interior becomes a metaphor for the psyche. Of course, simply to live is to 'leave traces' in material and psychological senses. As Walter Benjamin stressed in discussing bourgeois homes of the 1880s, the interior was fundamentally altered by its occupants' 'impression' (1986: 155–6).

The above observations are indicative of the ways in which nineteenth-century culture, in response to modernity, acknowledged a new, unstable interdependency between the body and space; between the inner psyche and outward aesthetics. This provides a useful context for consideration of Ann C. Colley's essay 'Bodies and mirrors: the childhood interiors of Ruskin, Pater and Stevenson'. Moreover, the notion of 'traces' within, and of, the interior has been developed in the twentieth century by theorists who have emphasised the relationship between the dwelling-place and the formation of self-identity: 'To say that mortals *are* is to say that *in dwelling* they persist through spaces by virtue of their stay among things and locations. And only because mortals pervade, persist through, spaces by their very nature are they able to go through spaces' (Heidegger, 1997: 107). Notably, spatial and architectural metaphors describing structures of thought have been used by Sigmund Freud, in relation to 'dream-work', and by Michel Foucault in *The Order of Things* (1970). Colley is also drawing on this 'body' of knowledge in her comparison of three nineteenth-century autobiographical texts as models of how consciousness of one's physical being, specifically as it related to the rooms of childhood, illuminates the interiors of home. These autobiographical texts are impelled by 'the desire to recover – to resurrect – the child within the rooms of home' – rooms partly defined as the domain of the Imaginary; a pre-linguistic and pre-Oedipal gap when the child first imagines itself as a coherent, individual identity (Sarup, 1992). Colley's essay reminds us that the body was both a container (with an interior) and contained *within* the domestic interior (Stewart, 1993: 104) and that, marked by its childhood experiences of domestic space, it had stories to tell about that space.

The formation of domestic space as a liminal space (itself a contradiction) had, then, a direct bearing on how nineteenth-century individuals articulated *privacy* in psychological terms. Additionally, and interdependent with this, the 'frontiers' of the intimate, private world had to be negotiated in physical, very tangible terms. As a 'specifically modern phenomenon' (Reed, 1996: 7), domesticity was characterised in terms of privacy and comfort, although, equally, the 'domestic' space might be a site of antagonism (Sidlauskas, 1996: 67–8); of quarrels and hidden anxieties.

In this context the spatial order of the domestic realm can be read as a means of controlling sensual 'appetites'.[5] In an obvious sense space within the house was organised, or at least characterised, in terms of the extent of human traffic, noise levels, smells and dirt – the public was situated at the heart of the private. Privacy could then be defined as protection against other bodies' dirt and odours, although desire for this had to be negotiated with the surveillance of social reformers (and sanitary requirements such as ventilation), particularly where the inhabited rooms of the poor were concerned.[6] Alain Corbin, most obviously, has discussed the change in 'collective psychology' which led to the 'medicalization of private space' (1986: 162) and to the ways in which intimate spaces – corners, recesses – presented an 'aesthetic of olfaction' (169) relating to both private space and the individual body.[7] This model of thinking can usefully be applied to individual case-studies in nineteenth-century Britain and America. Corbin writes: 'Nothing is more revealing of social distance and the fierceness of antagonisms than the repulsion and the desire which flowed from these bodies trapped in homes where all privacy was lacking, pathetic theatres where fantasy so impregnated daily life that it is probably vain to insist on attempting to separate them' (1995: 69). If there is no private space within the home as 'prison', the body becomes a site of both fear and desire (the sexualised space).

The desire for privacy as produced by an increasingly heterogeneous population and the effects of urban overcrowding is analysed by S. J. Kleinberg. While middle-class homes were designed, externally and internally, to 'ward off' urbanisation, working-class tenement rooms tended to integrate, rather than segregate, people, and doors and windows opened onto the street. In working-class urban neighbourhoods, lack of privacy meant that 'family quarrels became public property', although neighbours tried to protect themselves by *not* getting involved in domestic quarrels. Kleinberg demonstrates that, nonetheless, aspiration to own a *home* of one's own cut across class and racial divides. The question of privacy and the problem of 'nearness', as opposed to distance, between the classes is also addressed in Martin Hewitt's essay, 'District visiting and the constitution of domestic space in the mid-nineteenth century'. The domestic space is never just private; it is a sign for public and cultural interaction, a space which 'outsiders' or strangers can enter, a site of encounter. Hewitt takes the specific case of district or domestic visiting in mid-nineteenth-century Britain in order to establish the degree to which the working-class urban home as 'thoroughfare' was a middle-class construct. In analysing the figuration of 'thoroughfare' in middle-class accounts of district visiting, Hewitt discusses doorstep etiquette and instances when the threshold was policed by the working-class inhabitants. Hewitt ultimately assesses the extent to which historians can piece together evidence of a working-class sense of their own privacy; of their ability to 'define their own home as separate from public or communal space, and hence control access to it'.

In negotiating any sense of privacy or the private as it related to the nineteenth-century domestic space, voyeurism was always an issue. Space could be defined or carved out for the body, whether in constructing class or ethnic identities or a demarcation along gendered lines. This process of 'othering' was, of course, contingent on maintaining a 'distance' in the face of the ever-present threat of a *lack* of privacy in domestic and urbanised domains. The essays in this volume are concerned with the ways in which someone's domestic space is constructed for them by somebody else. Yet, as a number of the essays also demonstrate, there is discomfort in the individual's experience of the 'gap' between the unfamiliar and the familiar, between the adult body and the childhood space it recalls; between what is and what was. Domestic space, in the individual memory or in historical reconstruction, is inevitably coloured by nostalgia – a nostalgia for the oneiric richness of childhood space, for something lost in the gaps in time where domestic tasks are performed or in fragments such as workbags or rag rugs, which, as Carolyn Steedman argues, bear traces of an actual history. As Steedman, crucially, asks in 'What a rag rug means', 'whose dream is this?' Steedman is particularly concerned with the working-class interior as the object of the (middle-class) writer's desire, a desire to 'write the self through others who are not like you'. In this context we might recall Guy Mannering's remark in Walter Scott's novel *Guy Mannering* (1815): 'It is disgusting to see the scenes of domestic society and seclusion thrown open to the gaze of the curious and vulgar' (quoted in Tristram, 1989: 260). Mannering is commenting on the domestic debris, the leavings and objects of a domestic space, on show at an auction. To try to read these objects, or to stand *outside* a house and see in through its windows 'is to write a story of lives one does not know' (247).

Yet voyeurism cuts both ways, or nostalgia for a domestic space is not necessarily comfortable. An interior and the objects within it, as the essays that follow discuss, can be unpredictable in various ways; the material one deals with can prove unstable, like the rag rug which Steedman suggests 'cannot to its own edges keep'. Discomfiture is experienced by the voyeur on both sides of the window – the observer and the observed – and on both sides of any historical divide. The attempt to define a physical domestic space is necessarily about recreating a historical space – and it involves contradictions and tensions. As Manfredo

Tafuri comments, 'That such a battle is not totalizing, that it leaves borders, remains, residues, is also an indisputable fact' (1987: 8) – which itself is part of a historiographical project.

Notes

1 Our interest here is in offering strategies for reading the nineteenth-century domestic space, rather than in attempting a comparative study of national differences concerning the domestic space.

2 For historiographical surveys of US and British investigations into the 'separate sphere' of nineteenth-century women, see Kerber, 1988, and Hall, 1992, respectively.

3 The debate about private and public space within history, social theory and cultural anthropology is summarised in Helly and Reverby, 1992.

4 Jacques Derrida links deconstruction with writing in terms of spatiality; both open up a path (or eternal possibilities). 'One lives in writing. Writing is a way of living.' See Derrida (1986), 'Architecture where the desire may live', interview with E. Meyer, reprinted in Leach, 1997: 321.

5 For discussion of the relationship between privacy, sexuality, gender and the architecture of the house, see Wigley, 1992.

6 For discussion of working-class domestic interiors in nineteenth-century fiction, see Tristram, 1989: 100–8.

7 For further discussion of the body as a threat to the purity of domestic space see Poovey, 1995. The fourteenth-century treatise by Henri De Mondeville first mentioned the body as a house with an interior and openings which needed constant surveillance. See Wigley, 1992: 358.

Bibliography

Agnew, J.-C. (1989), 'A house of fiction: domestic interiors and the commodity aesthetic', in S. Bronner (ed.), *Consuming Visions: Accumulation and Display of Goods in America 1880–1920,* New York, Norton.

Ames, K. L. (1992), *Death in the Dining Room and Other Tales of Victorian Culture*, Philadelphia, Temple University Press.

Benjamin, W. (1986), 'Paris, capital of the nineteenth century', in *Reflections,* trans. E. Jephcott, New York, Schocken Books.

Berg, B. (1978), *The Remembered Gate: Origins of American Feminism, the Woman and the City*, New York, Oxford University Press.

Bourdieu, P. (1977), *Outline of a Theory of Practice*, trans. R. Nice, Cambridge, Cambridge University Press.

Brah, A. (1996), *Cartographies of Diaspora: Contesting Identities*, London, Routledge.

Bronner, S. (ed.) (1989), *Consuming Visions: Accumulation and Display of Goods in America 1880–1920,* New York, Norton.

Brown, G. (1990), *Domestic Individualism: Imagining Self in Nineteenth-Century America*, Berkeley, University of California Press.

Callan, H. and Ardener, S. (1984), *The Incorporated Wife*, London, Croom Helm.

Colomina, B. (1992), 'The split wall: domestic voyeurism', in B. Colomina (ed.), *Sexuality and Space*, Princeton, Princeton Architectural Press.

Corbin, A. (1986), *The Foul and the Fragrant: Odor and the French Social Imagination*, Leamington Spa, Berg.

Corbin, A. (1995), *Time, Desire and Horror: Towards a History of the Senses*, Cambridge, Polity.

Cowan, R. S. (1989), *More Work for Mother: The Ironies of Household Technology from the Open Hearth to the Microwave*, London, Free Association.

Davidoff, L. and Hall, C. (1987), *Family Fortunes: Men and Women of the English Middle Class 1780–1850,* Chicago, University of Chicago Press.

Dickerson, V. (1995), *Keeping the Victorian House*, New York, Garland.

Falk, P. and Campbell, C. (eds) (1997), *The Shopping Experience*, London, Sage.

Forty, A. (1995), *Objects of Desire: Design and Society since 1750*, London, Thames and Hudson.

Foucault, M. (1997), 'Of other spaces: utopias and heterotopias', in N. Leach (ed.), *Rethinking Architecture: A Reader in Cultural Theory*, London, Routledge.

Frank, E. Eve (1979), *Literary Architecture: Essays Towards a Tradition*, Berkeley, University of California Press.

Girouard, M. (1979), *The Victorian Country House*, New Haven, Yale University Press.

Grier, K. (1988), *Culture and Comfort: Parlor-Making and Middle-Class Identity*, Washington, Smithsonian Institute Press.

Hall, C. (1992), 'Feminism and feminist history', in C. Hall, *White, Male and Middle Class: Explorations in Feminism and History*, Cambridge, Polity.

Halttunen, K. (1982), *Confidential Men and Painted Women: A Study of Middle-Class Culture in America*, New Haven, Yale University Press.

Halttunen, K. (1989), 'From parlor to living room: domestic space, interior decoration, and the culture of personality', in S. Bronner (ed.), *Consuming Visions*, New York, Norton.

Heidegger, M. (1997), 'Building, dwelling, thinking', in N. Leach (ed.), *Rethinking Architecture: A Reader in Cultural Theory*, London, Routledge.

Helly, D. O. and Reverby, S. (eds) (1992), *Gendered Domains: Rethinking Public and Private in Women's History*, Ithaca and London, Cornell University Press.

Higonnet, M. and Templeton, J. (eds) (1994), *Reconfigured Spheres: Feminist Explorations of Literary Space*, Amherst, University of Massachusetts Press.

Kerber, L. (1988), 'Separate spheres, female worlds, woman's place: the rhetoric of women's history', *Journal of American History*, 1, 9–39.

Langland, E. (1995), *Nobody's Angels: Middle-Class Women and Domestic Ideology in Victorian Culture,* Ithaca and London, Cornell University Press.

Lauretis, T. de (1987), *Technologies of Gender: Essays on Theory, Film and Fiction*, London, Macmillan.

Leach, N. (ed.) (1997), *Rethinking Architecture: A Reader in Cultural Theory*, London, Routledge.

Logan, T. (1995), 'Decorating domestic space: middle-class women and Victorian interiors', in V. Dickerson, *Keeping the Victorian House*, New York, Garland.

Marcus, J. (1994), 'Registering objections: grounding feminist alibis', in M. Higonnet and J. Templeton (eds), *Reconfigured Spheres: Feminist Explorations of Literary*

Space, Amherst, University of Massachusetts Press.

McClintock, A. (1995), *Imperial Leather: Race, Gender and Sexuality in the Colonial Contest*, London, Routledge.

McCracken, G. (1988), *Culture and Consumption: New Approaches to the Symbolic Character of Consumer Goods and Activities*, Bloomington and Indianapolis, Indiana University Press.

Mertes, C. (1992), 'There's no place like home: women and domestic labor', in J. Fuenmajor, K. Haug and F. Ward, *Dirt and Domesticity: Constructions of the Feminine*, New York, Whitney Museum of American Art.

Miller, D. (1987), *Material Culture and Mass Consumption*, London, Basil Blackwell.

Mohanty, C. T. (1988), 'Under Western eyes', *Feminist Review*, 30, 61–88.

Moore, H. (1986), *Space, Text and Gender*, Cambridge, Cambridge University Press.

Pascoe, P. (1990), *Relations of Rescue: The Search for Female Moral Authority in the West 1874–1939*, New York, Oxford University Press.

Pater, W. [1873,1893] (1998), *The Renaissance: Studies in Art and Poetry*, ed. A. Phillips, Oxford, Oxford University Press.

Poovey, M. (1995), *Making a Social Body*, Chicago, University of Chicago Press.

Reed, C. (ed.) (1996), *Not At Home*, London, Thames and Hudson.

Romero, L. (1997), *Home Fronts: Domesticity and its Critics in Antebellum United* States, Durham NC, Duke University Press.

Ryan, M. (1981), *Cradle of the Middle Class: The Family in Oneida County, New York 1790–1865*, Cambridge, Cambridge University Press.

Salvaggio, R. (1988), 'Theory and space, space and women', *Tulsa Studies in Women's Literature*, 7, 261–82.

Sarup, M. (1992), *Jacques Lacan*, London, Harvester Wheatsheaf.

Sidlauskas, S. (1996), 'Psyche and sympathy: staging interiority in the early modern home', in C. Reed (ed.), *Not At Home*, London, Thames and Hudson.

Silverstone, R., Hirsch, E. and Morley, D. (1992), 'Information and communication technologies and the moral economy of the household', in R. Silverstone and E. Hirsch (eds), *Consuming Technologies: Media and Information in Domestic Spaces*, London, Routledge.

Simmel, G. (1997), 'Bridge and door', in N. Leach (ed.), *Rethinking Architecture: A Reader in Cultural Theory*, London, Routledge.

Smith-Rosenberg, C. (1971), 'Beauty, the beast and the militant woman: a case study in sex roles and social stress in Jacksonian America', *American Quarterly*, 23, 562–84.

Spain, D. (1992), *Gendered Spaces*, Chapel Hill, University of North Carolina Press.

Stewart, S. (1993), *On Longing: Narratives of the Miniature, the Gigantic, the Souvenir, the Collection*, Durham, NC, Duke University Press.

Tafuri, M. (1987), *The Sphere and the Labyrinth: Avant-Gardes and Architecture from Piranesi to the 1970s*, Cambridge, MA, MIT Press.

Tristram, P. (1989), *Living Space in Fact and Fiction*, London, Routledge.

Vicinus, M. (ed.) (1977), *A Widening Sphere: Changing Roles of Victorian Women*, Bloomington, Indiana University Press.

Wigley, M. (1992), 'Untitled: the housing of gender', in B. Colomina (ed.), *Sexuality and Space*, Princeton, Princeton Architectural Press.

Wilson, E. (1977), *Women and the Welfare State*, London, Tavistock.

Wilson, E. (1991), *Sphinx in the City*, London, Virago.
Wolff, J. (1990), *Feminine Sentences: Essays on Women and Culture*, Cambridge, Polity.
Wright, G. (1980), *Moralism and the Model Home: Domestic Architecture and Cultural Conflict in Chicago 1873–1913*, Chicago, University of Chicago Press.

What a rag rug means

Carolyn Steedman

> Tearless, their surfaces appear as deep
> As any longing we believe we had;
> If shapes can so to their own edges keep,
> No separation proves a being bad.
>
> (W. H. Auden, 'Objects', 1966)

This essay started out as an error of transposition. However, the tense of the title – 'means' rather than 'meant' – was always correct. It is about what a rag rug means, rather than what a rag rug meant (though it is about that too); about the rag rug as an obscure object of desire for all those who read the past, in their various ways, but particularly about historians as the readers in question.

The error of transposition is its introduction. I started thinking about the rag rug when I remembered the second chapter of Elizabeth Gaskell's *Mary Barton* (1848) in which, as evening falls, the Bartons and the Wilsons are returning from their May-time walk in the countryside.[1] Back in Manchester, 'among the pent-up houses', the darkness seems to have come sooner than it would have done in the fields they have just left. Mrs Barton takes the front-door key from her pocket and, 'on entering the house-place it seemed as if they were in total darkness, except one bright spot … a red-hot fire, smouldering under a large piece of coal' (49). Soon the stirred fire illuminates the whole room and, with the addition of a candle, we see its dimensions, its appurtenances, its furnishings and its decorations. It is an immensely detailed description of an interior space made up of: a window, a ledge, blue-and-white check curtains; geraniums on the sill; plates, dishes, cups, saucers, glassware; a japanned tea-tray, a crimson tea-caddy. This is a space crammed with furniture, though some of it is broken and only made of deal in the first place. The firelight provides depth, brightness and – the author seems to tell us as much – the intense interior glitter of the Victorian tale for children, when we first enter any old giant's castle, or this cottage in the woods, or that little house. From this warm, richly coloured room, doors lead to a little back kitchen, where the functions assigned to the shelves evoke pantries and storerooms, sculleries and larders (though there is, in fact, only the one little back kitchen). There is a staircase, so we know that we are in a house and not a one-level dwelling: that we are not here in one of those places that Bachelard called oneirically incomplete, in which 'the different rooms that compose living quarters jammed into one floor all lack one of the fundamental principles for distinguishing and classifying the values of intimacy' ([1958] 1994: 27). We are emphatically *not* in a dwelling that, by this criterion, fails to provide the working material for dreams.

I shall return to Bachelard and to the poetics of space in general and of this kind of space in particular. But the immediate concern has to be the fact that *there isn't a rag rug in the Barton parlour*. Rather, between the slating cupboard under the stairs, which the Bartons use as a coalhole, and the fireplace is 'a gay-coloured piece of oil-cloth laid'. No rag rug; and yet I *remember* a rag rug.

The process of my misrecollections is in fact quite easy to reconstruct: I once wrote a paper in which I connected Elizabeth Gaskell's description of the Barton parlour – 'simple and heart-wrenching detail upon domestic detail called up to make us understand a simplicity and sadness in this form of life', I wrote in 1986 – with a passage from Richard Hoggart's *Uses of Literacy* (1957) where, I said, 'a rag rug comes to symbolise a great and enduring simplicity of working class life' (Steedman, 1992: 197). I simply forgot the hundred and ten years between the two texts and put the rag rug down on the Barton parlour floor.

The passage from Hoggart that I transposed belongs to a long section called 'There's No Place Like Home', which details in a manner strikingly similar to Gaskell's 'a good [working-class] living room' ([1957] 1958: 20–6). There *are* moments of historicisation and chronicity in these pages of *The Uses of Literacy*, when Hoggart reminds the reader that what he writes is 'largely based on memories of twenty years ago'; but they are followed by immediate disavowal, for example, in the typical statement that 'the basic pattern of working class life remains as it has been for many years'. The rag rug (Hoggart calls it a clip-rug) comes at the end of his depiction of the house as a cluttered and congested setting, 'a burrow deeply away from the outside world'.

Its sounds shape the inwardness and harmony of this house: the quiet noise of the wireless and the television; 'intermittent snatches of talk'; the thump of the iron on the table; the dog scratching itself; the rustle of a letter being read.[2] And then Hoggart observes:

> In a few of the more careful homes this unity is still objectified in the making of a clip-rug by the hearth. Clippings of old clothes are prepared, sorted into rough colour groups and punched singly through a piece of harding (sacking). Patterns are traditional and simple, usually a centre circle or diamond with the remainder an unrelieved navy blue ... or that greyish-blue which mixed shoddy usually produces ... The rug will replace at the fireplace one made a long time ago. (23)

The rag rug of my *imagination* lasted the ninety years between Manchester in the 1840s (the fictional time of *Mary Barton*) and the Hunslet community of the 1930s that Hoggart recalled in the 1950s; and, while the aetiology of my error would no doubt be fascinating (especially to myself), I think that, in order to proceed, it is best to see the transformed oilcloth on the Barton floor as a *likely rug* and Hoggart's remembered rug as the personification of the way of living that he actually says it is: a feature of the poetics of a timeless and dehistoricised working-class life, available for use by historians and cultural critics of the twentieth century. As a poetics, it was partly derived from works like *Mary Barton* – that is, from social observation translated into fictional realism (in the industrial novel) and from – I strongly suspect – the gothic vision which informed the writing of so many of Dickens's metropolitan interiors. However, though the kind of restless bricolage of the fairy-tale that I am thinking of does appear in his writing (I think particularly of the Boffin's kitchen in chapter five of *Our Mutual Friend* (1864–65), Dickens *doesn't really do it*: firstly, those interiors (chapter five of *Barnaby Rudge* (1841), chapter six of *Dombey and Son* (1846–48) chapter three of *David Copperfield* (1849–50)) are not really working class and more significantly – a point to which I shall return – there is *usually somebody in them*. But for the visual depth that Dickens's writing seems to promise, but not – in this instance – quite deliver, and for the delight provoked by seeing it *for the first time*, there is always Henry Mayhew's sudden, swift surprise at an interior with the wall over the fireplace entirely 'patched up to the ceiling with little square pictures of saints' (1851: 47–8, cited in Rubinstein, 1974: 115–21).

There is no rest for the eye in these descriptions, however lovingly they may be detailed. Hoggart emphasises the harmony of the 1930s terrace house by dwelling on the pattern of the rug, the 'centre circle or diamond with the remainder an unrelieved navy blue (except for the edging)' (23). But the rag rug is irreducibly a thing made from the torn scraps of other things, from rags indeed. It returns us, no matter what coherence and peace Hoggart gives it in his mind's eye, to Mayhew's vision in *London Labour and the London Poor* (1851), of a vast metropolis, an entire way of life built upon the scavenging of the poor: bones retrieved for boiling down, dog shit collected from the street, mud dredged for tiny fragments of metal, rag yards heaped with old clothing on its way to becoming some other kind of object, some other sort of thing.[3]

We must remember, in transposing Hoggart's rug from the 1930s to the late 1840s, that his working-class interior was the product of longing. It was made partly of a nostalgia for his own past, from the oneiric richness of his own childhood space. It is useful to counterpoise Hoggart's dream of the rag rug with another extremely rare first-hand account of living in a working-class interior, that is, with Leonora Eyles's *The Woman in the Little House* (1922), in which she records:

> For five years of my life I was never alone for a single instant; in bed, in the kitchen, shopping, gardening, always someone very near to me, touching me most of the time. I felt sometimes as though I could come to hate the crowding people who were really so dear to me. Is it in one of these momentary spasms of impatient desire to get alone for a few minutes that murders are sometimes done? (54)

I shall reluctantly leave that alternative story, in which blood soaks the rag rug, taking from this conjunction of Hoggart with Eyles two points: that there is bound to be a distinction between the sexes in relation to the little house and all that is symbolised by the rag rug before the hearth; but that we are never likely to find out very much about that difference because voices *from* the working-class interior are an extraordinary rarity. All the descriptions we have are from observers, from those who penetrate the maze of greasy streets and step through the door of another kind of space. It is observation of those spaces and places of the nineteenth century to which our attention must now come.

Historians have provided us with a poetics of this kind of encounter, observation and imagining (unwittingly, I think: historians do not in the normal course of events do this sort of thing). I think first of all of Alain Corbin's work, which directly addresses *the ways of seeing* the homes of the poor evolved by the middle classes. In *The Foul and the Fragrant* (1986) he reports that 'the flood of discourse on the habitat of the masses' reached new dimensions after the 1832 cholera morbus epidemic (151–2). Using French (and particularly Parisian) evidence, he traces in some detail the ways in which the sanitary reformer's denunciations of the odour and excrement of the quarters of the poor were used by popular novelists to inscribe a new form of shock that made its effect on the sensory borderline between smell and vision: 'The odor of stagnant urine, congealed in the gutter, dried on the paving, encrusted on the wall, assailed the visitor who had to enter the wretched premises of the poor' (152).Corbin then goes on to provide an epitome of the journey to the lair, a journey that can be read (for Britain as well as France) in countless government reports, reports of charity organisations and reports by investigative journalists from the 1830s onwards. It is the mode in which modern historians of working-class life write – of course – because they have learned their rhetoric from the nineteenth-century sources themselves. David Rubinstein's book *Victorian Homes* (1974) is still the most useful compilation of such contemporary observations. And there is Corbin's epitome:

> The only means of entry was through low, narrow, dark alleys ... Gaining access to the poor man's stinking dwelling almost amounted to an underground expedition ... The narrowness, darkness and humidity of the small inner courtyard into which the alley opened made it look like a well, the ground carpeted with refuse ... Inside the dwelling, congestion, a jumble of tools, dirty linen and crockery, prevailed ... In particular, writings focused on the aspect of narrowness. The crampedness of the sleeping area, the depth of the yard and the length of the alley created in the mind of the bourgeois ... the impression of suffocation (152–3).[4]

Corbin also tells us that in all this complex of writing 'the cage rather than the den was the dominant image' (152). However, these powerful pages of his book suggest the imprisonment of the dungeon, not the animal cage, for Corbin evokes cage as prison – as underground prison, without air (151–7, 152–3).

I once found Margaret McMillan using this particular poetics of the working-class lair for overtly political purposes, as late as 1919. It is worth quoting from her writing because of the striking formality of vision (if it can be agreed that this vision was indeed made formalised through the processes of official and fictional writing, from the mid-nineteenth century onwards). McMillan was making her usual plea to the Labour Party and its sympathisers, to rescue the child of the slum by placing him in a garden, specifically in the garden of her open-air nursery school in Deptford. She usually did this, as in the following passage from *The Nursery School* (1919), by actually insisting on the child's enduring contact with the dark place that spawned him:

> Dennis lives in a … street [that] is a huddle of houses with dark, greasy lobbies and hideous black stairs leading down into cellars. It is so dark that when one goes down one sees nothing for a few moments. Then a broken wall and a few sticks of furniture appear and a dark young woman with glittering eyes looks down at us. Dennis is a great pet in the Nursery. On his firm little feet he runs all round the big shelter and garden … he breaks into a kind of singing on bright June mornings … his eyes alight with joy. In the evening his older sister comes and carries him back to the cellar. (82)

It is the cellar, the greasy walls, the stained and broken ceiling that endure in the imagination. Corbin calls the section of his book quoted from above 'Cage and Den'. These are the spaces poeticised and used for rhetorical purposes, despite the wealth of alternative description from the nineteenth century available for historical description. In fact, many a social investigator climbed a broken and stinking stair to find a small whitewashed room of endearing neatness, very close to the stars; or followed a child, fictional or real, through into the foetid courts and alleys that generated it – to find, not malodorous horror, but a floor scrubbed 'three or four times a week' by Mayhew's Little Watercress Girl (1851: 151–2), or a 'poor upper room' – Nelly's lodging in Mrs Sewell's ballad of 1861, *Our Father's Care* – where 'A small fire is burning, the water is hot, / The tea is put into the little teapot, / And all things are carefully set in their place' (14). Nevertheless, it is the lair we must consider, the small enclosed space between and beneath and at the end of something else: enclosed. Mayhew reported on the poetic dichotomies of this space quite as much as he did on an actual costermonger's dwelling in the first volume of *London Labour and the London Poor*: 'Although these people were living, so to speak, in a cellar', he reported:

> still every endeavour had been made to give the home a look of comfort. The window, with its paper-patched panes, had a clean calico blind. The side-table was dressed up with yellow jugs and cups and saucers and the band-boxes had been stowed away on the flat top of the bedstead. All the chairs, which were old fashioned mahogany ones, had sound backs and bottoms. (48)

It only lacks the rag rug.

What kind of space is this?

We know – not only from Bachelard, but mainly from him – all about 'the poetic depth of the space of the house', for the house is 'one of the greatest powers of integration for the thoughts, memories and dreams of mankind' ([1958] 1994: 6). He gave the name toponanalysis to 'this auxiliary of psychoanalysis' – that is, to 'the systematic psychological study of the sites of our intimate lives'. It is the house, its many rooms and levels, its stairways and recesses, that allows the topoanalyst 'to start to ask questions: Was the room a large one? Was the garret cluttered up? Was the nook warm? How was it lighted?' We may ask these questions too, for it is not houses that we have been considering, but *rooms* in houses – neglected, dirty houses – rooms in cellars, or rooms at the far reaches of a broken stair. Bachelard continued his questions about these spaces within houses, asking: 'How, too, in these fragments of space, did the human being achieve silence? How did he relish the very special silence of the various retreats of solitary daydreaming?' (8–9) We know the answer to that one even though, lacking evidence from those who lived in narrow cluttered rooms, we have to wait until the twentieth century for a voice to talk about the lack of aloneness of the little house.

As already observed, Bachelard considered that some dwellings were oneirically incomplete, incapable of providing material for the dream-work or even for daydreaming: 'the different rooms that compose living quarters jammed into one floor all lack one of the fundamental principles for distinguishing and classifying the values of intimacy.' Here he was finding the Parisian apartment wanting; but we must suppose that the large numbers of Victorian poor who lived with their family and others in one room were also deprived of the 'fundamental principles for distinguishing … intimacy' (27).

Overcrowding was not officially defined until 1891, as a room containing more than two adults. Children under ten counted as half by this measure and babies not at all. According to John Burnett (1978), 11.2 per cent of the population of England and Wales – about three and a half million people – was 'overcrowded' in 1891 (142–3). There are no reliable statistics on house-building for the first half of the nineteenth century and, as Enid Gauldie (1974) suggests, we have to steer a course between the statistical suppositions that census figures allow, suggesting that building kept pace with the increased demand for housing (the census shows that the average number of persons per inhabited house held steady between 1801 and 1831 and actually dropped very slightly in 1841) and the overwhelming evidence deposited by the slum visitor, that working-class districts were becoming more overcrowded (82–92). We must assume that throughout the middle years of the nineteenth century many more than 11.2 per cent of the population experienced oneiric deprivation.

And yet: the Barton parlour *is* the stuff of dreams, its furnishings those of the imagination – *someone's* imagination, though whose is not yet quite clear. If, accompanied by *The Poetics of Space*, we turn into the alley, cross the stinking court and enter one of these many single-room dwellings (or even allow that pleasant walk home the Bartons have on the level, in the clear light of day, along a street of half-finished houses and have a working-class woman put the key in the lock and open the door); if we do that with Bachelard's poetics of space in mind, then the objects we find in these numerous rooms present us with yet another puzzle.

Always, we see the objects in these working-class interiors as though for *the first time*. For Bachelard, the way in which quite ordinary objects are marked 'with the sign of "the first time"' by the writer is the highest form of poetic expression ([1958] 1994: 27). Using Rilke's *Fragments of an Intimate Diary*, he suggests that when objects are lit in this way *as for the first time*, they transmit a light to their surroundings just as, in the case in point, their evanescence fills the Barton parlour with radiance once the glowing eye of the fire is made to blaze and cast its illumination over the multitude of objects in the room. According to Bachelard, this intimate light is particularly manifest in things 'that are cherished', and he suggests that polishing, the giving of a bright appearance to things, is the best mark of cherishing:

> Objects that are cherished in this way really are born of an intimate light and they attain to a higher degree of reality than indifferent objects, or those that are defined by geometric reality. For they produce a new reality of being and they take their place not only in an order but in a community of order. (68)

When the working-class interior is the object of the writer's desire, its multifarious bric-a-brac gleams and glitters in this way. Further, the objects in the Barton parlour, ranged on the mantelpiece and towering up in the shelves of the open cupboard, while not possessing the oneiric depth of those 'objects *that may be opened*' (Bachelard, [1958] 1994: 85) like the caskets and boxes to which Bachelard draws our attention, are nevertheless objects that curve themselves outwards (or inwards), that present their interior as well as their exterior to the world: cups, glasses, dishes. The phenomenology of earthenware, glassware and china does indeed allow the most interesting elaboration of Bachelard's thesis, for these everyday objects present inside and outside together, as on a continuum created by the uses to which they are put; they contain and emanate the has-been-opened. It is worth noting as well that Gaskell has John Barton remember and grieve for his dear, dead wife in relation to these household objects. He remembers loving her, in her use of them (57).

The question remains: whose dream-work is this? And there is still, for the moment, the provisional answer to that question: that wherever we may come to locate the dream we can be certain that it is *not* in the mind or heart of the fictional or real inhabitants of the rooms we are considering.

The overwhelming impression for the reader is that, in these clean and itemised interiors, one has entered a fairy-tale. But it is not just the warmth, the fire filling the cluttered space with heat and light, each flame reflected back by the myriad surfaces, that we should note. It is the *smallness* of the house – this narrow room and the littleness of the objects depicted – that should give us pause. Bachelard mentions the fairy-tale as the beginning of his chapter on the 'miniature', and starts by discussing those objects that are 'so easily made smaller through literary means'. He understands the role of the reader and, of course, above all, of the writer in this process, perhaps even signalling that it is writing itself that has the major part to play in miniaturising the world. 'Is it possible' he asks 'for the conscious[5] – of both writer and reader – to play a sincere role in the very origin of images of this kind?' – for it is indeed the case that everything is made smaller in imagination, in the mind's eye (148).

The attraction of the miniature object, the deep pleasures of littleness, have been noted by literary scholars attempting to create a poetics of relative size and smallness (Armstrong, 1990: 403–16; Liebs, 1988: 56–60; Millhauser, 1983: 128–35; Stewart, 1993: 37–69). Claude Lévi-Strauss considered that miniaturisation was the very foundation of the aesthetic (1966: 22–5). But perhaps Susan Stewart's work is the most useful here, not only because the title of her book *On Longing* (1993) inscribes so clearly the desire involved in making small the world, but also because she understands the relationship of pleasure in the miniature with childhood and history. She writes that 'the miniature, linked to nostalgic versions of childhood and history, presents a diminutive and thereby manipulatable, version of experience, a version which is domesticated and protected from contamination' (69). Extraordinary insights and a reading of littleness that is historically located; a reading that forces us to think of the ways in which the pleasures of interiority and smallness inscribed in Elizabeth Gaskell's (and Henry Mayhew's and many others') description of the neat fairy-tale parlour emerged in a particular historical period and for – this point will be returned to – particular historical purposes.

But none of these theorists of littleness does what Bachelard so eloquently did in 1962. His overall turn of thought, announced in the introduction to *The Poetics of Space*, is to delineate the house by the structure of individual memory and the return in the imagination to the security of childhood. Much of the exegesis that follows in *The Poetics of Space* is to do with the way in which 'childhood remains alive and poetically useful within us' (16). And yet, when Bachelard comes to concentrate on the miniature in chapter seven of his book, he puts to one side the proposition that 'the tiny things we imagine simply take us back to childhood, to familiarity with toys and *the reality of toys*'. He dismisses this idea by telling us that 'the imagination deserves better than that' (he means: the imagination deserves a better kind of explanation than this). 'In point of fact', he claims, 'imagination in miniature is natural imagination which appears at all ages in the daydreams of born dreamers' (149). The question now forces itself: why does Gaskell poeticise that interior in this particular way? And why – by means of metonymy – does she do what she does to the people who enter the house-place just before us, who step over the threshold after Mrs Barton's turn of the key, but who then strangely disappear, so that what we are left to contemplate is the stillness and unpeopled nature of the fairy-tale house (the one belonging to the Three Bears that Goldilocks enters is the most obvious example to hand)? However, Bachelard disapproved of metaphor so much that he surely would disapprove of any recourse to metonymy as a device explanatory of the dream process.

Why? Why desire for this parlour, these things, this life, in a room emptied of people, though usually (in the time of social reality) full of them? The silence is held within the cups, glasses, teapots, boxes, tables and chairs that send forth their light into the room. Why desire, then, for a life that is actually emptied out of the picture we are presented with, as the ghosts of Gaskell's imagination fall silent on the threshold and we step into the little room?

We must pursue childhood a little further. Childhood – this has been established elsewhere – was brought into being in western culture as ideation, as idea, as memory, as image, at the same time as history was brought into being; and the poetic depth of childhood has been attested to by many literary scholars (Steedman, 1995). But, in connection with the adult desire for the working-class interior, these theses need further elaboration by consideration of a remembered child's use of the poetic space of the working-class interior.

It is Manchester in the late 1850s. The remembered child – it is

Frances Hodgson Burnett writing her nauseatingly entitled *The One I Knew Best of All* (1893) – lives in the Square. The chapter referred to is entitled 'Islington Square', a 'sort of oasis in the midst of small thoroughfares and back streets, where factory operatives lived' (62–79). The Square is cut off from these surroundings by iron gates, but the child (even more nauseatingly referred to as The Small Person) finds infinite delight in getting out, straying into a forbidden back street and luring 'a dirty little factory child into conversation' (65). Even *in* the Square the surrounding streets provide entertainment:

> "A row in Islington Court!" or, "A row in Back Sydney Street. Man beating his wife with a shovel!" was a cry which thrilled the bolder juvenile spirits of the Square with awesome delight. There were even fair little persons who hovered shudderingly about the big gates, or even passed them, in the shocked hope of seeing a policeman march by with somebody in custody. (69)

But none of this provides the dream-work. Something else does. In a quite extraordinary scene the child brings the desired working-class interior into her own house, as shadow play, as dream. Burnett describes the Nursery floor and one room at the rear of the house in particular, which 'looked down upon the back of the row of cottages in which operatives lived. When one glanced downwards it was easy to see into their tiny kitchens and watch them prepare their breakfasts and eat them too.' The narrative voice continues:

> Imagine then, the interest of waking very early one dark morning and seeing a light reflected on the ceiling of the Nursery bedroom from somewhere far below. The Small Person did this once and after watching a little, discovered that not only the light and the window itself were reflected, but two figures which seemed to pass before it or stand near it. (76–7)

The child wakes her sister: 'It's a man and a woman … Back Street people in their kitchen. You can see them on our ceiling. *This* ceiling; just look.'

The children whisper about what they see on the screen above them: the loaf in the woman's hand, the man washing his face at the dresser. They know that '"they're factory people and the man's wife must be getting his breakfast before he goes to work. I wonder what poor people have for breakfast."' 'Ah the charm of it!', continues Burnett:

> The sense of mystery and unusualness … How could one go to sleep … when the Back Street woman was awake and getting her husband's breakfast? One's own ceiling reflected it and seemed to include on it the family

> circle ... What each figure was really doing when it was near enough to the window to be reflected, what it did when it moved away out of the range of reflection and what it was possible they said to each other, were all things to be excitedly guessed at. (78)

The chapter closes with Burnett recalling:

> It became a habit to waken at that delightful and uncanny hour, just for the pleasure of lying awake and watching the Woman and the Man. That was what they called them. They never knew what their names were, or anything about them ... but the Small person was privately attached to them and continually tried to imagine what they said. She had a fancy that they were a decent couple, who were rather fond of each other and it was a great comfort to her that they never had a fight. (79)

It was all a very great comfort to those social investigators and novelists who wrote the working-class interior in the way I have described and the child's particular achievement in this case is to people the strange, magical interior of her reverie, have the Man and the Woman move across the screen, preparing food, eating it, washing at a dresser (though they do not – cannot – speak and their conversation is only to be guessed at).

I do not think I can say much more than this at the moment. Except this: I have spent some time recently trying to understand the means by which, with the development of a modern class society, working-class people, their image and their appurtenances, were inscribed to tell other people's stories: to tell some kind of story of the bourgeois self. This is another kind of argument, starting now rather than finishing. I would draw attention to – for example – the paradoxes and impossibilities of the servant's Character and the way in which the adolescent poor of eighteenth- and nineteenth-century England could be said to have been given the first itemised and written character in those prosaic letters of recommendation. I would point to the first extensively written 'childhoods' in English literature, in which what happens to the character as a child is understood to shape what happens in its future fictional life. I would point with never-failing astonishment to Defoe's *Moll Flanders* (1722) and to Jemima, from Wollstonecraft's *The Wrongs of Woman, or, Maria* (1978), to the fact that these characters are not only working class, but also women to boot, and have the first written childhoods in the literature. I would point to the constant surprise on recognising that Wollstonecraft has the bourgeois heroine *only able* to tell her own childhood and girlhood, and only able to interpret her own story, through a previous articulation of Jemima's terrifying tale of rape, poverty, prostitution and service. Maria only tells her story after Jemima has told hers. As readers we simply *cannot have* Maria's narrative, in any shape or form, without its framing by Jemima's. In textual terms, there is no story of the self for Maria without Jemima's being in place first. And we must pause to wonder, I think, about what was going on in the long revolution, which formed modern classes and our ways of seeing them (Steedman, forthcoming).

All I can suggest at the moment is that perhaps the working-class domestic is read and written out of the same obscure desire: that desire means you understand and write the self through others who are not like you. You want to enter that little space with all its miniature bricolage and, in doing so, you will take something away, though I do not yet know what that thing is. What I am certain of is that this has absolutely *nothing at all* to do with the people who actually, in time and circumstance, occupied the cruel habitations. Which is why I like the rag rug and my mistake about it: for the rag rug is made from the torn fragments of other things: debris and leavings, the broken and torn things of industrial civilisation. The rag rug carries with it the irreducible traces of an actual history and that history *cannot be made to go away*; but ways of writing it and wanting it (and what it represents) are actually somebody else's story.

Coda

Why isn't there a rag rug in the Barton parlour? It seems that there ought to be one, laid before the fire. Clip, peg or rag rug-making is an old domestic craft. Hooked or progged rugs (a progger is the implement – in appearance rather like a fat awl – used for pulling the piece of rag through the hessian backing) were simple copies of expensive looped and cut-pile carpeting. The flexibility and give of the rag rug was in any case a good choice for covering the uneven brick and stone floors of working-class interiors, better than carpeting would have been, could it ever possibly have been afforded (Shipley Art Gallery, 1988: 8).

The history of domestic production in nineteenth-century Britain is very uncertain and we know very little about the regional development of rag rug-making. Existing accounts suggest that developments in textile production and in the ready-to-wear clothing market gave great impetus to the practice. Cotton had been commonly worn in Britain in the seventeenth century.[6] Jute-hessian sacks were easily available in the 1830s. Mainly produced in Scotland, they were distributed across the UK as containers for loose foodstuffs and could probably be obtained from any grocer's shop or dry-goods merchant, anywhere, in the 1840s. In any case, the Lancashire sacking trade had developed in the mid-eighteenth century. In his tour of the county in 1771, Arthur Young noted the vitality of the Warrington sailcloth and sacking manufacture and that it was largely the province of women and girls (Rose, 1996: 5–6, citing Young, 1771: 163; Young, 1770, 3: 211–12).

And surely, in Manchester in the 1840s, there *should* be such a rug on the Barton's house-place floor. The production of woven cotton cloth, in this great centre of cotton production, rose expedientially in the 1840s. Total UK exports of cotton piece goods doubled between the late 1830s and 1850 (Mitchell and Deane, 1962: 182). The earlier century witnessed a growing localisation of the cotton industry in Lancashire (Farnie, 1979: 45–77; Rose, 1996: 13–26). By the 1840s, some 70 per cent of those employed nationally in the production of cotton lived in Lancashire. Counting the ten major Lanchashire concentrations of cotton manufacturers, Manchester was superseded only by Oldham in the number of its factories in the 1830s and 1840s (Rose, 1996: 13, 17; Baines, [1935] 1966: 386).

It appears, however, that the bags of loom ends and ready-cut spoiled cloth that, by the 1890s, could be purchased from the mills were not available fifty years before. By the early 1900s, according to some authorities, ready-stamped hessian could also be purchased by the yard, along with commercially produced hooks and proggers. A *length* of cheap – because flawed – cloth is not what you want for making a rag rug. You want bits and pieces, a variety of colours and textures, otherwise there would be just that unrelieved, solid colour of the border of Hoggart's rug. The tailor and the dressmaker were probably a source for bits and pieces long before the side-door of the mill. (And yet: Mary Barton is apprenticed to a dressmaker. *Why* doesn't she bring home bundles of off-cuts, bits of selvage, the awkward little pieces that remain, however economically you place the pattern?) Or perhaps, by looking to Lancashire, we are looking in the wrong place for the development of the rag rug. Over the Pennines or in the woollen districts up round Rochdale the industry was older, looms were not always the latest in modern technology that Lancashire aspired to, there was a much bigger variation in size of unit of production, a wider variety of size of loom (for broadcloth and narrow cloth) and theft was 'accepted as an integral part of outwork systems by merchant manufacturers' (Rose, 1996: 11). In short, where wool was woven there were perhaps many more opportunities for spoilage and wastage and the sale and purchase of remnants and off-cuts.

But the truth of the matter (and of the rag rug's absence from the Barton parlour floor) probably lies in the history of an industry other than textiles. After 1860 usable and commercially viable substitutes were found for cotton rags in paper manufacture but the large-scale, bulk import of wood pulp was a development of the later century (Coleman, 1958: 337–44: *The Times*, 10 October 1865: 10). In the very early 1860s, the first machinery designed to render old cotton fit for spinning came into production, so the consequent diminution in demand for cotton rags by the paper trade came in tandem with a new demand from the cotton industry. The technology had been available for woollen cloth rendering since 1813, but it was cotton that was needed prior to the 1860s, for the making of paper (*The Times,* 27 April 1863: 10; Thornton, 1960: 7).

From the middle of the eighteenth century cotton rags were at a premium and UK paper manufacturers imported vast quantities from abroad to fee the voracious appetite for paper. Prices rose to a peak in the early 1850s and a report to the Board of Trade in 1854 noted 'the great and increasing scarcity of the raw material used in paper making'. The official from the Department of Art and Science compiling the Report went on to observe that the cause of the scarcity was not just the 'growing thirst for literature' but also a raw material that was 'the product of wear and tear of a substance of very advanced manufacture' – that is, cotton. Even a partial stoppage in the cotton or linen trades (he mentioned recent lock-outs in Wigan and Preston) could account for scarcity and a rise in prices (Coleman, 1958: 338; British Parliamentary Papers, 1854, 65: 494 – 5, 505; *The Times,* 20 February 1860: 7, 22 March 1860: 12; 26 March 1860: 6; Rag Tax, 1863: 5).

All those involved in any form of tailoring or dressmaking had been exhorted, for at least the previous half century, to save every scrap of cotton and linen cloth possible. In 1799 *The Times* 'particularly recommended to Ladies and every person employed in Needlework, not to burn even the smallest pieces which they may cut', for:

> The Rags annually collected in this kingdom amount in weight to several tons. Doubtless a much greater quantity might be preserved by the care of individuals. – The paper Manufacturers would not then depend on the uncertain importation from foreign countries for an article which could be easily produced in our own. (17 December: 4)

There's romance in the rag of course, as Mrs Paull acknowledged in the title to her temperance tract of 1876, *The Romance of a Rag*, but even at this late date, when rags were no longer at the premium of unique raw material, the rag that tells the tale of a family and a hand-me-down dress ruined by a drunken working-class father (and which at the end of a process of severe purification becomes a temperance pledge card!) becomes paper, not reconstituted thread for cotton spinning (Paull, 1876: 53–82).

Nearly all our knowledge of the rag rug is framed by a romance. It comes from the period that oral history and a historiography of the 1960s and 1970s has located as the origin of the 'traditional working class'[7] (Hobsbawm, [1979] 1984: 176–213; Roberts, 1984: 128, 131, 151; Walker and Walker, 1987: 27–30; Shipley Art Gallery, 1988: 10–12). In this terrain of the historical imagination, the rug is connected with flat caps, pigeon-fancying, fish and chips, the kind of domestic interior that Hoggart described in *The Uses of Literacy* and the great monolithic industries (coal, steel, textiles) that gave birth to such a culture. But even Elizabeth Roberts's informants, speaking from the heartland of industrial Lancashire and remembering the period 1890–1940, never recall purchasing ready-cuts for the peg rugs they made. Rather, they remember cutting up 'old coats, they were kept specially'.[8]

We should return to the economy that Mayhew described, built on the scavenging, exchange and trading of tiny things. The rag rug has to do more than anything else, perhaps, with the second-hand clothing market, that half-hidden motor of an industrial economy that Beverly Lemire has described as a:

> well-established, organised system of redistribution, founded on the demand of those in more straightened circumstances ... The identification of the characteristics of this second tier of demand are crucial for an understanding of the British home market in the eighteenth century. (1991: 61–76, 62)

In the eighteenth century the second-hand trade in clothes was 'a key intermediate trade' for those in 'straightened circumstances' and for anyone who wanted to raise a bit of ready money. By the nineteenth century and the period of *Mary Barton*, it was the consumer economy of the poor and very poor, who – perhaps – found a domestic use for the final tatters of the seventh-hand shirts and shifts in which they clothed themselves, though it does seem that up until the 1870s even a small quantity of rags was worth more on the open market to the vendor than the value of a painstakingly-made floor covering could have been. Offering advice to the United States on the making of hooked rugs as part of a programme of national regeneration through handicrafts, the American Ivan Crowell suggested that 'roughly a square yard of worn clothing will make a square foot of hooked rug' (Crowell, 1945: 7). The value of even a tiny quantity of rags was one of the messages of Mrs Paull's *Romance of a Rag* (1876: 68).

We could suggest, then, that the rag rug has its origins in the metropolis or, more widely, in centres of commerce, trade and distribution older than Manchester, where the trade in second-hand clothing first established itself: South, not North. Any maybe we shouldn't be looking at the (absent) rag rug *at all*, but rather at what is actually *there* in the parlour of Gaskell's dream, which is that 'gay-coloured piece of oil-cloth' (49). This is the badge of the Barton's modernity; it symbolises the fact that they are doing quite nicely and suggests that their neat house-place does not have a broken, uneven, cracked brick floor that would need the soft contours of the rug, but rather that it is well made-up, even and smooth, able to take the relative stiffness of canvas coated with oil-based paint (Temple Newsam House, 1987: 101–11). Nor was oil-cloth particularly cheap and its maintenance demanded a well-ordered domesticity (Calder, 1977: 88–9; Temple Newsam House, 1987: 110–11).

And beyond even this – the absent rag rug, the present oil-cloth – is the question of whether this is the thing to start or end with at all. This room, this space is Gaskell's dream after all: her fiction. We should note the particularities of her interior, the glowing enchantment of its surfaces, textures and details and then pay attention to what she said of its origins and of the novel as a whole. She was one of the first voluntary district visitors of the Manchester and Salford District Provident Society and after the publication of her novel, told a fellow worker that:

> The one strong impulse to write 'Mary Barton' came to her one evening in a labourer's cottage. She was trying hard to speak comfort and to allay those bitter feelings against the rich that were so common with the poor, when the head of the family took hold of her arm and grasping it tightly said, with tears in his eyes: "Ay, ma'am, but have ye ever seen a child clemmed to death?" (Sharps, 1970: 56)

She probably started to write in the last months of 1845 at the suggestion of her husband, 'to divert her mind from the morbid thoughts which [then] assailed her', for she had lost her little boy Willie, just ten months old, in August that year (Sharps, 1970: 52; Uglow, 1993: 152–5). She asserted that it was John Barton's tragedy rather than the love interest and melodrama provided by his daughter's tale that should be read as the centre of the novel (Sharps, 1970: 57–9). Barton's story inscribes a tragedy and he is one of the few working-class tragic heroes in the literature because he is Elizabeth Gaskell's story, her dream and her compensation. What she took away from the labourer's cottage in which she tried to speak comfort was herself and a new way of understanding her own story, of parenthood, love and loss.[9]

What had she just said to the man who responded (in the moment when the story is born) '"Ay, ma'am but have ye ever seen a child clemmed to death?"' – Surely not that she had recently lost a child? The etiquette of talking to the poor – the nice reticence about one's own, always more comfortable, sorrows – was surely exercised here. There is certainly nothing in her correspondence or other personal writing to suggest that she ever – could ever have – behaved in such a boorish and thoughtless way. More likely she had said something general, as she would in *Mary Barton*, that the trials of the well-to-do are as great as those of the poor and, as Mr Carson has it rather more specifically right at the end of the novel, when he exclaims:

> How in the world can we help it? We cannot regulate the demand for labour. No man or set of men can do it. It depends on events which God alone can control. When there is no market for goods, we suffer just as you can do. (456)

But the separation between Gaskell and her interlocutor and between her and her invention John Barton proved (to use W. H. Auden's formulation) 'a being bad'. The hand pressed on another in sympathy, eyes and hearts meeting across the wastes of class relations, are acknowledgement of that separation.

The things in the little room of Gaskell's imagination have surface and depth only out of her longing. But they keep their shape, which is the shape of *what they are*, no matter who imagines them, because they are things with histories of their making, purchase, consumption and, in the Barton case, as tragedy tightens its grip and the household goods are sold one by one, their dispersal. And the systems of Cottonopolis – economic and social – stretching far beyond its boundaries into the great world of trade and commerce, colonialism and slavery and all the human relationships made and sustained out of those systems, are what make the separation that the novelist strives to dissolve but that remains in place, between Gaskell and her dream, between Gaskell and the labourer who gripped her arm, between John Barton and the Manchester masters who are to blame for it all.

Auden's deliberate phonemic ambiguity, in the verse used as epigraph to this essay, will tell us as much. Are these objects, things that shed no tears, or things untorn? In the case of this particular object, there is no doubt, for what makes up the rag rug that isn't there is – rags. The pieces of cloth are torn and they make up the rug that cannot to its own edges keep: it intrudes in the dream of the novelist, the dream of the historian, the dreams of all the sympathetic visitors to those heart-wrenching rooms on the other side of the border. It is the object that mediates and that promises the capacity to see what is oneself and what is not oneself but that, unlike the 'blankets, rags and other soft objects' of the object relations theory poeticised by Auden, cannot allow a final disengagement from itself (Davis and Wallbridge, 1983: 69–72; Winnicott, 1974: 1–30). The rag rug is the truth of the novel, the history it cannot escape, and its tragedy.

'The Paper Makers' Grievance' of 1863, expressed in their campaign against the taxes on rags, outlined a grand system of the world in which the waste of an industrial civilisation was caught in the same great cycle as cultural production: 'Civilisation invents various and abundant clothing – the wear of clothing terminates in the production of rags – Rags are transmuted into Paper – Paper supplies the incessant Press and the various activities of the Press sustain and extend Civilisation.' This was a congratulatory description, for was it not the case that where 'society is most civilised there will be most Rags for the Paper Maker and most demand for his paper … the Continent makes more Rags than it makes Paper … England makes proportionately much more Paper than the Continent, and does not get enough of its own Rags' (Rag Tax, 1863: 5)?

But there should be no self-congratulation for the historian reading the nineteenth-century domestic space and making the mistake of carpeting it with a rug that in fact couldn't be made in an economy where such a tiny number of things circulated again and again among so many people; where scarcity and technological underdevelopment created a shortage, not of the poor, but of the traditional symbols of the poor – their rags; and where even a handful of tattered clothing was worth a trip to the rag merchant, reckoned as it was until the late nineteenth century, as half a loaf of bread.

Notes

1 References in the text are to the 1970 Penguin edition.

2 In the Barton parlour, Elizabeth Gaskell has Alice Wilson note the same 'com-

fortable sounds of a boiling kettle and the hissing, fizzling ham' (53).

3 For the strange dislocations of perspective that come from Mayhew's classificatory and statistical obsessions, see Himmelfarb, 1984, 312–54.

4 The other entrances to working-class interiors in *Mary Barton* are managed by Gaskell in the way Corbin describes but, in the case of Alice Wilson's cellar ('perfection of cleanliness') and that of the destitute Davenports, there is practically nothing (mouldy straw and one chair) to arrange in the mind's eye, certainly no disordered jumble as in Corbin's. The interiors are sparse, to show two varieties of poverty (51–2, 97–105).

5 'La conscience – celle de l'écrivain, celle du lecteur – peut-elle sincèrement etre en acte à l'origine même de telles images?' (Bachelard, 1957: 40). This should surely be translated as 'consciousness'.

6 'By the late seventeenth century, cotton was commonly found in the humblest peddlers' packs and its place as a cheap alternative to linen was firmly established' Levitt, 1996: 155. Levitt cites Margaret Spufford, *The Great Reclothing of Rural England: Petty Chapmen and their Wares in Seventeenth-Century* England (London, Hambledon), 1984, 92.

7 The wartime injunction to Make Do And Mend gave some impetus to a history of the rag rug, but its most thorough treatment was in the American folklore movement of the early twentieth century. Here the rag rug was given the most diverse and spectacular of world histories: attributed to Vikings, belonging 'absolutely to America, none ever having been found in the Old World', `wrapped in a veil of mystery' and – in one account – with the power to dispel 'Chaos' and bring about its 'antonym, order, Heaven's primary law' (Crowell, 1945: 1; Foley and Waugh, 1927: 4; Phillips, 1925: 9. See also Bowles, 1927; Miall, 1938; Hawker-Smith, 1940).

8 Agnes (Kate Walker's mother) remembered – presumably of the 1930s – that worn 'outer garments went into the rugs, the underwear was used as cleaning rags and the woollens were unpicked and knitted up again' (Walker, 1987: 28).

9 John Hawley points out that, on questions of political economy, class consciousness and working-class political activism '*Mary Barton* may well have been written to console, not the workers, but the middle classes from which Gaskell came' (1989: 23–30, 28).

Bibliography

Armstrong, F. (1990), 'Gender and miniaturization: games of littleness in nineteenth-century fiction', *English Studies in Canada,* 16, 403–16.

Auden, W. H. (1966), *Collected Shorter Poems, 1927–1957*, London, Faber.

Bachelard, G. (1957), *La Poétique de l'éspace*, Paris, Presses Universitaires de France.

Bachelard, G. [1958](1994), *The Poetics of Space*, trans. M. Jolas, Boston, Beacon.

Baines, E. [1835] (1966), *History of the Cotton Manufacture in Great Britain*, London, Cass.

Bowles, E. S. (1927), *Handmade Rugs*, Boston, Little Brown.

British Parliamentary Papers (1854), Copy of the correspondence between the Departments of the Treasury and Board of Trade, in regard to the Scarcity of Materials in the Fabrication of Paper'; and 'An Account of the Total Quantity of

Rags Imported into the United Kingdom and the Total Quantity Exported from the United Kingdom, in each Year, from 1801–1853 inclusive', 65, 491–5, 505.
Burnett, F. H. (1893), *The One I Knew Best of All,* London, Frederick Warne.
Burnett, J. (1978), *A Social History of Housing 1815–1970*, Newton Abbot, David and Charles.
Calder, J. (1977), *The Victorian Home*, London, Batsford.
Coleman, D. C. (1958), *The British Paper Industry 1495–1860: A Study in Industrial Growth*, Oxford, Clarendon Press.
Corbin, A. (1986), *The Foul and the Fragrant: Odor and the French Social Imagination*, Leamington Spa, Berg.
Crowell, I. (1945), *Design and Hook Your Own Rugs*, New York, Macmillan.
Davis, M. and Wallbridge, D. (1983), *Boundary and Space: An Introduction to the Work of D. W. Winnicott*, Harmondsworth, Penguin.
Ellison, T. [1886] (1968), *The Cotton Trade of Great Britain* , London, Cass.
Eyles, M. L. (1922), *The Woman in the Little House*, London, Grant Richards.
Farnie, D. A. (1979), *The English Cotton Industry and the World Market*, Oxford, Clarendon Press.
Foley, E. and Waugh, E. (1927), *Collecting Hooked Rugs*, New York, Century.
Frykstedt, M. C. (1980), 'Mary Barton and the Reports of the Ministry to the Poor: A new source', *Studia Neophilologica*, 52, 333–6.
Gaskell, E. [1848](1970), *Mary Barton: A Tale of Manchester Life*, Harmondsworth, Penguin.
Gauldie, E. (1974), *Cruel Habitations: A History of Working-Class Housing 1780–1918*, London, Allen and Unwin.
Hawker-Smith, B. (1940), *Thrifty Rug Making: Including Surrey Stitch Rugs. With a Foreword by Lady Dowson*, London, Pitman.
Hawley, J. C. (1989), '*Mary Barton*: the view from without', *Nineteenth-Century Studies*, 3, 23–30.
Himmelfarb, G. (1984), *The Idea of Poverty: England in the Early Industrial Age*, London, Faber.
Hobsbawm, E., [1979, 1981](1984), *Worlds of Labour: Further Studies in the History of Labour*, London, Weidenfeld and Nicholson.
Hoggart, R. [1957] (1958), *The Uses of Literacy*, Harmondsworth, Penguin.
Kahler, E. (1971), *The Inward Turn of Narrative*, Princeton, Princeton University Press.
Lemire, B. (1991), *Fashion's Favourite: The Cotton Trade and the Consumer in Britain 1660–1800*, Oxford, Oxford University Press.
Lévi-Strauss, C. (1966), *The Savage Mind*, London, Weidenfeld and Nicholson.
Levitt, S. (1996), 'Clothing', in M. B. Rose (ed.), *The Lancashire Cotton Industry: A History since 1700*, Preston, Lancashire County Books.
Liebs, E. (1988) 'Between *Gulliver* and *Alice*: some remarks on the dialectic of GREAT and SMALL in literature', *Phaedrus*, 13, 56–60.
McMillan, M. (1919), *The Nursery School*, London, Dent.
Mayhew, H. (1851), *London Labour and the London Poor,* London, George Woodfall.
Miall, A. (1938), *Make Your Own Rugs*, London, Woman's Magazine Handbooks, 4.
Millhauser, S. (1983), 'The fascination of the miniature', *Grand Street*, 2, 128–35.
Mitchell, B. R. and Deane, P. (1962), *Abstract of British Historical Statistics*, Cam-

bridge, Cambridge University Press.

Paull, M. A. (1876), *The Romance of a Rag and Other Tales*, London, Kempster.

Phillips, M. L. (1925), *Hooked Rugs and How to Make Them*, New York, Macmillan.

Rag Tax (1863), *The Rag Tax: The Paper Makers' Grievance and How to Redress It, for Private Circulation*, London, privately printed.

Roberts, E. (1984), *A Woman's Place: An Oral History of Working-class Women 1890–1940*, Oxford, Blackwell.

Rose, M. B. (ed.) (1996), *The Lancashire Cotton Industry: A History since 1700*, Preston, Lancashire County Books.

Rubinstein, D. (1974), *Victorian Homes*, Newton Abbot, David and Charles.

Sewell, M. (1861), *Our Father's Care: A Ballad*, London, Jarrold.

Sharps, J. G. (1970), *Mrs Gaskell's Observation and Invention: A Study of Her Non-Biographic Works*, Fontwell, Linden Press.

Shipley Art Gallery (1988), *Ragtime: Rugs and Wallhangings*, Tyne and Wear Museums Service.

Steedman, C. (1992), *Past Tenses: Essays on Writing, Autobiography and History*, London, Rivers Oram.

Steedman, C. (1995), 'Inside, outside, other', *History of the Human Sciences*, 8:4, 59–76.

Steedman, C. (forthcoming), 'Modernity's suffering self: other people's stories', in T. Blowers (ed.), *Autobiography: Strategies for Survival*.

Stewart, S. (1993), *On Longing: Narratives of the Miniature, the Gigantic, the Souvenir, the Collection*, Durham, North Carolina, Duke University Press.

Temple Newsam House (1987), *Country House Floors*, Leeds, Leeds City Art Galleries.

Thornton, R. and Sons (Dewsbury) Ltd (1960), *A Story of Woollen Rag Sales 1860–1960*, London, Harley, 1960.

The Times (1799), 'High price of paper, on account of the scarcity of rags', 17 December.

The Times (1860), 'The budget and free trade in rags', 20 February.

The Times (1860), 'Meeting of paper manufacturers to consider export duties on foreign rags, 22 March.

The Times (1860), 'Rags from India', 'Importation of Foreign Rags', 26 March.

The Times (1863), 'Machine to render old cotton rags fit for spinning', 27 April.

The Times (1865), 'M. Canrinade's substitute for rags in making paper', 10 October.

Uglow, J. (1993), *Elizabeth Gaskell: A Habit of Stories*, London, Faber.

Walker, A. and Walker, K. (1987), 'Starting with rag rugs: the aesthetics of survival', in G. Elinor, *et al*. (eds), *Women and Craft*, London, Virago.

Winnicott, D. W. (1974), 'Transitional objects and transitional phenomena', in *Playing and Reality*, Harmondsworth, Penguin.

Young, A. (1770), *A Six Months Tour Through the North of England*, 4 vols, London, W. Strahan.

Bodies and mirrors: the childhood interiors of Ruskin, Pater and Stevenson

Ann C. Colley

Years after they had left their childhood behind them, John Ruskin, Walter Horatio Pater and Robert Louis Stevenson continued to reflect upon the homes in which they had passed their early lives. In particular they thought about the rooms of their childhood. When they described these spaces, they did not simply re-present the contours and things that had composed the drawing-room of 28 Herne Hill in London, the interiors of the house in Enfield or the day nursery and bedrooms of 17 Heriot Row in Edinburgh. Instead, they considered how their physical being had related to the walls and windows of childhood.[1] Conscious of how this relationship defines the sense of one's surroundings, they let their memories resuscitate the dialogue their bodies had once had with these interiors. They understood that it is the child's being that shapes and illuminates the interiors of home. Articles do not define interiors; bodies that move and feel their way among these objects do.

Three models of interiority

Although Ruskin, Pater and Stevenson are all sensitive to the defining function of the body, each, not surprisingly, experiences the phenomenon in a different way. The result is that their autobiographical texts (*Praeterita,* 1885; 'The Child in the House', 1878; *A Child's Garden of Verses, 1885*) offer three distinct models of how the consciousness of one's physical being illuminates the interiors of home. Ruskin's text speaks of the invisible body, Pater's of the aesthetic body and Stevenson's of the ubiquitous body.

The first model is Ruskin's. In his often grumbling, yet graceful, autobiography Ruskin describes the houses of his childhood: he writes briefly about 54 Hunter Street (London) and more extensively about the house at Herne Hill (four miles south of London). With a keen immediacy he describes the commanding views from their garret windows, the front and back gardens and the setting of the Herne Hill residence. But with their emphasis on 'prospect', these passages do not represent Ruskin's experience of the interiors of home, for they belong more to the public Ruskin, the figure whose carefully selected words guided the British around Venice and directed readers' eyes to a more 'truthful' view of the Alps. Instead, the sections in *Praeterita* that reveal more intimate moments are those in which he once more steps inside his childhood surroundings and considers his relationship to them. No longer preoccupied by how a shadow falls on a cathedral's tracery or by the continuity of a building's structural lines, he dwells upon a few intimate moments of home and recalls how he had passed his days 'contentedly' inside rooms, comparing the colours in the carpet or gazing at the patterns in the bed covers. He remembers how he had once stood by the windows watching a wasp on the window-pane or repeatedly looking at the iron post out of which the water carts were filled ([1885] 1989: 12, 34, 7).

Paradoxically, in all these intimate spaces of home the presence of the body is virtually absent. In *Praeterita* Ruskin makes it clear that he had not occupied these comfortable recesses and corners with the fullness of his physical being but rather as an almost invisible entity. As if replacing metaphor with synecdoche, Ruskin describes his younger self by focusing exclusively upon his eyes that reach out as far as they can and leave the rest of his body behind, unobserved and unmolested. Throughout his work, the eyes replace the physical body by standing in for it.[2] To observe was enough. Ruskin moved through the rooms and interiors of home as inside a frame supporting a glass that hides the body in its dimness while allowing the eyes to peer through its dusk. When he sat observing, his eyes wandered into the patterns of the floors and walls; he travelled within the portchaise and stared out of its window; setting out on holidays, he took his position on a 'little box' between his mother and father and enjoyed the prospect appearing piece by piece before him (23). Disappearing into the supporting brackets, his body released his eyes and gave him the freedom to stare, unnoticed, in 'rapturous and riveted' attention (50). This granted him a protective invisibility that allowed him to observe without being engaged by anything other than himself. He existed as the spectator, not as the observed. Later in life he was always to value those moments when he could take note of his surroundings away from people's sight and consciousness. For instance, in 1842, alone in Champagnole, Ruskin recalls that his 'entire delight was in observing' without himself being 'noticed' (155–6). Part of Ruskin's nostalgia for his childhood is to return to the monastic invisibility that allowed him the privacy of his visual ecstasy.

Pater's rendering of his childhood experiences in the semi-autobiographical portrait 'The Child in the House' ([1878] 1986) is naturally different from Ruskin's. Although Pater's interiors, like Ruskin's, radiate an almost monastic aura, they by no means resemble Ruskin's, for the body that inhabits and forms them has a distinctly different effect. It is a sensuous presence. And although for Pater the visual experiences are just as essential as they are for Ruskin, these visual moments are not detached or bodiless. They emerge from and return to a body through which images move along the nerves and bring vitality to his being. In Pater's interiors, therefore, the child's body is just as significant as it is in Ruskin's, but not because of its inquisitive invisibility; it is conspicuous because of its willingness to be affected by what lies outside of it. Here the haptic and the visual conjoin to create an impressionistic body.

When Pater portrays Florian Deleal, the young boy in 'The Child in the House', he dwells upon the boy's willing, though sometimes unconscious, acceptance of the visible, the tangible and the audible encircling him. Within, the winds from outside the house play on him and through the open windows the coming and going of travellers, the shadows of evening, the brightness of day, the perfumes from the neighbouring garden and the scent of the lime tree blossoms awaken his senses. The sensitive boy looks at the fallen acorn and the black crow's feathers that his sister has brought in from 'some distant forest' and discovers intimations of places beyond – these 'treasures' speak the 'rumour of its [the wood's] breezes, with the glossy blackbirds aslant and the branches lifted in them' (229).

The outside and the inside come together in his body that risks being wounded by the tyranny of the senses and the surrendering of its boundaries – something the sheltered Ruskin could not expose himself to. From over the high garden wall, sentiments of beauty and pain float into Florian's consciousness and penetrate what Pater calls the 'actual body' (232); the cry of his aunt on the stair when she announces his father's death strikes and quickens him; the wasp in the basket of yellow crab-apples stings him (Ruskin, recall, only watched the wasp at his window.) The receptive Florian listens to the voices of people below speaking of the sick woman who 'had seen one of the dead sitting beside her' and then brings the ghostly figure into his own space so that the *revenant* sits 'beside him in the reveries of his broken sleep' (234). Similarly he goes outside so that he may bring what is there inside. He passes through the garden gate, fills his arms with red hawthorn blossoms (the scent of which has already reached him) and returns to arrange these brilliant flowers in 'old blue china pots along the chimney piece' (231).

Later, in two other imaginary and semi-autobiographical portraits, 'Emerald Uthwart' ([1892] 1986) and *Marius the Epicurean* ([1885] 1986), Pater echoes many of the details describing Florian's experiences within his home. In these texts the children breathe, feel, touch, move and see with their bodies as Florian does. No eye, as in Ruskin's case, leaves the body to reside in the half-concealed recesses of a drawing-room. The young and solitary Emerald is a child who, within the context of home, responds to the sights and sounds surrounding him – to the 'rippling note of the birds' and to the flowers in the garden that yield a sweetness when the 'loosening wind' unsettles them (344). When flung open, the windows in the attic where he sleeps admit the scent of roses, and the faint sea-salt air envelops him as he sleeps under 'the fine old blankets' (345). Similarly, the child Marius in the solitude of his early dwelling feels the sea wind that blows from the distant harbour, inhales the scent of the new-mown hay that the sea air sweeps into his room and takes pleasure in the view of the purple heath.

The affect of these children's sensuous bodies and consciousness is complemented by the interiors of home. Like Florian, who sees and touches what is outside the boundaries of his body, these interiors, as if they were bodies themselves, extend and incorporate what is beyond them – what is outside the windows or the enclosing walls. These interiors do not shut themselves off; they resist exclusiveness. Like a shuttle in a loom they move continuously inside and out of each other. In Florian's childhood home, for instance, the staircase moves the reader from floor to floor and up to a broad window, out to the swallow's nest that hangs beneath the sill and then back down into the house and out again on to the open, flat space of a roof that offers a view of the neighbouring steeples. Interiors and exteriors mingle. They pass through the intermediary spaces – the windows and gates left ajar – to meet and lie over and press against each other. In this manner the child's body and the rooms of home engage in an exchange. In a sense, each passes into the condition of the other.

The rooms of Stevenson's childhood reveal a third possibility, another way the body's effect converses with and gives shape to its surroundings. This time, though, it is neither Ruskin's curious invisibility nor Pater's receptive body that defines or intermingles with the interior;

instead, it is the moat of sickness encircling the child's body that structures the spaces of home and creates the sense of the ubiquitous body.

Stevenson, who began writing his childhood poems during a particularly difficult time with his health, returns to those interior spaces in *A Child's Garden of Verses* ([1885] 1969). He re-enters the rooms that recall the fevers, the severe bronchial infections, the earaches and, eventually, the haemorrhaging that from the age of two kept him for long periods in bed. Confined, the young Stevenson periodically missed school and passed his days 'exiled' from the company of other children. As his biographers have pointed out, Stevenson never forgot what he called the 'terrible long nights' through which he lay awake, in his words, 'troubled continuously by a hacking, exhausting cough, and praying for sleep or morning from the bottom of my shaken little body' (Daiches, 1973: 10).[3]

The interiors described in *A Child's Garden of Verses* recall the scenes of Stevenson's early confinement. The poems take place in the night nursery; they inhabit the land of the counterpane; they climb the stairs; they go into the walled garden and they look through the broad window of 17 Heriot Row. In a sense, each verse is a room shaped by the sick body's desire to escape from itself. The poems and the spaces they describe offer release from the enclosures of the body's frailty. Like the children in one of the verses, who break through a breach in the wall and go down to the mill ('Keepsake Mill'), or like the river that flows 'out past the mill, / Away down the valley, / Away down the hill' ('Where Go the Boats?'), out 'A hundred miles or more' into foreign lands – to Babylon, Malabar, Africa and Providence ('Pirate Story') – and like the swing that takes the child up high so he can look over the garden wall and 'see so wide' ('The Swing'), these poems reach beyond to places afar; they break through their limits and climb the cherry tree to look abroad ('Foreign Lands') (36, 28, 57).

In these poems the interiors of home do not isolate the convalescing child. Through his desire to be rid of what threatens to exile him, the ailing child shapes the rooms and enclosed gardens so that they carry him to places beyond. The young Stevenson convincingly substitutes one object for another; he transforms the chair, the stairs, the bedclothes, the windows and the flickering of the coals' embers into vessels of escape. The bedroom chairs stuffed with pillows become ships; a basket in the sun turns into a pirate's boat; the counterpane assumes its own topography of hills, dales and plains and the sheets merge into seas. These interiors liberate the sick body from itself.

Most of all, though, the desire of the sick child to find release from himself creates situations in which the child identifies with other children and, in that way, becomes part of a ubiquitous body so that he can for a while be less alone, excluded and strange. Within these rooms is a larger landscape that collapses the distant into the contiguous and, simultaneously, expands the immediate into the distant. The child senses, although he cannot see them, the presence of other children whose activities are similar to his. These children may live away in the far East or in the West beyond the foam of the Atlantic Sea ('The Sun Travels') and they may eat 'curious' food rather than 'proper meat' ('Foreign Children'); nevertheless, the sick child senses that they share a common physical rhythm: all 'dine at five' ('Foreign Lands'); like him, but in an inverted pattern, they go to bed and at dawn they awake and dress ('The Sun Travels') (29). These parallels form the larger, more inclusive body so that all children, even when confined and alone, belong to an unseen, unconscious, yet animated intertextuality of being that is theirs. Just as the sickly Stevenson once looked out of the nursery window, through the darkness of the night, to see the lit windows where other sick 'little boys' were also waiting for the morning, the child in the verses finds comfort in inclusiveness (Daiches, 1973: 10–11). He knows there are others ready to receive and understand him, so that, for instance, when he launches his boats, he is aware that children 'A hundred miles or more' away will bring them into shore ('Where Go the Boats?') (Stevenson, [1885] 1969: 36).

Because of this sense of ubiquitousness, the potentially lonely and isolated 'I' of the poems' interiors frequently joins the more inclusive 'We'. In 'A Good Play', 'Pirate Story', 'Farewell to the Farm', 'Marching Song', 'Happy Thought', 'The Sun Travels', 'The Lamplighter', 'My Bed is a Boat', 'Keepsake Mill' and 'Picture-Books in Winter', the child attaches his being to others so that 'we' are afloat, 'we' swing upon the gate, 'we' march, 'we should all be as happy as kings', 'we' play round the sunny gardens, 'we' are very lucky and 'we' see how all things are. It is, of course, this metamorphosis that empowers the child in *A Child's Garden of Verses*. Like the shadow that follows or jumps ahead of the child, his sick body is almost always a silent, threatening presence among the verses' lines. Yet, within the context of the poems' transfigured interiors, the child is able to reach beyond himself and connect with others and join the ubiquitous body of childhood. Through play and fantasy, the child alters the rooms of home and releases the suffering 'I' from the fragility of itself and thus realises the possibilities of a more encompassing and restorative 'we'. Stevenson's child, in a sense, brings to life one of the most vital experiences of interiority – the understanding that an interior does not exist for its own sake but, instead, for the desire of reaching something or going somewhere.[4]

Rooms without mirrors

In all these models of interiority, many of the familiar 'landmarks' of the inside are visible: the windows, the doors, the staircases and the fireplaces. In none, though, is there the usual mirror – an absence that is significant, since mirrors and looking-glasses were considered an important fixture in the Victorian household. Continuing the eighteenth-century interest in mirrors as both essential and decorative household furnishings, English designers and manufacturers in the nineteenth century developed them for the home market and abroad. Consequently, in upper-class and middle-class homes mirrors hung above fireplaces, pier-glasses and oval mirrors in decorative frames took their place among pictures on the wall, mirror wardrobes and English cheval glasses stood in people's dressing-rooms, and convex mirrors that had become universally fashionable served as useful and ornamental items of furniture. If one looks, for instance, at photographs of Stevenson's childhood home in Edinburgh, or if one opens the pages of his *Dr Jekyll and Mr Hyde* (1886), one cannot help but notice the looking-glass: the large mirror in the drawing-room and the cheval glass in Dr Jekyll's study. And if one peruses Victorian paintings of nineteenth-century interiors, one's eye cannot ignore the mirror. Depictions of interiors such as Joseph Clarke's *The Labourer's Welcome* (n.d.), William Powell Frith's series concerning *The Road to Ruin* (1887), Frederick Daniel Hardy's *The Young Photographers* (1863), George Goodwin Kilburne's *Poor Relations* (1875), Sir William Quillar Orchardson's *The First Cloud* (1887) and *Mariage de Convenance* (1886), Walter Dendy Sadler's *Sweethearts* (1892) and Joseph Jacques Tissot's society paintings expose the significant presence of the looking-glass within the homes of the upper and middle classes and, to a lesser degree, in the working-class cottages. In these works, both elaborate and modest mirrors stand on dressing-tables and hang above the mantelpiece or from a wall.

However, unlike these paintings that draw attention to the mirror, Ruskin's, Pater's and Stevenson's depictions of their early homes ignore the mirror's existence. The mirror's reflecting and revealing eye is notably absent, for the child in their texts does not require its integrating attendance – its way of 'digesting' and making complete the area and contents of a room, its way of bringing interiors and exteriors together.

For example, in Clarke's *The Labourer's Welcome*, the small mirror hanging among the pictures reflects and frames the image of the returning husband as he walks through the cottage door. In this way the mirror mingles what is out of view – the exterior – with what is directly before the viewer's eyes inside the cottage. In addition, from these writers' perspective, the child has no need of the mirror's deflecting, interrupting images that comment upon the presence of something other than what is in view. And, most important, neither does the child require the mirror suspended above a mantelpiece or the looking-glass hung inside its gilded frame to affirm his sense of belonging – to feel his own materiality. The body and the interior it defines and inhabits exist without the confirmation of the mirror. The looking-glass world is irrelevant. The child does not need to see its image in the mirror to gain a sense of its totality, to understand, rightly or wrongly, a feeling of coherence or to develop a sense of self that distinguishes it from others.[5]

For these reasons the confirming, surveying and integrating mirror is not a focal point in these autobiographical texts, as it is in August Leopold Egg's *Past and Present I* (1858), Charles Hunt's *My 'Macbeth'* (1863), or Frederick Daniel Hardy's *Playing at Doctors* (1863). In these paintings the mirror, placed dead centre, reveals how the various subjects relate to their interiors, to the outside and to each other. The grand mirror in *My 'Macbeth'*, for instance, radiates like a halo around the artist, confirming and enclosing his success. The small convex mirror in *Playing at Doctors* parallels the family's benevolence and with that the experience of belonging and inclusion. It overlooks the temporary untidiness of the children's play and in doing so emphasises the unruffled security of home. The convex mirror in this painting is of the kind that was extremely popular in Victorian households. With its gilt cavetto moulding studded with balls surmounted by an eagle displayed with a gilt ball suspended from its beak, the mirror's frame would have been familiar to the viewers.[6] And, of course, in *Past and Present I,* the mirror simultaneously unfolds the past and the future. Within its rococo frame, the glass not only reveals what has been, but also shows what is to be. Its reflected images lead to the open door and to emptiness – to a space devoid of objects and the security of home. Caught in adultery, the 'fallen' wife lies prostrate outside the mirror's surveillance, exiled from its field of vision and soon to be ostracised from her husband's society and the household in which the mirror hangs. Significantly, once she is exiled from home, no mirror confirms her space. In the immediate sequence to the first painting, *Past and Present II*, the mirror is darkened and in the last of the series, *Past and*

Present III, of course no mirror appears, for the wife no longer has a room to be in.

The childhood interiors of Ruskin, Pater and Stevenson exclude the mirror because it is not needed either to confirm or to exile those who inhabit what would have been caught in its field of reflection. The child in these interiors does not make a spectacle of the self – the self is not something to be seen. The disembodied, 'invisible' Ruskin, for example, is not something to be looked at. On the contrary, as pointed out earlier, he is the one who does the looking. His eye, not the mirror's, is the mediator, the interpreter, the surveyor. Ruskin's child does not engage reflection; instead, with his own eye, the 'true eye', he looks down into what lies before his field of vision and absorbs the world through sight (Emerson, 1993: 89). Indeed, he overlooks the reflected image. For instance, when the young Ruskin watches his father shave, he observes his actual father and ignores the image in the shaving mirror that must have been there. He moves his attention instead from his father to the watercolour drawing that hangs above the dressing-table and waits for his father to tell stories about the picture's subject. He does not let the mirror trip him. Ruskin describes the moment:

> I was particularly fond of watching him shave; and was always allowed to come into his room in the morning (under the one in which I am now writing), to be the motionless witness of that operation. Over his dressing-table hung one of his own water-colour drawings ... It represented Conway Castle, with its Frith and, in the foreground, a cottage, a fisherman and a boat at the water's edge. When my father had finished shaving, he always told me a story about this picture ([1885] 1989: 28–9).

The reflected image promises no narrative to the curious child.

In his adolescent poetry and prose of the 1830s, Ruskin did occasionally speak of reflection; however, it is either to disparage the mirror or to engage a form of seeing that the ordinary mirror – the one that hangs in a room – does not permit. For instance, in 1837, when Ruskin was in residence at Christ Church, Oxford, and suffering from Adèle-Clotilde's refusal to return his affection, he wrote a poem he entitled 'The Mirror' (1837). In the poem Ruskin speaks of the mirror's inability to include her 'loveliness' within its frame. He himself plays no part on its reflecting surface. He stands outside as the spectator-surveyor who passes judgement on the looking-glass and finds it guilty of inconstancy for, unlike him, it has no memory with which to retain the 'living vision' of her beauty (Cook and Wedderburn, 1903, 2: 20). Its reflection is merely transitory.

Other poems, such as 'On Skiddaw and Derwent Water' (1830) and a passage from *The Poetry of Architecture* (1838), also speak of reflection. In these texts lakes and small bodies of water become looking-glasses through which to view the landscape. These are not the Claude glass – the tinted convex mirrors carried by picturesque tourists – for when Ruskin looks into the water's reflection, he does not limit himself to what images the surface reveals, nor does he turn his back (as was the practice of those holding the Claude glass) on what he is staring into. Instead, especially in *The Poetry of Architecture*, he lets the images reflected in the water draw his eye down to what is underneath and fall unfathomably into 'the blue sky' (Cook and Wedderburn, 1903, 2: 90). In a sense, this natural mirror creates an illusion; it draws the eye inside and, with it, Ruskin's being; it does not leave his body standing, separated and gazing. The image is no longer a reflected one. Ruskin quickly bypasses that more superficial state so that his eye may actually enter the landscape and be a part of its immediacy. So intent is Ruskin to rid himself of the idea of 'mirror', in fact, that in the passage from *The Poetry of Architecture*, he instructs his reader to eradicate the 'edge' of the water – to keep it out of sight. Ruskin does not want to think of the conventional mirror; at this moment he does not desire a framed reflection.

Pater's Florian also inhabits a non-reflecting space. He is neither a spectacle to be looked at nor a participant in a world that makes a spectacle of what is in it. He knows images not through their reflection but by the way the visual experiences interpenetrate with his body. The image for Pater's child, therefore, is not so much to be seen as it is to be felt. It does not dwell exclusively outside of his body merely to be observed, for, almost compulsively, the child opens his arms to gather, to hold and to take in to himself what he sees. Like the young Florian who collects the hawthorn blossoms, the child brings these images close to his body. When he touches their brilliance, he transforms what before was a purely visual moment into a haptic experience, the sensations of which work their way into the nature of his being.

Stevenson's child displays yet another form of the unreflected image. His young boy looks out; others do not look back at him. He is not a spectacle (the lamplighter goes about his rounds and ignores the child standing at the window). In addition, he is a child who resides somewhere beyond the conventional visual field. In the half-light of his evenings, in the darkness of his nights and in the metamorphic fantasies of his play, the reflecting images of mirrors are irrelevant. Shadows overwhelm them and so does a circumference of experience and distance too large for the confining, duplicating arena of the looking-glass. Even when the young boy, in *A Child's Garden of Verses*, looks down into the 'Looking-Glass River', it is not his disappearing reflection in the darkening water that arrests him. When the ripples disturb the smooth surface and the water turns black, the child does not bemoan the loss of his image; instead, he laments the slipping away of an opportunity to see down into the river's depths and imagine himself there, united with its mysteries. He desires to look through, not into, the looking-glass, to engage the less visible. He wants to see – and be – beyond what is given.

Because of their disregard for the conventionally reflected image, these children do not participate in the mirror's community that necessarily separates the self from itself and imposes a moment of estrangement or divergence – what is commonly called 'otherness'. In Ruskin's, Pater's and Stevenson's texts, the child communes primarily with himself. Whatever 'otherness' exists, whether in the form of a mirror image or in the form of other people, does not take him away from himself nor cause him to question his identity. On the contrary, the child and his body are connected in various ways to each other and to what surrounds them. Stevenson's child might for a minute feel isolated and want Leerie, the lamplighter, to pause and look at him standing in the window, but on the whole he, like Ruskin's and Pater's child, lives in the community of his own mind and inside the frame of his own body. The consequence is that what might, as in a reflected image, be always 'over there' is not; it is also 'here', attached in some way to the child. The young Ruskin, secure and conceited, 'occupies the universe' and knows he is its 'central point' (Ruskin, [1885] 1989: 27). Only his eyes mediate between the inside and the outside. Through their censorship and acuity, they eradicate what otherwise could be disturbing distinctions between the child's sense of himself and his surroundings. Led by his eye and his ear, the child easily experiences the intertextuality of the inside and the outside.

Similarly, Pater's Florian does not reside within a world irretrievably disrupted by its otherness. Florian does not step back to look at himself, for he is too entwined in the continuous weaving of his own sensations that connect and harmonise with his surroundings. Threads of what lie outside and inside continuously intermingle to bind the self. This continuous overlapping of his bodily sensations with what lies outside of himself smudges experience so that, ultimately, no fissures separate him from what otherwise would be alien. The boy in Stevenson's verses, because he attaches himself to what exists beyond the immediate, succeeds in smearing many of the boundaries that usually separate the 'there' from the 'here' and the introspective from the visual self. The reflexive 'I' is not necessarily a factor in any of these children's early lives.

For these young subjects, then, the looking-glass world seems irrelevant. Contrary to what theorists like Henri Wallon, Jacques Lacan and Maurice Merleau-Ponty suggest, for these children the mirror, whether real or metaphoric/symbolic, is not the necessary attendant to their sense of identity and relation.[7] Without becoming unnecessarily involved in the intricacies of these theories, it is sufficient to point out that Ruskin, Pater and Stevenson are not, for instance, participants in Lacan's mirror phase; their sense of their own unity does not depend upon the illusory wholeness that the mirror image initially projects or allows. In addition, they do not require the mirror to experience a discrete separation from others. The looking-glass does not catch the young Ruskin, Pater and Stevenson and cause them to turn round, look at the other and engage the disturbing world of objectification. Nor does the mirror cause these children to cope with what Merleau-Ponty terms 'the unsuspected isolation' that reveals itself when the child suddenly notices two subjects facing each other in the reflection (1964: 119). For them, consequently, the subsequent work to reclaim a wholeness that the reflected image has divided is irrelevant. Their embeddedness in themselves and their interiors obviates that necessity. In their youth, because they are not spectators of themselves, the mirror is not a factor in the relationship with themselves, their rooms and with others. The mirror is simply not present.

It is only when Ruskin, Pater and Stevenson have become adults and left behind the rooms of their childhood that the spectre of the mirror appears and the discrepancies of experience penetrate. Interiors and exteriors separate, and the body, even though it may share the same memory with its childhood self, requires a mirror image of itself. Now, like Stevenson's Mr Hyde, the individual must consult the mirror to look at himself and see who he is. Ruskin, Pater and Stevenson must pick up the looking-glass of their autobiographical texts in an attempt to reintegrate or reclaim themselves. Ruskin, disoriented by attacks of madness, puzzled by the realisation that no one outside of himself either parallels or complements his sensibility, and finding himself to be, in his own words, more 'curious' than he thought, turns to the mirror of his text for affirmation ([1885] 1989: 221). He leaves the arena of the 'subjective me' and enters the framed, self-conscious space of the 'specular I' (Merleau-Ponty, 1964: 136). No longer is he the *camera lucida* – the lens or the eye. In *Praeterita* he is now the observed. Looking at the past, he stands outside of himself.

A similar sense of alienation presses upon Pater. Overwhelmed by feelings of fragmentation, sensitive to the divisiveness emerging from the succession of selves that rarely overlap but leap ahead, and anxious that the thickening walls of experience are closing in around him, he too turns to the mirror of the autobiographical text to arrest what is fleeting and, perhaps, for a while, to draw closer to what is now an 'otherness'. Pater creates the mirror of his imaginary portraits which objectify his sense of having become a spectator of himself. Through the imaginary, semi-autobiographical portrait of Florian, Pater attempts to return, as an adult, to the affirming harmony of childhood. As if anticipating Gaston Bachelard who, in *The Poetics of Reverie: Childhood, Language and the Cosmos* (1971), suggests that reverie enables one to re-enter the childhood that has been abducted by the shadows and forgetfulness of experience, Pater, through his dreams, comes through from the back of the looking-glass into the rooms of his childhood (the opposite of what Alice does) and turns to look through the mirror of his text at what had been there. Like Leonardo da Vinci in Rome, he brings his former, more cohesive self back to life by surrounding his subject with mirrors (the reflecting, interpenetrating style of 'The Child in the House') that reveal all sides of the young Florian. In a sense, Pater's semi-autobiographical portraits recall the procession in *Marius the Epicurean*, in which mirror-bearers follow the image of the goddess Iris. The bearers hold the mirrors at an angle so that the goddess's image and the faces of the worshippers lined up in the street advance towards one another (61). Like these ritual mirrors, the text brings Pater closer to his ideal – it lets him approach the icon of his childhood.

Even the adult Stevenson, who has endeavoured to stay within the sphere of his childhood, must resort to the mirror of his autobiographical text. He must create the looking-glass of his poems through which he tries to set his eyes on the child reflected in their frame and to replicate what had once been his playful world. Just as one used to hold a mirror under the nostrils of a failing life, Stevenson, like Ruskin and Pater, places his verses under the breath of memory in order to reveal the evaporating moments of the past.

Although these textual mirrors function as sanctuaries from forgetfulness, they are inadequate, for, just as nostalgia paradoxically distances a person from what he or she desires, the mirror separates the subject from its own reflection. These texts cannot replicate the cohesiveness of childhood. Rather than reintegrate the self, they expose the gaps between what is and what was. They surrender to the fact that the child has grown up and gone away. Furthermore, like mirrors, these texts hold their images within a frame that exiles the peripheral, or what connects the image to its surroundings. The mirror segregates rather than integrates. In this way, of course, its images contradict the cohesiveness that the one who holds up the mirror desires. Allowing one image at a time, the looking-glass fails to admit the blending of the one into the other – the continuous overlapping that is part of the past's becoming.

Given the distinctive constitution of Ruskin's, Pater's and Stevenson's childhood, however, the principal failing of the text as mirror is that it is compelled to make visible, through language, what had been invisible to them. This is where the poignant discrepancy lies for, as I have previously suggested, it was the unselfconscious 'invisibility' of the bodily experience that was distinguishing and that created, for them, the wholeness which subsequently split into the fragments and objects of the spectral, adult self. For Ruskin, this invisibility was the bodilessness that could see; for Pater it was the body that never saw itself but lived in its sensations, and for Stevenson it was the unseen presence of the 'we'. Now all of this invisibility must be eclipsed by the reflected image; it must be objectified through the written word. Ruskin, Pater and Stevenson have now to look at themselves. Yet what choice is there, for, outside the less public and tangible alternatives of reverie and longing, the textual mirror is the one authoritative space left?

Full of longing, Ruskin undertakes his autobiography. As if trying to replicate the moments when, after a long trip abroad, he would first catch sight again of Herne Hill, sixty-two years later he re-enters, through his writing, the 'sacred and comfortable' interiors of his early years ([1885] 1969: 52). He returned physically to the nursery of Herne Hill to compose much of *Praeterita and* wrote its Preface on 10 May 1885, the day that would have been his father's hundredth birthday. Mainly, though, he travelled towards home by rereading himself, by looking again at his past and sorting old journals and letters. As in Velasquez's *Las Meninas*, these 'mirrors' restored visibility to that which had been out of view (Foucault, 1973: 8). This reviewing, however, had little to do with the narcissism that the cartoonist of Mr Narcissus Ruskin in the 18 December 1880 issue of *Punch* found in Ruskin's continual references to himself (Spear, 1984: 199). The activity, rather, reflected his despair, for, the more the darkness of his manic episodes threatened to envelop him, the more he desired the relative peace of reflection and needed to re-enter the interiors of the past. Outside of these mirrors' frames stalked that which threatened to destroy him. The moments that he had hoped to keep invisible, out of sight, might suddenly make themselves visible.

Significantly, Ruskin's first attack of madness (in 1878) was marked by terrifying delusions in which 'the Evil One', in the form of a large black cat, sprang at him from behind a mirror and 'commanded him to commit some fearful wrong which he was powerless to resist' (Rosenberg, 1961: 113). At the same time, then, that the retrospective mirror was offering Ruskin a safe itinerary, it was also taking its revenge for his selectivity and reminding him that, although he might try to evade the painful and disturbing events of his life, he might still unexpectedly come face to face with their visibility – outside the mirror's frame.

Like Marius who leaves home only to seek to regain it, Pater, throughout his imaginary portraits, travels towards the sanctuary of home. Influenced by what he calls 'the enchanted distance fallacy', Pater idealises home ([1885] 1986: 58). Home becomes the fixed point of time within the bewildering flux of the disappearing present. In a sense, home actualises the myth of unity that Pater explores in his *The Renaissance* ([1877] 1978) for, within its rooms, the child lives less separated from himself. He is, perhaps, his own twin, and in being so brings to life the introductory fable of Amis and Amile – the two friends whose 'inward similitude' binds them inseparably (9). The inward and the outward require no translation, for the intermingling of the inside and the outside creates a fabric of boyhood that folds the various elements together. In this manner, the child personifies the modulated union of landscape and person that Pater finds so attractive in the Venetian painters and which comes close to the condition of music (153).

Now, though, about thirty years later, Pater, excluded from the harmony of childhood, must translate the more idyllic past into the perpetual flight of the present by tilting the mirror and catching the reflected image with his words. He has no alternative. And neither does the exiled Stevenson. Finding himself separated from what had been an integral part of him and experiencing the physical and psychical distance between him and home, Stevenson creates small mirrors out of each verse and, for a moment, presses close to their reflective surfaces. But, because of the mirror, instead of being the subject he must now be the one who perceives. Visibility replaces being. As the poet he must step outside the child's room and illuminate what before he had no need to see. The isolation in the poems is, perhaps, not the child's but that of the solitary figure who was once a child.

The desire to recover – to resurrect – the child within the rooms of home impels these autobiographical texts. As though soliciting the aid of the Medusa's head uncovered near Marius's childhood villa, Ruskin,

Pater and Stevenson attempt to revivify what is lost. Like Asclepias, who with two phials of Medusa's blood (drawn from the veins of her left side) raised the dead, they with their ink resurrect the past. But Medusa's petrifying gaze cannot destroy them, for the text's deflecting mirror protects them from an unmediated confrontation with their former selves. Perhaps, after all, there was no need in a period before a 'fit of craze' for Ruskin to crush the head of a viper that had just crossed his path and to announce that he had obliterated for himself 'the last lock of Medusa's hair' (Hunt, 1982: 397–8). Perseus's shining shield (the mirror) had already done the deed.

Paradoxically then, in the end, the distorting, segregating, alienating mirror image saves Ruskin, Pater and Stevenson. Like nostalgia itself, this mirror keeps them away from a direct sighting of the past and, through that act, prevents what lives in their memory from dying. Their mirrors urge the eye away from the stare of the direct experience that hardens, stultifies and even destroys its subject (recall the myth of Orpheus). The only way, then, to try to get back into these interiors that originally had no mirrors is to add one later, walk back with it through the rooms of childhood and attempt to blend into its reflection.

Notes

1 Their orientation anticipates those like Maurice Merleau-Ponty who argue that it is not through thought, absented from body, that one knows one's surroundings, but through one's 'bodily situation' – that one is conscious through the body's position in space (1964: 5). Their point of view also looks forward to twentieth-century architectural theorists such as Kent Bloomer, Charles Moore and Robert Yudell, who insist that one measures and orders the world from one's own body, that the body is in 'constant dialogue' with the buildings surrounding it (1977: 57). Ruskin's, Pater's and Stevenson's sensitivity to the relationship of their bodies to their surroundings might, in some way, reflect the emphasis placed upon the child's body in nineteenth-century guides on raising a child. See 'Physiological Bodies' in Steedman, 1995.

2 As if conscious of this substitution, Ruskin recalls the time he 'frightened' his mother 'out of her wits' by announcing that his eyes were coming 'out of his head' (Ruskin, ([1885] 1989: 38). Many critics, of course, have remarked upon the importance that Ruskin attached to the act of seeing.

3 Of all the photographs and paintings of Stevenson, none captures his fragility more than John Singer Sargent's 1885 portrait – painted the year *A Child's Garden of Verses* appeared – in which Stevenson's lank and almost transparent body moves through the shadows into darkness. His long thin fingers touch his face and his leg as if having to confirm their actuality.

4 For a discussion of this principle, see Tafuri, 1987.

5 In these last sentences I am obviously reacting to the emphasis Jacques Lacan places upon the mirror stage in childhood. For a discussion of this mirror stage, see Sarup, 1992: 62–6, 82–4.

6 For information on the convex mirror, see Wills, 1965: 35–6.

7 See 'The Child's Relations with Others', in Merleau-Ponty, 1964; 'The Mirror Stage as formative of the function of the I as revealed in psychoanalytic experience', in Lacan, 1977; and Wallon, 1928.

Bibliography

Bachelard, G. (1971), *The Poetics of Reverie: Childhood, Language and the Cosmos*, Boston, Beacon Press.

Bloom, H. (ed.) (1985), *Modern Critical Views: Walter Pater*, New York, Chelsea House.

Bloomer, K., Moore, C. and Yudell, R. (1977) *Body, Memory and Architecture*, New Haven, Yale University Press.

Colvin, S. (1980), 'Robert Louis Stevenson', in J. Calder (ed.), *Robert Louis Stevenson: A Critical Celebration*, Totowa, New Jersey, Barnes and Noble.

Cook, E. T. and Wedderburn, A. (eds) (1903), *The Complete Works of John Ruskin*, 39 vols, London, George Allen.

Daiches, D. (1973), *Robert Louis Stevenson and His World*, London, Thames and Hudson.

Emerson, S. (1993), *Ruskin: The Genesis of Invention*, Cambridge, Cambridge University Press.

Foucault, M. (1973), *The Order of Things: An Archaeology of the Human Sciences*, New York, Vintage.

Helsinger, E. K. (1982), *Ruskin and the Art of the Beholder*, Cambridge, MA, Harvard University Press.

Hersey, G. L. (1982), 'Ruskin as an optical thinker', in J. D. Hunt and F. M. Holland (eds), *The Ruskin Polygon: Essays and the Imagination of John Ruskin*, Manchester, Manchester University Press.

Hewison, R. (1976), *John Ruskin: The Argument of the Eye*, Princeton, Princeton University Press.

Hunt, J. D. (1982), *The Wider Sea: A Life of John Ruskin*, London, Dent.

Lacan, J. (1977), *Écrits: A Selection*, trans. A. Sheridan, New York, Norton.

McGrath, F. C. (1986), *The Sensible Spirit: Walter Pater and the Modernist Paradigm*, Tampa, University of South Florida Press.

Merleau-Ponty, M. (1964), *The Primacy of Perception*, ed. J. M. Edie, Evanston, Illinois, Northwestern University Press.

Monsman, G. C. (1967), *Pater's Portraits: Mythic Patterns in the Fiction of Walter Pater*, Baltimore, Johns Hopkins University Press.

Monsman, G. C. (1980), *Walter Pater's Art of Autobiography*, New Haven, Yale University Press.

Pater, W. H. (1986), 'The Child in the House' [1878] and 'Emerald Uthwart' [1892], in W. E. Buckler (ed.), *Walter Pater: Three Major Texts*, New York, New York University Press.

Pater, W. H. [1885](1986), *Marius the Epicurean: His Sensations and Ideas*, ed. I. Small,

Oxford, Oxford University Press.

Pater, W. H. [1877] (1978), *The Renaissance*, intro. L. Evans, Chicago, Academy.

Rosenberg, J. D. (1961), *The Darkening Glass: A Portrait of Ruskin's Genius*, New York, Columbia University Press.

Ruskin, J. [1885] (1989), *Praeterita: The Autobiography of John Ruskin*, intro. K. Clark, Oxford, Oxford University Press.

Ruskin, J. (1903), 'The Mirror' [1837] and 'On Skiddaw and Derwent Water' [1830], in E. T. Cook and A. Wedderburn (eds), *The Complete Works of John Ruskin*, vol. 2, London, George Allen.

Ruskin, J. (1903), *Modern Painters* 5, in E. T. Cook and A. Wedderburn (eds), *The Complete Works of John Ruskin*, vol. 7, London, George Allen.

Ruskin, J. (1903), *The Poetry of Architecture* [1838], in E. T. Cook and A. Wedderburn (eds), *The Complete Works of John Ruskin*, vol. 1, London, George Allen.

Sarup, M. (1992), *Jacques Lacan*, Toronto, University of Toronto Press.

Spear, J. L. (1984), *Dreams of an English Eden: Ruskin and his Tradition in Social Criticism*, New York, Columbia University Press.

Steedman, C. (1995), *Strange Dislocations: Childhood and the Idea of Human Interiority 1780– 1930*, Cambridge, MA, Harvard University Press.

Stevenson, R. L. [1885] (1969), *A Child's Garden of Verses*, New York, Airmont.

Tafuri, M. (1987), *The Sphere and the Labyrinth: Avant-Gardes and Architecture from Piranesi to the 1970s*, trans. P. d'Acierno and R. Connolly, Cambridge, MA, MIT Press.

Wallon, H. (1928), 'La maladresse', *Journal de Psychologie Normal*, 25, 61–78.

Wills, G. (1965), *English Looking-Glasses: A Study of the Glass, Frames and Makers 1670– 1820*, New York, Barnes and Co.

Yudell, R. (1978), 'Body movement', in K. Bloomer, C. Moore and R. Yudell, *Body , Memory and Architecture*, New Haven, Yale University Press.

Political pincushions: decorating the abolitionist interior 1787–1865

Lynne Walker & Vron Ware

The extent of British women's involvement in the antislavery campaigns that spanned 1780–1870 has deservedly been the subject of important feminist research in the last decade. In particular, the extraordinary details of women's campaign work has enabled historians to complicate the idea that middle-class women had no opportunity to take part in public political debate, and that their influence was mainly confined to the private, domestic world centred around the home. While in broad agreement with this work, we adopt a different perspective in this essay, taking as our starting point the material culture of abolitionism and its presence within the antislavery household.

We were initially intrigued by the way that women participated in and identified with the abolitionist movement through the decoration of their homes and bodies with emblems of slavery. Our extensive research in museums, archives and private collections in Britain, supported by recent historical work in this field (Midgley, 1992; Oldfield, 1995; Yellin, 1989), has enabled us to call attention to a wide range of material objects used, produced and circulated among women during these campaigns, and thus explore how women brought the subject of racial slavery into the fabric of their homes and their everyday lives. Far from confining women's agency to networks of domesticity, however, we use this material to argue that the decoration of the female body and home, the combination of the personal and the political, and the elision of the private and public spheres challenged binary gendered divisions of space and culture. These practices not only mapped the home as a legitimate arena for women's political action, but produced a power base within nineteenth-century domestic space for related activities in the previously masculine preserve of the public realm. These abolitionist tactics also became the model for women reformers' activities in the second half of the nineteenth century, most notably the campaign for women's suffrage. At the same time, we suggest that the antislavery images and objects that were popular with women deserve to be examined as important elements in the changing nature of British racism in the nineteenth century.

Just as many of the objects themselves take on different meanings when viewed in different contexts – the museum showcase, the reconstructed home, the private legacy of family treasures – so we were wary of approaching the domestic interior as a space that could be examined from a single point of view. The emerging discipline of 'home history' was helpful in suggesting ways to combine the study of objects and interiors using the methodologies of design history, with a social historical perspective to allow a more fluid and complex relationship between people and things in the cultural ecology of everyday life. Our essay sketches the parameters of women's involvement in abolitionism during this period within the context of the movement as a whole. However, in addressing the rather volatile meanings of what can seem disarmingly innocent household objects, we were also concerned to demonstrate that they could be used to discuss the changing representations of 'race', racism and its racialised subjects, white as well as black. In a deliberate attempt to capture this contingent relationship, we decided to introduce the main elements of our research by evoking a multi-dimensional construct of the historical home, using examples from tourism, art and literature.

Crossing the threshold

We begin by entering a house, as voyeurs or, rather, detectives, looking for material evidence left by one of the most famous abolitionists of them all. The house in which Harriet Beecher Stowe lived in retirement with her husband Calvin and their adult twin daughters is lovingly maintained as a tourist shrine. It is set in what was once a community of writers and reformers in Hartford, Connecticut, along with a museum and another house that belonged to Stowe's friend and neighbour, Mark Twain. Just before we cross the threshold, however, the assembled party of visitors is briefed on how to behave inside the house. Nothing must be touched; we can look and, of course, ask as many questions as we like.

As we proceed through the front door and into the first room, herded by the rope barriers, half listening to the biographical prattle of the guide, it dawns on us how deeply unsatisfying it is to look on a person's domestic space as an exhibit. There is little sense of it being a lived-in home, despite the information about who slept where and even where Stowe did her writing. Instead, we are presented with a form of discursive practice involving a clearly gendered order expressed through the immaculately clean arrangement of domestic space: furniture, pictures, rugs, wallpaper, objects, both handmade and mass-produced.

At the same moment that we decide to recognise this as discourse, we also begin to accept that we are intruders and to enter the spirit of the occasion. Although the nature of the museum tour raises important and uncomfortable questions about how to reconstruct imaginatively the inside of a middle-class Victorian house, we have come to explore the home of a female abolitionist and to raid it for facts and feelings about how women with strong political views decorated their homes. If we are here to view, to 'read' the contents of the house, then that's what we'll do. Like Goldilocks, we want to try all the beds and chairs that are inviting us to sit down before the owners return. We begin to look more closely at the objects and to question the guide more persistently. The information that we receive is both educational and disturbing.

In the front parlour, the room reserved for formal occasions, we ask whether Harriet Beecher Stowe would have had any objects or images that expressed her abolitionist views. Our eyes fall suspiciously on a small statue of a man attending a girl lying on a couch. From the guide's helpful answer we learn several things: that the figures are indeed Uncle Tom and Little Eva; that there are several other similar examples in the house; that they belong to a genre of objects known in the trade as 'Tomitudes' (see figure 1); that these Tomitudes were frequently sentimental and mawkish, mass-produced in the second half of the nineteenth century to cater for consumers who knew and cared little about the brutal histories of the slave system. Most disturbing of all, we discover that Stowe had frequently expressed her antipathy to these objects and would never have allowed them to pass through the front door, let alone grace her walls and table tops. Though no doubt intended as a tribute to Stowe's enduring impact on historical representations of racial slavery, the presence of Tomitudes in the woman's home alongside her allegedly cherished possessions seems an insult to her memory.

We are shocked and surprised to be presented with a view of the house as it would have been, when this significant detail (inadvertently discovered) casts doubt on the integrity of the whole reconstruction. It is all the more ironic considering that Stowe was responsible, along with her sister Catharine Beecher, for influencing a large number of American

1 'Tomitude', Uncle Tom and Little Eva, earthenware figure group, *c*. 1855.

women in appropriate ways to organise and decorate their interiors. In 1869 the sisters published a household manual entitled *The American Woman's Home; or, Principles of Domestic Science: being a guide to the formation and maintenance of economical, healthful, beautiful and Christian homes*. In a chapter on 'Home Decoration' they advise:

> There are few of the renowned statues, whether of antiquity or of modern times, that have not been accurately copied in plaster casts; and a few statuettes, costing perhaps five or six dollars each, will give a really elegant finish to your rooms – providing always that they are selected with discrimination and taste. The educating influence of these works of art can hardly be over-estimated. Surrounded by such suggestions of the beautiful, and such reminders of history and art, children are constantly trained to correctness of taste and refinement of thought and stimulated – sometimes to efforts at artistic imitation, always to the eager and intelligent inquiry about the scenes, the places, the incidents represented. ([1869] 1944: 94)

This extract underlines the extraordinary power of household ornaments both to represent and construct unambiguous messages about cultural identity. Even though the book appeared at the end of the period we are considering, the flavour of these words of wisdom helps to set the scene for our discussion of the abolitionist interior. Above all, the somewhat tasteless presence of the Tomitude in the home of Harriet Beecher Stowe today serves as an important reminder that, when we look back at the past, it is always tempting to pop in a few extra ornaments to show how much more we know now than they did then.

Depicting the feminised interior

We move now to a picture of another interior, this time rendered in paint by a woman in 1843, nine years before the publication of *Uncle Tom's Cabin* in Britain and almost thirty years before Stowe moved into her Hartford home. The picture shows a room in Hollington House, East Woodhay, Hampshire and is from a series of watercolours by the amateur artist, Charlotte Bosanquet (see figure 2). It is an illustration of a typical middle-class drawing-room characteristic of the 1830s and early 1840s, 'tastefully' decorated with a white marble fireplace, pale, rose-pink walls, a white ceiling and apple green curtains and upholstery (Lasdun, 1981: 53). A woman sits reading in a chair next to a large round table with her back to the window for light. On this occasion, our well-informed guide is J. C. Loudon, whose much-read *An Encyclopaedia of Cottage, Farm, and Villa Architecture and Furniture* describes the drawing-room as: 'the

2 Charlotte Bosanquet, 'Drawing Room, Hollington House', East Woodhay, Hants, 1843.

sitting-apartment of the ladies … distinguished by the elegance of its proportions, decorations, and furniture' (1833: 796). As Leonore Davidoff and Catherine Hall have reminded us, Loudon was concerned with educating the middle classes in the canons of good taste, in which women were to play a special role (1987: 191): 'The arrangement of the multitudinous furniture and ornaments must be left to the taste of the lady of the house; none but a lady can do it' (Loudon, 1833: 797). The picture invites us, the public, to consume the image of a woman alone with her private thoughts.

In this painted room, we read the semblance of timeless order signified by stillness. The view of the green landscape through the window frame is as immovable as the paintings carefully hung on walls or the room's seated occupant. Everything is as it should be seen: 'a few busts, or curious small sculptures' (Loudon, 1833: 797) are called for, a lady's work table and desk, decorative china, and an album of prints open for 'instructive diversion' (Lasdun 1981: 52). Loudon recommended such an arrangement for the drawing-room to avoid the 'dismal effect of idleness, everything should be arranged … in the drawing-room, as if the person using the room[s] had been employed in some way' (Loudon, quoted in Lasdun, 1981: 46). This aesthetic prescription for an elegant drawing-room included moral elements and values which represent the middle-class work ethic and were important aspects in the formation of the middle class, producing 'tasteful' but moral decoration of domestic space to distinguish the industrious middle class from the idle aristocracy (Morgan, 1994:146; Lasdun, 1981: 52).

Unlike the reconstruction of Harriet Beecher Stowe's house, the details in the watercolour cannot be rearranged by subsequent generations of relatives and historians anxious to fiddle with the ornaments in the interests of what is commonly known as heritage. The objects depicted in Charlotte Bosanquet's drawing-room (the display case, round table, album, writing materials, books, paintings, engravings, ceramics, work table and other accoutrements for needlework and sewing) are significant because they testify to the increasing power of consumption enjoyed by the middle class since the eighteenth century. They also work actively to construct the social identity of the family that owns Hollingworth House and the wider class to which it belongs. We are fortunate to have not just our own hindsight, but also the expertise of Loudon as our contemporary guide to remind us of how deliberately moral and political messages could be inscribed on and through the domestic in the nineteenth-century home, especially the feminised space of the drawing-room, with its 'tasteful' and 'discriminating' furnishings and ornaments. The whole picture is thus a strong statement in the emerging discourse of a gendered order expressed through notions of ownership and affluence, and through the accentuation of domestic order and control, and the pursuit of diligence and morality.

Reading Mrs Jellyby: a/skewed femininity

Our third scene, which we find in *Bleak House*, Dickens's classic interpretation of mid-century Victorian society, is altogether different, not least because it represents a diametrically opposed disorder – a domestic disorder associated here with the project of 'civilisation' in Africa. This time we enter the house of the philanthropist Mrs Jellyby, looking through the eyes of the youthful Esther Summerson. Before we read about the state of the interior, however, we are warned that our host is a very remarkable woman. So great is her devotion to public work – at this moment a project to cultivate the coffee berry on the banks of the Niger and send two hundred 'superabundant' families from England to civilise the natives of Borrioboola-Gha (Dickens, [1853] 1986: 82) – that she shows no trace of concern when one of her smaller children tumbles down stairs. Esther observes that she is evidently too busy to brush her hair and that she fails to notice that she has dropped her shawl, exposing the fastenings of her dress that do not manage to meet up at the back. These eccentricities are remarkable, but less shocking than the condition of the room: 'The room, which was strewn with papers and nearly filled by a great writing-table covered with similar litter, was, I must say, not only very untidy, but very dirty' (85).

Seated at the desk is Mrs Jellyby's daughter, who also suffers from dishevelled hair and inadequate dress but, as it turns out, is a seething victim of her mother's obsessive philanthropy. Humiliated and miserably neglected, the daughter seeks out the visitors later that night and bursts out: 'I wish Africa was dead!' (92). This sentiment is reiterated again as another measure of Mrs Jellyby's dysfunctional femininity by her 'mild and bald' husband who is so dispirited by domestic disorder that his sole communication to his daughter on the night before her wedding is: 'Never have a Mission, my dear child' (477). The rest of the house differs little from the first room. Dirt, disorder, neglect and discomfort rule, children run wild and the servants treat the visitors with contempt.

Mrs Jellyby is a wicked parody of the do-gooder who is so caught up in her own charitable impulse that she actively harms those around her. The reader is expected to recoil at the disgraceful state of her house, at the jumble of revolting objects that lurk incompatibly in the cupboards, at the idea of eating half-cooked food prepared on filthy surfaces, and at the prospect of cold, dusty, draughty bedrooms and dark and precipitous staircases. The host is insensitive and self-righteous and apparently has no idea of the misery she inflicts on her family. The moral framework of philanthropy permitted middle-class women to hold interests outside the home which, in Mrs Jellyby's case, leads her to fixate on 'the momentous importance of Africa, and the utter insignificance of all other places and things' (87). This philanthropic interest in Africa results in, or is perhaps caused by, a completely skewed femininity, devoid of all supposedly natural instincts.

Imaging abolition

Our task now is to consider all the unnamed women in uncelebrated houses who made it their mission to free the slave. We want to consider ways in which women participated in and identified with the antislavery movement through the decoration of their homes and bodies with emblems of slavery and slogans of emancipation. By compiling an inventory of the kinds of material objects produced, used and circulated during these campaigns, we want to explore how women brought the subject of racial slavery into their domestic space. This discussion arises out of a fascination with the objects themselves – certainly with the process of tracking them down – and the way in which they represent the changing nature of British attitudes to race and racism in the period in question. This enquiry also connects up with broader debates about the genealogy of feminist practices and strategies, and with the formation of new subjectivities and identities in the late nineteenth century.

One of the most haunting and enduringly powerful images of the slave trade is the diagrammatic plan of a slave ship used to transport enslaved Africans across the Middle Passage (see figure 3). According to Oldfield, the drawing was based on the dimensions of an actual slave ship, the *Brooks* of Liverpool, and depicted its lower deck 'as if viewed from above, "with Slaves stowed on it, in the proportion of not quite one to a ton"' (1995: 163). In 1789, well over a thousand copies were distributed by abolitionists in the Plymouth area where the idea had originated. Weeks later, the London Committee produced a more detailed version, adding a similar plan of the quarter deck, with longitudinal and cross sections of the whole ship. The engraving was produced in various formats, from posters to leaflets to framed prints, and found its way into many abolitionist homes across the country from the end of the eighteenth century. The London Committee, which financed the printing, distributed more than eight thousand in one year (Oldfield, 1995: 167).

This print, along with many other visual images of the brutality of racial slavery, is just one example of the way that political opinions could be represented inside the home itself. Propaganda was not just hung on walls, however. Abolitionist texts and images were often inscribed in the decoration of the drawing-room: represented in the furnishings and fabrics (see figure 4), depicted on transfer-printed china on the tables (see figure 5), portrayed in illustrated books shelved there, printed on stationery for the mistress's writing table and even worn on the body itself (see figure 6). Ownership of these images and artefacts suggested an antipathy to slavery and the technology of the slave trade, a belief in the fellow humanity of those racialised as black, and in the right to hold individual opinions. We are interested in exploring the difficulties that arise when the image of the slave ship or the suffering of slaves depicted in antislavery prints and artefacts is inserted into the nineteenth-century interior, into a space already charged with meaning.

3 Plan of lower deck of slave ship, engraving after the 'Brooks' of Liverpool, detail, 1788, with seal of the London Committee for the Abolition of the Slave Trade, distributed free by Plymouth committee; similar prints were sold by ladies' antislavery societies.

4 Chair seat cover (originally), canvas-work panel of a kneeling slave and verse with floral border, n.d.

5 China plate with abolitionist motifs and mottoes, early nineteenth century (1830?). China was commercially available and some was sold through women's antislavery groups.

First, there is the problem of historical interpretation – of 'reading the nineteenth-century domestic space' – which we have tried to address above. In some ways we are helped here by the emerging discipline of 'home history'. This approach, outlined by Thomas J. Schlereth in the introduction to an edited collection called *American Home Life, 1880–1930: A Social History of Spaces and Services* (Foy and Schlereth, 1994), moves on from the purely antiquarian, collectors' tradition, embraces histories of art and design, but emphasises the social histories of the period and perceives the spatiality of the interior as a complex dynamic between environment and social relations: 'The social history orientation aspires to understand domestic routine as well as design scheme. It is concerned with housing as well as houses; often its researchers are more interested in a home's inhabitants – parents, boarders, servants, in-laws, children, guests – than its physical habitat' (5).

6 Slave medallion, black on yellow jasper, impressed 'Wedgwood', late eighteenth/early nineteenth century.

Although we will pursue this approach in the course of this essay, we are also concerned to address another problem raised by the juxtaposition of political propaganda with the image of conservative domestic order. How does an image or a statement from one discourse become transformed once it is viewed as part of another? In other words, did the figure of the suffering slave become domesticated and depoliticised once it was hung on the walls of the bourgeois Victorian home? Or, alternatively, did the home become self-consciously politicised by the introduction of propaganda? We want to argue that both things can be seen to happen: the critical representations of racial slavery were to some extent sanitised and sentimentalised but they were also domesticated in the sense of made normal, legitimate, knowable, and their presence was capable of signifying powerfully subversive messages. The strong moral imperative of antislavery images and artefacts allowed for rules to be broken; even the Quakers, who held deep religious objections to displaying images, were said to have made an exception by hanging the framed engraving of the slave ship in their homes (Oldfield, 1995: 165–6).

Nevertheless, an obsession with the horrors of the slave ship or the humiliation of women slaves may have watered down or at least obscured a radical political analysis of slavery. For example, the frequent presence in antislavery imagery of a female figure representing Britannia as a liberating icon minimises or, at a certain point, precludes such an analysis offered by antislavery imagery. As Moira Ferguson points out, the logical extension of the antislavery argument to 'championing African self-determination' was abandoned when texts depicted 'silent victims who depend upon outside intervention' and when the 'civilising mission' of British colonialism, and British womanhood, was 'transvaluated into a pro-emancipation mission' (Ferguson, 1992: 257). This embrace of stereotypical imagery permitted abolitionists to avoid the accusation of being unpatriotic or unwomanly by associating themselves with Britannia, the feminised emblem of nation (based on eighteenth-century allegorical paintings) and enabled them to press their case, manipulating visual and material culture to their own political ends (Tickner, 1987).

The phrase 'home history' is useful partly because it reminds us of the contingent and changing nature of the spaces that different classes have called home. The increasing importance of the drawing-room in early Victorian Britain, for example, raises questions about where abolitionists might have hung their prints of the slave, about how women's increasing participation in the movement affected domestic space, and about the type of abolitionist artefacts produced and their arrangement in the home for decoration, use and propaganda. In late eighteenth-century households, framed prints were normally hung in the entrance hall and in the dining-room (Oldfield; 1995: 163), spaces that were considered part of the male domain, while propaganda items which were made at this date for women were associated with the female body and its adornment. Most famously and importantly, the industrialist and antislavery campaigner, Josiah Wedgwood, produced a cameo bearing the image of a shackled slave kneeling in supplication under the words: 'AM I NOT A MAN AND A BROTHER?' (see figure 6). By the end of the eighteenth century, it had become commonplace for women opponents of the slave trade to wear Wedgwood bracelets, hairpins and pendants (Oldfield, 1995: 156–8). This fashionable femininity is represented and reproduced in other late eighteenth-century objects, such as scent bottles and patchboxes, in which stylish beauty spots were kept, which were decorated with the kneeling slave, associated with the female body and intended for ladies' dressing-tables (Transatlantic Slavery Gallery, Liverpool).

However, 'after 1828 [when] women visibly dominated the movement' in Britain (Ferguson, 1992: 261), not only did the gender of the subjects depicted in antislavery artefacts become feminised, portraying female subjects and themes, but the objects themselves became more closely associated with the home and with its most 'feminine' space, the drawing-room (see figure 2). Simple and homely items connected with domestic activities and female interests, such as flower stands, pincushions and sheet music, were produced for women through ladies' antislavery societies (Birmingham Female Society 1825–31). In addition, a range of engravings in albums and portfolios which were often displayed in the drawing-room, as well as in frames hung on walls, were widely circulated by these women's groups.

In the feminised space of the drawing-room, guests were entertained and instructed at antislavery tea parties where 'slave-free' East Indian tea was drunk (Ferguson, 1992: 261) out of china decorated with abolitionist texts and images (see figure 5). In the drawing-room, sewing circles, as well as individual needleworkers, embroidered antislavery sentiments and images on fabrics that were used to decorate the home, such as the seat cover shown in figure 4, and ladies' antislavery groups filled suitably decorated workbags with printed abolitionist propaganda (see figure 7) for persuasion and display, while the hearts and minds of male

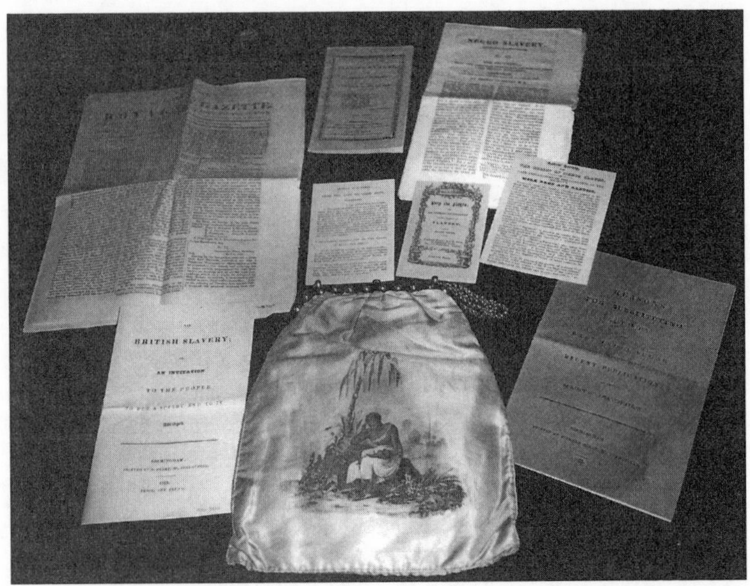

7 Antislavery 'workbag' and pamphlets, in the form of a silk purse with abolitionist image printed and poem (verso) in black, produced and sold by the Birmingham Female Society for the Relief of Negro Slaves, 1827–28.

family members and friends were addressed through readings from antislavery pamphlets and poems. Women's antislavery groups were established in, and run from, drawing-rooms (Birmingham Female Society, 1847: 16) which were also employed as meeting sites (16).

Women's antislavery arguments were also developed by playing on the characteristic nineteenth-century desire to collect and display objects in the home. At this time, as Mark Girouard has pointed out, more people than ever 'were collecting more and more objects, partly because there was more money all round, partly because large numbers of mass-produced decorative objects were available at comparatively little expense, partly because collecting something or other became in the nineteenth century a widespread craze.' Girouard concludes that accumulating objects symbolised escapism and security in the face of 'doubt, despair, fear of revolution, dislike of the way the world was changing', as well as 'the desire to be in fashion' (Girouard, cited in Lasdun, 1981: 20). We, however, see these cultural practices of collecting, display and fashion, which tactically referenced the accepted, indeed fashionable, decorative language of the middle-class interior, as also potentially helping to facilitate a challenge to the status quo.

These are just a few aspects of the different social histories that need to be taken into account in this exercise. However, in order to understand the significance of these kinds of images as political propaganda outside the home as well as inside, we need to expand this interpretation of 'home history' beyond the dynamics of design and domestic routine to investigate the nature of abolitionism as a social movement. Although the campaign against slavery attracted more supporters in the nineteenth century, organised abolitionism began in the last quarter of the eighteenth century. The Wilkite agitations of the 1760s introduced a new material culture of popular protest with the manufacture of objects such as inscribed medallions, prints, badges, pewter and ceramics. This helped to commercialise politics in a way that we would recognise today. When the Society for the Abolition of the Slave Trade was founded in London in 1787, the first manifestation of organised resistance to the institution of racial slavery in the Caribbean and the brutalities of the Atlantic slave trade, it inherited a legacy of campaigning methods and styles that were highly appropriate for a new public eager to consume the fruits of industrialisation. One result of this was that 'the movement began to acquire its own visual culture, a culture that was at once dynamic, immediate and malleable' (Oldfield, 1995: 155).

By the 1830s the antislavery movement had to compete with many other causes against a background of increasing urbanisation and the development of an impoverished and exploited working-class population in British cities. Many abolitionists were simultaneously involved in other reform movements, such as the Anti-Corn Law League or Chartism. At the same time, conflict within these groups often developed, and splits within their ranks demonstrated a powerful conservative lobby that attempted to control the more radical elements. Overlapping involvement in different reform movements was not, however, always tolerated, and some campaigners held strong objections to what they perceived as the self-righteous hypocrisy of the antislavery movement. It was not uncommon for radicals like William Cobbett to try to disrupt antislavery meetings on the basis that they distracted attention from evils closer to home.

Linking domestic space and the public weal

Since the publication in 1992 of Clare Midgley's invaluable *Women Against Slavery: The British Campaigns 1780–1870*, it has become more difficult to summarise the ways in which British women campaigned for the ending of racial slavery in the West. Not only were women from many different parts of the country actively involved, motivated by different social and political sensibilities, but they also devised and performed a wide range of activities that were important precisely because they made links between the confined space of the home and the wider world of international politics. Apart from the agency of women in campaigns themselves, it is also important to consider the complex dynamics of gender, class and race in abolitionist discourse that their involvement and enthusiasm helped to generate.

For our purposes here, it seems appropriate to separate women's involvement in the antislavery movement into two periods, before and after the setting up of the first women's organisation. The first period, 1787–1792, saw an increasing number of women in London and provincial towns expressing their support for the work of the Society for the Abolition of the Slave Trade. In London alone approximately 10 per cent of the total number of subscribers (about two hundred) were women (Oldfield, 1995: 137). Although women were discouraged from signing petitions – one of the chief tactics of the movement at this early stage – their involvement in the campaign throughout the country was evident from subscription lists of local committees, reports of meetings and the correspondence of leading abolitionists. Middle-class women were also able to contribute legitimately to the growing antislavery literature by expressing their sentiments in poetry and fiction (Ferguson, 1992). More recent research has shown that women played an increasingly important role in promoting the tactics of abstention and consumer boycotts (Midgley, 1996: 137–67). Abstention had begun with individual Quakers in Britain and America refusing to consume or trade in goods produced by slaves; by the 1790s it was widely recognised in Britain as a key weapon in informing the public about the evils of slavery and motivating people to reject its products – specifically sugar (see figure 8) and cotton. It was vital that women, as housewives and the primary preparers of food, were persuaded of their moral duty to ensure that their families did not ingest the fruits of such an iniquitous system. As Midgley argues, 'The abstention campaign was the keystone of a wider movement to convert Britain into a nation of antislavery households, to create an antislavery culture with deep domestic roots' (1996: 143).

In 1824 the movement was revitalised when Elizabeth Heyrick published a pamphlet entitled 'On the Reasons for Immediate Not Gradual Emancipation; Or, an Inquiry into the Shortest, Safest, and Most Effectual Means of Getting Rid of West Indian Slavery'. Heyrick represented

8 Sugar bowl, inscribed in gilt lettering 'EAST INDIA SUGAR not made by SLAVES', brown glazed stoneware, *c.*1822–34.

a growing frustration with the reformist position of campaigners such as Wilberforce, who, following the abolition of the slave trade in 1807, were alarmed at the prospect of insurrection in the colonies. Her arguments, which centred on the need to boycott slave-grown produce in order to achieve immediate and complete emancipation, were widely circulated among abolitionists in Britain and within the new movement in America. Heyrick put her theories into practice in her home town of Leicester where she carried out a door-to-door survey of households, finding support for the idea of a consumers' boycott.

It was also around this time that women were attending meetings in such large numbers that it was thought expedient to form separate organisations. In 1825 the Birmingham Female Society for the Relief of Negro Slaves began life in the home of Lucy Townsend, drawing in women from a wide area, including Heyrick herself. Other groups sprang up in the North and South of England, as well as in Scotland, Wales and Ireland, channelling the energies of many women who had been silenced or overshadowed by their menfolk in mixed gatherings. The network provided by this proliferation was also an important factor, as members exchanged information and discussed tactics, which ranged from collecting petitions for Parliament, instigating boycotts of sugar and cotton, and making and selling workbags filled with instructive literature for the home, to fundraising and numerous other campaigning strategies. Many of these groups developed significant links with similar organisations in America which resulted in the exchange of ideas, mutual support and the circulation of antislavery artefacts across the Atlantic.

In joining antislavery organisations, many were fulfilling the comfortable expectations of their class and gender by performing acts of philanthropy that allowed them to define their own femininity in relation to other kinds of women. Professing to care for the wronged Negro slave was often seen as a proper expression of woman's innate spiritual superiority, while her work in her home and local community was seen as the logical extension of a charitable impulse. William Wilberforce's cautious endorsement of women's contribution to the movement outlines the boundaries within which their participation was deemed welcome:

> We would remind every lady in the United Kingdom that she has her own sphere of influence, in which she may usefully exert herself in this sacred cause; and the effect of that influence, (even if it were quietly and unobtrusively confined to the family circle, or to the immediate neighbourhood), in awakening sympathy, in diffusing information, in imbuing the rising race with an abhorrence of slavery and in giving a right direction to the voices of those on whom, under Providence, hang the destinies of the wretched slaves. (cited in Ware, 1992: 113)

Deeply domestic

During this period, gender, space and morality were often elided by antislavery writers and reformers, such as Hannah More, Catharine Beecher and Harriet Martineau, who developed ideas about the home as a site of moral education. In the home, women's roles as moral guardian and mother were acted out, ethical behaviour was taught and gender roles absorbed by children, for instance, through reading children's books or learning children's hymns. Antislavery campaigners commandeered these expectations and resources, most effectively perhaps in Anna Laetitia Barbauld's *Hymns in Prose for Children* (1781) which were 'so popular that at her death in 1825 the *Christian Reporter* charged parents with being "deficit in the first of duties" if they did not utilize the hymns to instruct their children' (Ferguson, 1992: 132). The mother and child motif appeared on many abolitionist artefacts, such as the Birmingham group's workbags, which depict a slave mother and her sick child (see figure 7), and which were inscribed with Barbauld's hymn:

> Negro woman who sitteth pining in
> Captivity and weepest over thy sick
> Child; though no one seeth thee,
> God seeth thee; though no one pitieth thee,
> God pitieth thee; raise thy voice forlorn
> And abandoned one; call upon him
> From amidst thy bonds for assuredly
> He will hear thee. (Victoria and Albert Museum)

Normally, workbags would have contained pieces of embroidery, the lady's principal accomplishment, which was employed to inculcate femininity and its virtues, such as propriety, perseverance and attention to detail (Parker, 1984). Antislavery workbags were filled instead with propaganda pamphlets, cards and reproductions from various sources, which included abolitionist poems such as Hannah More's 'Slavery' of 1788 (reprinted in the mid-1820s), extracts from Jamaican planters' newspapers detailing 'in their own words' the horrors of slavery in the colonies; and a pamphlet of 1827 on 'Reasons for substituting East India for West India sugar' (Victoria and Albert Museum). Today, the surviving evidence indicates that many women were well informed about the details of the slave economy and were able to mount powerful arguments against the institution when necessary, arguments that were economic as well as moral.

The album of the Birmingham antislavery group, compiled in 1828, reveals fascinating details of its members' attitudes towards their self-appointed 'mission to the slave'. Women were exhorted to identify with the powerlessness of female slaves by addressing each other in a religious discourse that emphasised their own weakness and frailty as women. They frequently alerted those within their own circles of acquaintance to 'remember those in bonds as bound with thee and those that suffer adversity, as being herself also in the body' (Hebrews 13: 3). As well as relying on written texts, abolitionists produced powerful graphic images of women slaves that asserted a shared femininity that was being desecrated by the institution of slavery. In 1826 the Birmingham group made use of Wedgwood's famous medallion, 'AM I NOT A MAN AND A BROTHER?' by printing a picture of a kneeling manacled female slave asking 'AM I NOT A WOMAN AND A SISTER?' on the front of their first album. This adapted image quickly became effective propaganda in its own right (Yellin, 1989: 3–26).

Changing representations

Engravings contained in the 1828 Birmingham album and printed on china and workbags show black women being humiliated by the lust and brutality of white male slave drivers (Victoria and Albert Museum), or being torn apart by grief and anguish as husband and children are sold before their eyes. By the 1820s prints depicting scenes such as these were commercially available, as well as reproductions of paintings dealing with the horrors of the slave trade (Oldfield, 1995: 167–71).

Nevertheless, this visual culture of antislavery politics cannot be read as though its effects were unchanged during the course of the overall campaign. While these often sentimental images of the suffering negro were fashionable in the late eighteenth century, it is important to remember that this same period saw the development of a European racial science that sought to rationalise visible physical differences between people through the invention of racial types. In the first half of the nineteenth century new disciplines such as ethnography, anthropology and biology explained and rationalised existing social and economic inequalities by identifying supposedly natural hierarchies of race, gender and class. (Stepan, 1982; Schiebinger, 1993). The common bond of humanity – or sisterhood – that provided abolitionists with such ready ammunition in the 1780s already looked very different thirty years later when Saartje Bartman was being displayed on a public stage as the Hottentot Venus. Although abolitionists took court action against her capture and obscene exploitation, the government supported her owners, claiming that Bartman's contract with them stated that she had left South Africa of her own free will.

By the mid-nineteenth century any expression of common humanity and social equality between black and white could be read as a political statement that went against the grain of an increasingly populist racism. In 1859 African-American abolitionist Sarah Remond addressed a group of women in Warrington who then presented her with a watch inscribed with the words: 'Presented to S. P. Remond by Englishwomen, her sisters' (Ware,1992: 78). This encounter, movingly described in the pages of the *Warrington Times*, was significant because relatively few members of the middle class met either former slaves or free blacks, and, by the 1850s, were largely dependent on books such as *Uncle Tom's Cabin* for their information. Although Stowe was well received in Britain, and her book adopted as an effective tool in the antislavery movement, her fictional characters lent themselves only too well to caricature and parody in the second half of the century – a phenomenon of which, as we have already noted, she became uncomfortably aware. As Midgley writes, 'abolitionists in the eighteenth century were effective in shifting the images of blacks as commodities to blacks as victims' (1996: 143). We would suggest that it is important to turn to the wider context of imperialism in the second half of the nineteenth century to understand how the representation of black men and women were no longer represented as victims but as figures of fun and ridicule. The Tomitude was quite at home in the British drawing-room (Beddoe, 1996: 1) and in the American parlour, reinforcing rather than challenging racist notions of what it meant to be black. The enduring power of the kindly subservient slave provides further evidence of the international networks of culture through which notions of race circulated, often facilitated by women.

A transatlantic view

Following the abolition of British slavery in the Caribbean in 1838, the situation in America demanded more attention from British abolitionists. By this time there were well-established links between individual women and groups in the two countries and ideas and tactics were regularly exchanged and discussed. An illustration of this important relationship can be seen in the annual Boston Antislavery Fair, to which British women sent a significant amount of handmade and purchased goods to help raise money for the movement. A list of articles on sale in one year included pen-wipers, engraved with the motto 'Wipe out the blot of slavery'; needle-books ('May the use of our needles prick the conscience of slaveholders'); watch-cases ('The political economist counts time by years; the suffering slave reckons it in minutes'); and a quilt with this poem stitched on the central star: (quoted in Chambers-Schiller, 1994: 260)

> Mother! when around your child
> You clasp your arms in love,
> And when with grateful joy you raise
> Your eyes to God above –
> Think of the Negro-mother.
> When her child is torn away –
> Sold for a little slave – oh then,
> For that poor mother pray!

More detailed study of the annual fair itself provides extraordinary evidence of sustained fundraising and educational work carried out by

American women with support from female abolitionists from all over the British Isles.

Although there are records of British women whose commitment to abolition was connected to a broader politics for social and political change – Chartist sympathisers and early campaigners for women's rights such as Anne Knight and Elizabeth Pease (who also worked with her father to end indentured labour in India) – it is safe to say that most women remained within their classed and gendered worlds. A few made connections between their own subjugation as women and that of the black slave in the Caribbean, but nothing like on the same scale as their counterparts across the Atlantic. When American women's rights activist Lucretia Mott visited Britain with Elizabeth Cady Stanton for the 1840 International Antislavery Convention, she remarked in her journal that British women seemed to be no better than 'drudges' whether they organised separately or together with men (Ware, 1992: 80–7). The decision of the mainly British and conservative body of this conference to exclude women from the debate was symptomatic of prevailing dogma about appropriate spheres of organising for men and women, which few British campaigners sought to challenge directly. However, the boundaries of men's politics and the local, domestic world of women and family were not so clearly drawn as this might imply.

In Britain, the moral conviction articulated through the construction of a 'transracial' and spiritually pure femininity was inscribed on artefacts that served both functional and decorative purposes in the home. By displaying images on walls and slogans on everyday household objects, these women were not merely conforming to acceptable notions about confining their activities to the domestic world. They were also contesting and extending ideas about woman's place and women's role, often traversing and transgressing the private/public boundary as they sallied forth from their homes to canvass for signatures and support, collect money, distribute and sell abolitionist goods, attend meetings and fairs and promote boycotts. Choosing 'slave-free' food and clothing meant women researching and involving themselves in issues of production and consumption. Some spoke of the need to free the home of 'pollution' by slave-grown products. Now we would recognise this as being intensely 'political' and important in the development of consciousness of social and economic relations in the wider world. We would argue that these activities of middle-class women, and the discourse of female moral agency that they helped produce, were influential in determining both radical and conservative notions of femininity, class and race – what it meant to be British and specifically a British woman – in the first half of the nineteenth century. At the same time the gendered dynamics of abolitionism altered the social mapping of the home and its living spaces.

By the mid-century, in spite of its continuing campaigns and its important contacts with women's abolitionist groups in America, the British antislavery movement was winding down. Nevertheless, to its importance as the first political campaign in which women were involved in significant numbers must be added its role as a pre-feminist activity that informed later battles for women's rights. Later in the nineteenth century, feminists took much of their style and methods of campaigning from the antislavery movement in their struggles for women's rights, adopting the politicised home as a power base from which to organise and campaign (Walker, especially 1998; 1995). In many ways this is not surprising, since a significant number of feminist activists came from radical nonconformist backgrounds.

Conclusion

Investigating the abolitionist interior is a far more complex task than visiting a reconstructed home. In order to pursue this enquiry into the material culture of abolitionism within the antislavery household, it has been necessary to adapt the emerging discipline of 'home history'. With the feminised space of the drawing-room as our main focus, we have sketched out the distinctive patterns of women's involvement in abolitionism in the context of the wider movement, and drawn attention to the representation of black women and men within changing discourses of racial science. From another perspective, we have identified the importance of collecting, fashion and display in the context of the growing consumption of household goods. With this background, we have discussed the feminisation of antislavery artefacts and considered the impact and significance of the objects and images produced, exchanged and circulated by women during the period between 1770 and 1865. Finally we have tried to weave together disconnected disciplines to argue against the traditional historiographical framework of 'separate spheres' which has so effectively obscured the complexities of gender and class relationships in the nineteenth century and insulated middle-class women from any notion of political agency. In so doing we have attempted to depict the feminised interior as a dynamic social space, absolutely connected to the turbulent social and political relations of the outside world against which it was often defined.

Bibliography

Beddoe, S. (1996), *Black Britannia: Representations of Black People in the Willett Collection*, Brighton Museum and Art Gallery.

Beecher, C. E. and Stowe, H. B. [1869] (1944), *The American Women's Home; or, Principles of Domestic Science: being a guide to the formation and maintenance of economical, healthful, beautiful and Christian homes*, Hartford, The Stowe Day Foundation.

Bermingham, A. and Brewer, J. (eds) (1995), *The Consumption of Culture 1600–1800: Image, Object, Text*, London, Routledge.

Birmingham Female Society for the Relief of Negro Slaves (1825–31), Ledger Account Book 1825–1831, Birmingham Public Library Archives.

Birmingham Female Society for the Relief of Negro Slaves (1825–31), Album, *c*. 1828, Birmingham Public Library Archives.

Birmingham Female Society for the Relief of Negro Slaves (1825–31), Annual Reports, 1845–89, Birmingham Public Library Archives.

Chambers-Schiller, L. (1994), '"A Good Work among the People": the political culture of the Boston Anti-slavery Fair', in J. F. Yellin and J. C. Van Horne (eds), *The Abolitionist Sisterhood: Women's Political Culture in Antebellum America*, Ithaca and London, Cornell University Press.

Davidoff, L. E. and Hall, C. (1987), *Family Fortunes: Men and Women of the English Middle Class 1780–1850*, London, Hutchinson.

Dickens, C. [1853] (1986), *Bleak House*, Harmondsworth, Penguin.

Ferguson, M. (1992), *Subject to Others: British Women Writers and Colonial Slavery 1670–1834*, London, Routledge.

Foy, J. H. and Schlereth, T. J. (eds) (1992), *American Home Life 1880–1930: A Social History of Spaces and Services*, Knoxville, University of Tennessee Press.

Ladies Antislavery Associations, 5 (n.d.), Goldsmiths' Library, Senate House, University of London, in V. Ware (1992), *Beyond the Pale: White Women, Racism and History*, London, Verso.

Lasdun, S. (1981), *Victorians at Home*, London, Weidenfeld and Nicholson.

Loudon, J. C. (1833), *An Encyclopedia of Cottage, Farm and Villa Architecture and Furniture*, London, Longman, Rees, Orme, Brown, Green and Longman.

Midgley, C. (1992), *Women Against Slavery: The British Campaign 1780–1870*, London, Routledge.

Midgley, C. (1996), `Slave sugar boycotts, female activism and the domestic base of British anti-slavery culture', *Slavery and Abolition*, 17: 3, 137–6

Morgan, M. (1994), *Manners, Morals and Class in England, 1774-1858*, New York and Basingstoke, St. Martins Press and Macmillan.

Oldfield, J. R. (1995), *Popular Politics and British Anti-Slavery: The Mobilisation of Public Opinion Against the Slave Trade, 1787–1807*, Manchester, Manchester University Press.

Parker, R. (1984), *The Subversive Stitch: Embroidery and the Making of the Feminine*, London, Women's Press.

Schiebinger, L. (1993), *Nature's Body: Gender in the Making of Modern Science*, Boston, Beacon Press.

Stepan, N. (1982), *The Idea of Race in Science: Great Britain 1800–1960*, London, Macmillan.

Tickner, L. (1987), *The Spectacle of Women: Imagery of the Suffrage Campaigns 1907–1914*, London, Chatto and Windus.

Transatlantic Slavery Gallery, Maritime Museum, National Museums and Galleries on Merseyside, Liverpool, Patchbox Accession no. 1987.212.3.

Victoria and Albert Museum, Textiles and Dress Department, two printed silk work-bags and pamphlets, etc., sold by the Ladies Society for the Relief of Negro Slaves, *c*. 1827, Accession nos. T.227–1966 and T.20 to I–1951; antislavery pin-cushion, Accession no. T.1695–1913.

Walker, L. (1995), `Vistas of Pleasure: women consumers of urban space in the West End of London 1850–1900', in C. Campbell Orr (ed.), *Women in the Victorian Art World*, Manchester, Manchester University Press; a revised and expanded version of a talk given to the Design History Society study day, 'Cracks in the pavements: gender/ fashion/architecture', held at the Design Museum, 1991, and published under that title by Sorella Press, London, 1992.

Walker, L. (1996), `Well-placed women: spaces of the Victorian women's movement in London', in I. Borden *et al.* (eds), *Strangely Familiar: Narratives of Architecture in the City*, London, Routledge.

Walker, L. (1998), `Home and away: the feminist remapping of public and private space in Victorian London', in R. Ainley (ed.), *New Frontiers of Space, Bodies and Gender,* London, Routledge.

Ware, V. (1992), *Beyond the Pale: White Women, Racism and History*, London, Verso.

Yellin, J. F. (1989), *Women and Sisters: The Antislavery Feminists in American Culture*, New Haven, Yale University Press.

Inventory of antislavery artefacts included the following institutions and collections: Victoria and Albert Museum, London; Birmingham City Archives, Central Library; Friends' Library, London; Wilberforce Museum, Hull; Transatlantic Slavery Gallery, Maritime Museum, Liverpool; Durham Record Office; Brighton Museum and Art Gallery; Friends Historical Library, Swathmore College; Bristol Record Office; Ashmolean Museum, Oxford; Museum of the New World, La Rochelle; John Judkin Memorial Museum, Bath; Whitworth Art Gallery, Manchester; Harriet Beecher Stowe Center, Hartford; and various private collections.

Refracting the gaselier: understanding Victorian responses to domestic gas lighting

Sarah Milan

The invention of gas lighting was a dramatic innovation. After centuries of people using costly and labour intensive candles and oil lamps to light homes, gas lighting was represented as a cheap and convenient alternative. By the 1820s it had been extensively adopted to light factories, streets, theatres and shops, transforming the appearance of London and its nightlife. However, it was not until the 1870s that gas lighting became a familiar feature in the home.[1]

Studies of gas lighting have usually been limited to narrative accounts of the development of the gas industry and of technological progress, which emphasise that gas lighting was a radical improvement. The speedy introduction of street and factory lighting has been the focus of these studies but only fleeting attention has been given to domestic consumption which has been viewed as inexplicably slow to develop. An exception is Wolfgang Schivelbusch's *Disenchanted Night* (1988), which suggests that 'gas lighting really was excluded from the centre of the bourgeois home, the drawing room' as part of a rejection of industrialisation in the domestic sphere (72).[2] Here, as with other accounts, gas lighting's status as an immediate improvement on traditional light technologies is unquestioned. The importance of Welsbach's incandescent mantle, which, from the 1890s, greatly improved the usability of the new technology, has been recognised, but there has not been an accompanying assessment of the usability of gas lighting before this time. Until domestic consumption is explored in depth, conclusions cannot be drawn as to how Victorians responded to this new technology.

To identify and understand these responses, domestic gas lighting must be contextualised. Contextualisation should, I suggest, follow two approaches: the first might broadly be termed 'practical'. It needs to be established, as far as is possible, at what period there was significant use of gas lighting in homes that could afford it, when use became widespread and what was distinctive about its use. Its attributes as a light source and the impact it had on furnishings and air quality when compared with traditional technologies are also important. Finally, we need to consider whether gas lighting seemed a tangible improvement to contemporaries. This approach opens up the possibility that consumers may have been influenced by reasoned and strategic considerations when responding to the availability of a new product.

The second approach might broadly be termed 'symbolic' and uses the model of consumption studies which considers that all kinds of object – mundane, technical and ornamental – carry symbolic meanings as well as performing practical functions. This essay, in particular, explores the public spaces and contexts in which objects, in this case gas lighting, were used and understood. Furthermore, it considers that these spaces and contexts importantly contributed to the symbolic meanings of gas lighting in domestic space. Contextualisation provides a much richer account of the impact and reception of new technologies in the home. Instead of simply comparing consumer responses to technological developments, it is possible to explore the process by which new products become invested with cultural meaning as they enter public and domestic spaces.

Using gas light in the home

The general view that there was little use of gas lighting in the Victorian home until late in the century needs to be qualified. The scarcity of statistics showing the extent of domestic gas lighting use and the lack of detailed research in this area has led to reliance on satirical cartoons and industry pamphlets which express amazement that more people did not use gas in their homes. The research for the present study has focused on domestic gas lighting in London and has found evidence, ranging from engravings and photographs to advertisements and trade catalogues, which indicates that by the 1850s there was significant use of gas lighting in middle-class homes, including the drawing- and dining-rooms (see figure 9).[3]

During the years 1850–80 there was considerable consumer agitation against the price of gas charged by the metropolitan companies. The *Hackney and Kingsland Gazette* summed up the situation in 1874, declaring that '[f]ew questions have ever perplexed the community of London more than that of the ways of getting cheaper gas' (22 July).

14 Paris Guide ADVERTISEMENTS. 1855.

F. & C. OSLER,

44, OXFORD STREET, LONDON,

(MANUFACTORY, BROAD STREET, BIRMINGHAM,)

ESTABLISHED 1807,

Manufacturers of Glass Chandeliers, Glass Lustres,

TABLE GLASS, &c., &c.,

A SELECT AND EXTENSIVE STOCK, IN EVERY VARIETY OF PATTERN, OF

RICHLY-CUT CRYSTAL GLASS CHANDELIERS,

WITH GLASS BRANCHES, FOR DRAWING-ROOMS, &c.

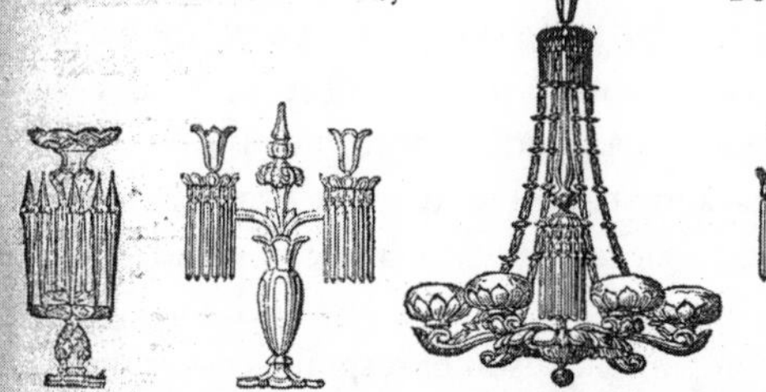

ELEGANT CRYSTAL GLASS CHANDELIERS FOR GAS,

(Made from "Registered" Designs); with Glass Branches, &c.; suitable for Drawing Rooms and Ball Rooms.

THEATRES, CONCERT, ASSEMBLY, AND BALL ROOMS, LIGHTED BY ESTIMATE, ON THE LOWEST TERMS.

A LARGE AND CHOICE ASSORTMENT, IN NEW AND BEAUTIFUL DESIGNS, OF

HANDSOMELY-CUT GLASS LUSTRES AND GIRONDOLES.

BEST CUT TABLE GLASS, IN EVERY VARIETY,

Including Wine Glasses, Decanters, Dessert Services, &c.

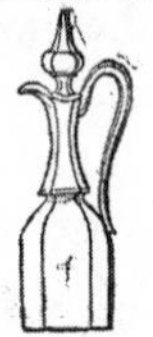

ORNAMENTAL GLASS, ENGLISH AND FOREIGN

(The latter selected and imported by Messrs. Osler) in the greatest variety.

CLUB, MESS, AND GENERAL FURNISHING ORDERS FOR GLASS PROMPTLY EXECUTED.

[13—Lo

9 F. & C. Osler, advertisement for crystal gaseliers and table glass, 1855. This advertisement was reproduced in the Art Journal Advertiser of May 1854 with the additional text: 'The more extensive use of Gas in private dwellings has induced Messrs Osler to direct their particular attention to the manufacture of this class of articles – which with a view to their general adoption, are offered at very moderate prices.'

Agitation was organised by private consumers and local authorities in the form of parliamentary lobbying and public meetings. However, despite the bad press that the gas industry continually received, the demand for gas lighting steadily increased. This had the effect of roughly halving the price of gas fittings (Timmins, [1866] 1967: 350–1).

In the early years, the choice of fittings and degree of usage seems to have been curtailed by concern for thrift and the greater expense of fittings. A rare gas rent book of the firm Messrs Spinney and Sons, which details Richmond customers' gas bills for 1838, indicates that gas might only be used in the winter or over the Christmas period. Some customers listed in the rent book used gas for just a day in a quarter, presumably for a special occasion, or to light a single space such as the billiards room. At this time most contracts were from sunset to sunrise, with customers specifying the hours they would burn gas and being billed accordingly. Meters to measure the exact amount used only became widely available in the 1850s and were an additional expense for the consumer who had to buy in all the gas apparatus.

When gas lighting was introduced into homes, it was not necessarily the case that it replaced candles and oil. Combined light technologies were usual, with gas being used in some areas, oil or candles in others. This suggests that consumers were aware of the various benefits (economic or otherwise) of the lighting options available. The placing of particular types of light fittings in various spaces also gives an indication of what their attributes were considered to be. A gas bracket or pendant in a passageway or kitchen had a different role from a gaselier or a candlelit chandelier in a parlour or drawing-room. Contrary to Schivelbusch's conclusion that gas was excluded from drawing-rooms, the extensive advertising of gaseliers suggests many people thought gas appropriate to the 'public' spaces within the home which were used to entertain visitors.

The materials from which gaseliers were made emphasise their public role: highly polished, variously coloured metal finishes or glass droplets were used to create glitter and sparkle and show jewels off to their best effect. In contrast, brackets and gas lamps, mostly for private evening use, often had opaline or ground glass globes tinted with blue, green and salmon to soften the light (King, *c*. 1872: 27).

One of the most distinctive features of gas lighting for its middle-class users was the ability it gave them to light interiors brightly. The gas itself was much cheaper than buying candles or oil, and for the first time middle-class households had the opportunity to light their houses extensively at comparatively little cost. The author of a domestic economy guide commented in 1854 that middle-class rooms were often lit much more brightly than was required 'for any ordinary occupation ... [Gas's] low price often leads to an abuse – the light from it is frequently and unnecessarily and injuriously strong' (Walsh, 1857: 133). The *English Woman's Domestic Magazine* advised readers on dinner parties in 1874 as follows:

> No matter what the season or what the hour that you fix upon your dinner, it must always be given by gas light, or, if you have not gas, by lamp and candlelight. Above all, let there be plenty of light. If it be daylight outside, you must close the shutters and draw the curtains. (185)

Ornate gaseliers to display the light were also highly popular. Authorities on design and taste such as Charles Eastlake, author of the popular *Hints on Household Taste* ([1869] 1878), were unanimous in their condemnation of gaseliers, which they considered the most over-elaborate and poorly made of all household furniture. Mrs Loftie, author of another household taste guide, vividly described the ostentatious appearance of gaseliers:

> Nothing can compete with the gaselier in tawdry deformity. Bronze and ormolu constructions of leaves and chains, dog's heads and mermaids, scrolls and china flowers, basket work and pebble knobs, Brummagen gone hopelessly mad and poisoning us besides. (1878: 39)

This taste for strong light and ornate gaseliers became an established and oft-noted feature of middle-class drawing-rooms. Ornate lighting clearly had an important social role in the nineteenth century which needs to be understood in relation to the situation before the availability of domestic gas lighting. Only the wealthy, usually aristocrats, had been able to afford to light their houses extensively at night. The middle classes usually ate supper in the late afternoon and relied on a central table lamp to read or sew by in the evening. Elite social occasions such as dinners and balls were distinguished by their use of hundreds of candles at enormous cost (Leeds City Art Galleries, 1992: 1). Even different types of candle and oil were accorded status depending on their expense and ability not to smoke or smell (Ford, 1988: 197): spermacetti candles and wax candles produced less smoke, were largely odour-free and the most expensive, and were therefore considered to be of the highest status; the lower quality candles and oil lamps that the middle class could afford were less highly regarded; and then there was the so-called 'dip of the poor' which involved dipping reeds into a coating of hot grease.

Between 1840 and 1860, then, as gas lighting was steadily entering more and more households, these status distinctions were being undermined and a rich display of light could no longer authentically signify great wealth. This may be the reason why the overwhelming majority of the aristocracy switched straight from candles and oil to electricity to light public rooms, rather than try gas, considering it, in the words of Lady Diana Cooper of Belvoir Caste 'vulgar' (cited in Rubinstein, 1974: 48–9). The popularity of very bright lighting can be understood, then, in terms of a pleasure in affecting grand displays of light which had previously been reserved for the elite. The fashion for strong gas lighting and elaborate fittings can be viewed alongside the middle-class taste for ornate home furnishings; pieces were prized which appeared highly luxurious.

However, perceptions of gas light changed during the course of the nineteenth century and were determined by fashion, taste, light fittings and the arrival of stronger light sources, notably electricity. In 1817, for example, *The Times* commented that the new light (on show at the Drury Lane Theatre) had the 'clearness of diamonds … yet chastened with such a mild radiance as not to glare or dazzle the eye by their brilliancy' (7 September). The *Examiner* of the same day agreed that the light was 'mild as it is splendid'. Later, the influence of the aesthetic movement in interior decoration in the 1870s and 1880s created a fashion for the softer dispersal of light through brackets arranged at intervals around the walls. The quality of gas light was then described as 'intense but hard' (Mrs Orrinsmith, 1878: 115). In the late 1880s, with the arrival of electricity, the popular phrase 'darkness visible', which had earlier been applied to candles and oil, began to be applied to gas light. What had been described as 'harsh', 'glaring' and 'stifling', now became described as 'intimate', and its ability to heat a room as well as light it was appreciated.

Gas lighting altered the appearance of interiors by lighting rooms much more brightly and diffusing the light throughout a room more effectively. This led authors of household decoration guides to urge readers to consider how their decoration schemes would look when lit by the new lighting (Orrinsmith, 1878: 117). Another effect of gas lighting on the interior was the deterioration of ceilings, furnishings and air quality. It can certainly be argued that all forms of artificial lighting caused some damage to the domestic interior in the nineteenth century. Oil and even improved candles (available from the 1850s) were not made to the standards available today, as they produced more dirt on walls and ceiling and were smellier than a comparative amount of properly combusted gas. Candles, in particular, were a difficult light source to manage, needing regular trimming to prevent guttering and black smoke. In addition, candles and oil lamps dripped wax and oil onto furniture, books, clothes and hair.

Gas lighting, if used and installed properly, would indeed have been a welcome improvement, but this was frequently not the case. The practical transition to using the new technology was itself problematic, with consumers applying their knowledge of using candles and oil to gas light. The main problem this caused was the increased heat in a room, as burning gas created much more heat than burning air. As one observer wrote in the 1850s:

> Our ordinary gas-burners are each equal to from six to twelve candles, and that two or three of them are often burnt in a small room, it will readily be understood that a greater amount of light is employed than is required … and great astonishment is expressed that the room is hot and oppressive. (Walsh, 1857: 133)

Gas lighting also created a distinctive and often unpleasant smell, although promoters did argue that this aided the detection of gas leaks.

Blacker ceilings from using gas was the most often reported complaint. These were caused partly by consumers burning more gas than necessary and by the quality of the gas itself. By 1866 it was widely appreciated that London gas was the worst in Britain. A House of Commons inquiry established that 'witnesses were unanimous in their statement of the dark condition of London as compared with Edinburgh, Glasgow, Manchester, Birmingham, Plymouth, Brighton' (*Journal of the Royal Society of Arts*, 1866: 526). Suburban newspapers of the 1860s and 1870s commented on 'the horrible blackness that disfigures their ceilings, and permeates their book cases and wardrobes … [and] the fumes that take the colour out of the shop goods and the gilding off pictures frames' (*Hackney and Kingsland Gazette*, 22 July 1874).

Articles and readers' letters in newspapers, together with official government testing of the purity of London gas, suggest that there was a reduction in quality between 1850 and 1866. In these years Parliament had responded to fierce public agitation over the high price of gas by setting regulations over price and illuminating power, but not over the sulphur content in the gas. It was the sulphur that caused higher degrees of pollution but which also enabled gas companies to produce better-quality by-products, such as ammoniacal liquor and tar. Such by-products were equally if not more profitable than supplying gas lighting. In 1872, at a meeting of London's Court of the Common Council to discuss further spending on lobbying Parliament against the gas companies, a member commented: 'When you needed your ceiling whitewashed once a year, now you have to have it done three or four times. The filth from the impurity of the gas is something so extraordinary.'[4] R. W. Edis in his book *Decoration and Furniture of Town Houses* (1881) recommends the use of plain deal or canvas plaster ribs to protect the existing plaster work, which could be painted regularly to undo the effects of 'gas which is generally impure and a disgrace to modern science and civilisation' (277).

The noxious gases in London's atmosphere, coupled with the products of combusted gas, such as sulphurated hydrogen, sulphuric acid and ammonia, not only damaged the interior but also polluted the air, smelt unpleasant and caused headaches. They also caused the deterioration of household plants. This may have led to hardier plants such as aspidistras being favoured to decorate the interior (Wainwright, 1979: 167–8) and the cultivation of plants in glass cases or under bell glasses. As F. W. Burbidge comments in *Domestic Floriculture, Window-Gardening and Floral Decorations* (1874), 'If much gas is used it is as well to content ourselves with a few interesting plants or ferns, and to give these the protection of a closed or Wardian case' (1).

The gas itself, and the excessive amount burned, were not the only causes of polluted interiors. The service pipes and other gas apparatus were installed by independent gas fitters who were often plumbers rather than trained fitters. Pipes which were badly laid led to vast quantities of gas escaping into the earth which, in the words of a witness from the 1870s, 'darkens the soil, and makes it so offensive that the emanations from it can hardly be endured, renders the basement rooms of houses uninhabitable from the poisonous action of the gas, and even dangerous from explosions, and taints the water with a filthy odour' (Liberty, 1913: 202). This pollution also led to explosions, causing Dickens to write humorously in *All the Year Round*:

> I have heard of a letter addressed to a leading water company, which ran somewhat in this form:
>
> 'Mr Blank presents his compliments to the Blank company, and wishes to know whether they supply gas or water. Mr Blank is led to make this enquiry, because one of his servants went to the cistern with a pitcher and a candle, and instead of procuring water, she blew up the roof of the wash house!' (12 October 1861: 58)

Once bad fitting had taken place there was a 'continual expense attached to keep them in anything like working order' and, whatever the standard of workmanship, gas lighting also required a high level of consumer maintenance and knowledge, being much more complicated to use than candles and oil (King, *c.* 1872: 18). George King's *Advice to Customers on Gas Economy or how to keep down high and extravagant gas bills*, written in the 1870s when significant improvements to gas apparatus had been made, is a painstaking and detailed account of the problems that could arise from the new technology and the necessary precautions against them. This suggests that, in the long term, having gas lighting was unlikely to save time or effort. Only a few of these problems can be discussed here.

The most popular type of meter, the 'wet' meter, had to be placed carefully below the level of the pipes and in a moderately cool temperature. If the temperature was too warm 'jumping lights' would result; if too cool the meter might freeze. King further adds: 'In no case should an inexperienced person disconnect or remove a meter when frozen. I have known meters so taken off by those who did not understand them, blown to pieces and much damage done' (5). 'Wet' meters needed water poured in and drawn off around every six weeks, and when unattended or malfunctioning could cause a sudden cut in the gas supply. A report to the British Association of Gas Managers presents a vivid picture of the trials of gas lighting: 'Occasionally the supply stopped suddenly, just as a dinner party was about to assemble and the host, instead of meeting his friends, had to tuck up his sleeves and set to work "watering" or at Christmas time "thawing" the meter' (1875: 61). The gas burner was crucial to supplying effective gas light, but this information was only widely disseminated in the 1870s. The government gas referee's report to the Board of Trade in 1860 concluded that good quality and appropriately situated burners could lead to an increase of 30 – 50 per cent more light, while gas bills remained the same and the atmosphere in the room was improved (*Journal of the Royal Society of Arts*, 1860: 578). There were many different sizes and types of burner and no single type or size could be bought to supply the whole house. Batswing burners, for example, were not recommended for rooms with low white ceilings unless the gas was of poor quality (King, *c.*1872: 10). The consumer had, then, to understand the purity of the gas (which was a matter of great debate) as well as judge which burner to use in a room.

The light fittings themselves, particularly water-slide gaseliers and pendants, provide a further example of the hazards of gas lighting. These fittings could be lowered or raised for a concentrated or diffused light and needed refilling between intervals of eight to twelve weeks. One advertisement from the *Illustrated London News* made use of recent accidents to sell its product:

> GAS EXPLOSIONS PREVENTED
>
> THE TERRIBLE GAS EXPLOSIONS at LIVERPOOL and ISLINGTON
>
> – If the PATENT SAFETY ATLAS SLIDING CHANDELIER had been used these terrible accidents could not have occurred. These chandeliers, which prevent all accidents of this or any similar character, may be had from all chandelier dealers and respectable Gasfitters, in town and country.
> No sliding chandeliers are safe but the Patent Safety Atlas. (27 November 1858)

It is apparent from King's consumer guide that an effective supply of gas was dependent, at least until the 1890s, on many different variables, not least the consumer's own considerable commitment to learning how to maintain and select the correct apparatus. Gas lighting required skilled maintenance and was not simple to use when compared with candles and oil. In the 1870s, in particular, it also caused substantial damage to the air quality and furnishings of the domestic interior. Both are surely important in explaining why gas lighting entered into the home less quickly than into public spaces where gas light's ability to draw in trade was an added incentive. However, there was widespread use of gas lighting, despite its complications and criticism, and the criticism that was voiced arose to a large extent from the tangible difficulties involved in using gas light rather than, as Schivelbusch suggests, from a reaction to industrialisation.

The social and symbolic meanings of gas lighting

Gas lighting's capacity to light whole streets and so extend the hours of daylight, together with its industrial origins, made it the most artificial and radical light technology yet invented. Street lighting was first viewed by some people, particularly clerics, as unnatural because it prevented the onset of darkness which was considered part of the God-given cycle of day and night.[5] As gas lighting became a familiar part of London life, it became associated with deceptive appearances and the industrialised landscape. This section will examine the public origins of these associations and discuss the related meanings that gas lighting held in domestic space.

Novels describing gas lighting are used here as sources to indicate the way in which public associations were utilised to convey the nature of domestic interiors and their occupants. The symbolic meanings that gas lighting carried in these texts suggest the cultural associations they may have held in Victorian society. The use of interiors in novels to convey the character and behaviour of individuals to readers depended, of course, on the existence of a shared set of meanings about particular objects.

Until the later nineteenth century there was little to distinguish the claims made for gas lighting from those made for quack remedies or fraudulent business schemes. Early in the century, gas lighting was associated with fraud and deception. Frederick Winsor, the first major gas lighting publicist, used displays (notably the temporary gas lighting of Pall Mall in 1806) and a barrage of pamphlets to recruit investors for his National Light and Heat Company. His publicity relied on unfounded and exaggerated claims – gas light was 'scentless, a cure for asthma, all pulmonary troubles and conducive to vigorous growth in plants, since it will generate the elements required for their sustenance in much greater proportion than even the most powerful action of solar rays' – which were quickly recognised to be completely false. Gas light, he added, would also 'create good humour, by uniting convenience, utility and pleasure' (1807: 1). Winsor was not alone in making such claims. The Gas Light and Coke Company's 'Operative Chemist', Frederick Accum, adopted the popular technique of using the form of a treatise or polemic to advertise his services and gas lighting's amazing attributes. His *Practical Treatise on Gas Light* (1815) declared that gas had the advantages of 'saving of labour, cleanliness, safety and cheapness ... like the light of the sun itself, it only makes itself known by the benefit and pleasure it affords ... The gas flame is entirely free from smell' (3). Even J. O. N. Rutter, an established gas engineer and author of many pamphlets on gas lighting's price and purity published from 1837 to 1865, presented gas lighting as an instant cure for the problem of artificial lighting, 'requiring no preparation on the part of the consumer' (1865: 9).

Dickens considered that the prominence of quacks in London and the suspicion they consequently generated was the reason why gas lighting received so little recognition and enthusiasm as a great invention:

> For one discovery that has lived through the practical test of application, and has really benefitted the world, a thousand have been the pet children of quacks and visionaries. Until the new comer makes good its claims to be considered something beyond the common herd, we save our time, our money, and our labour, by regarding it cautiously. (*All the Year Round*, 12 October 1861: 55)

Early critics of gas lighting were convinced that the invention was yet another fraudulent scheme to steal money from the public: charlatans were continually holding out '*golden prospects* to the unthinking though respectable part of the community, so as to involve them in the most abortive and absurd schemes, which have had no other effect than that of filling the pockets of these "projectors" at the expense of their deluded and often ruined subscribers' (Candidus, 1817: 12). The 1840s in particular was a period when many people lost their money by investing in risky or fraudulent business schemes, particularly concerning another modern industrial invention, the railway.

The gas companies were viewed with contempt throughout the nineteenth century. Popular criticism even manifested itself in drama when a play performed at the Crown and Anchor Tavern on the Strand in November 1832 (and said to be founded on 'fact') satirised the mismanagement and corruption of a Westminster gas company – among the characters, Frederick Winsor appears singing 'Hope told a flattering tale'. The striking degree of consumer agitation and contemporary comment, which particularly appears in suburban newspapers from the 1850s to 1880s, clearly shows that the general public's common perception was that the gas companies were deceiving customers. Indeed, as a gas factory tour guide complained to an *All the Year Round* reporter, 'popular prejudice was so strong we have difficulty getting a hearing' (16 March 1861: 43). It was the case, then, that, from the early years when gas lighting was first demonstrated to the public until the late nineteenth century, the new invention was regularly associated with businesses or people who tried to deceive the public. This was one way in which gas lighting was continuously linked with deception but there was also the related association gas lighting had with the superficial and the spectacular.

Winsor inadvertently encouraged this image with his regular demonstrations of gas lighting at the Lyceum Theatre during 1803 to 1804. These were accompanied by lectures on the theory of lighting with coal gas, delivered either by himself in his foreign accent (he was a Moravian refugee) or a native speaker. It became a popular amusement and curiosity, probably considered in the same way as exhibitions of 'mysterious' scientific instruments which had long been a feature of London's street and theatre entertainments. Exhibitions of gas lighting were also not new. Since the seventeenth century, displays of gas flame formed a magical evening entertainment: coal gas was collected from marshy ground in sheeps' bladders which were then pricked and a candle held to the hole to show the strange flame produced (*All the Year Round*, 12 October 1861: 55–9).

Most people's first experience of gas lighting in an interior in the early nineteenth century is likely to have been when they visited the theatre. During the 1810s, theatres competed against each other to be the first to use gas lighting in order to attract the crowds. Here, gas lighting was part of the theatrical spectacle and the same spectacular use can be observed in the lighting of Brighton's Royal Pavilion in 1819. During the period gas was installed, the Pavilion largely functioned as a pleasure palace for George IV. In addition to gaseliers and brackets being fitted in the interior, flaring gas jets were attached to the outside of windows and the glass ceiling to illuminate the coloured panes (Leeds City Art Gallerie, 1992: 28). The effect was an exotic play of light in keeping with the ornate, oriental design of the building. In municipal ownership after 1845, the Pavilion became a popular public attraction but, even when it had functioned as a home for royalty, the context for gas lighting had always been spectacular rather than domestic.

Gas lighting was also a distinctive part of London's developing commercial and night-time spectacle. By 1816 the Gas Light and Coke Company was estimated to have installed gas lighting in a thousand shop interiors. Retailers were said to use mirrors and gas lighting to enhance the appearance of goods and give the impression that stocks were bigger than they actually were, which promoted the idea that gas lighting created deceptive *appearances* as well as its being associated with business fraud. Responses to gas lighting were not only negative. In 1836 Dickens, for example, responded enthusiastically to the new gas-lit window displays in *Sketches by Boz*: 'under the canvas blind of a cheesemonger's, where great flaring gas-lights, unshaded by any glass, display huge piles of bright red, and pale yellow cheeses' (1995: 182–3). Theatres and shops had established the power of gas lighting to attract custom and, together with the use of plate glass, changed the face of retailing and increased its appeal. Emile Zola vividly indicated the impact of gas lighting and plate glass on traditional retailing in *Au Bonheur Des Dames* or *The Ladies' Paradise* (published in English in 1886), where the fictional Paris department store, based on the Bon Marché store, is the star of the piece. Even while it is viewed with dismay by the traditional and ailing mercers opposite, at night the store continues to enthral potential customers with its magnificent gaslit façade.

Gas lighting had initially been a curiosity or possible fraud. Subsequently, it was used to create impressive effects in theatres and shops. Both these contexts influenced the characterisation of gas lighting in the domestic space and the fictional representations of domestic interiors.

Above all, gas lighting was presented as possessing deceptive qualities. In *Our Mutual Friend* (1865), the Veneerings' dining-room is strongly gaslit and contains furniture which imitates more expensive pieces through the application of veneer (fine or fancy work) (6, 10). Both veneers and strong gas lighting shared a common property: they were ostentatious but false tokens of wealth in the mid-nineteenth century. Like veneers, gas fittings were criticised because they could appear to be expensive but were in fact made with rich surface finishes hiding inferior metal underneath (Eastlake, [1869] 1878: 146).

Dombey, another of Dickens's characters who favours ostentatious display, has his house completely redecorated and furnished for his new bride. Gas lighting is described as being 'the garish light [which] was in the long darkened drawing rooms' (*Dombey and Son* [1848] 1982: 341). Readers, as Richard Altick has written, would have read 'garish' as suggesting gas lighting (1991: 743). This characterisation of gas lighting was not objective. As we have seen, descriptions of the quality of gas light were often determined by shifting cultural perceptions. The descriptions played on the experience of the bright flaring lights of stages and shops, of gas lighting in public space. When transferred to domestic space this characterisation became a criticism of individuals: authors and readers linked Dombey's or the Veneerings' preoccupation with grand appearances with the ostentatious display of theatres and shops, and their competition for social position with the competition for custom. Both affected a grand 'show'.

Aside from shops and theatres, gas lighting was also strongly linked with gin shops and this too influenced fictional representation of gas lighting. Elaborate use of mirrors and gas lighting has led to these shops being termed 'gin palaces'. Flaring exterior jets were an identifiable sign of a gin shop and there was even a notorious ten-foot-high lamp outside one establishment which contained seventy jets (Dickens, 1995: 182–3). As is well known, since the eighteenth century, gin shops had become symbols of slack morals and the degeneration of family life. The great gas lights that now adorned their façades and drew customers into the shops no doubt formed a significant association in the public consciousness. This is played on for comic effect in Trollope's *Barchester Towers* (1857), where the newly-arrived Mrs Proudie decides to install several gigantic twelve-burner gaseliers in the Bishop's Palace. These are first used at her disastrous house-warming, when the Bishop's palace takes on the appearance of a gin palace ([1857] 1980: 88)!

There was a further public context for gas lighting which enabled

Victorian writers to convey meanings for gas lighting in domestic space. Made from coal in factories, gas lighting was as clear a product of industrialisation as the railways. Metal light fittings themselves, in particular gaseliers with their 'chain pulleys, and such mighty machinery', were also ostensibly 'products of industrialisation' (Orrinsmith, 1878: 117). Industrialisation could represent progress but also an unnatural control of, and effects on, the environment. Gas holders in particular represented both these negative and positive aspects. At the beginning of the nineteenth century, wooden brewer's vats were used to hold gas. These were then superseded by iron constructions which demonstrated a new 'industrial' aesthetic, in stark contrast with the surrounding buildings (*Illustrated London News*, 16 July 1878). It was only in the 1870s that gas holders began to acquire the cast iron pineapples, classical columns and beams that toned down this aesthetic (*Journal of the Institute of Gas Engineers*, July 1963: 356). Their appearance and their capacity to hold millions of cubic feet of gas, which was increased from year to year, was reported with amazement in the papers, and their safety was also often discussed, particularly on occasions when gas holders exploded. As gas works were as often situated in residential areas as away from them, many people viewed these explosions at close quarters. The most notable case took place on 4 November 1865 at the Nine Elms Gas Works in Battersea, and caused nine deaths. *The Illustrated London News* reported that:

> Those who saw the explosion described it as one vast upheaving of flame shooting high into the air, with a burst that shook everything around. People nearly a mile off were thrown violently down, and persons who were in houses and streets adjacent to the works received severe burns. (11 November 1865)

The unrestricted competition between companies for periods during the 1850s and 1860s (which led to as many as eight sets of gas mains being laid in a single street alongside water and telegraphic wires) increased the occurrence of explosions (Liberty, 1913: 189). One of the most notable occurred in 1880 when a rapid series of explosions led to the paving stones of Percy Street, Charlotte Street and Fitzroy Square being torn up, wrecking the houses 'without any visible or assignable cause'. This was thought by *The Times* to have 'added immeasurably to its [gas] terrors for the moment' (7 July).

Gas pipes and works not only caused fire and destruction but were also responsible for much of London's polluted soil, drinking water, river and atmosphere. According to the gas engineer, J. O. N. Rutter, gas works were connected in the public's mind with 'fierce fires, dirty processes and offensive odours' and there were many petitions against the erection of gas works in residential areas (Rutter, 1860: 30). There was also the Victorian domestic experience of rooms that I have already discussed: the black ceilings and hot, dry, smelly atmospheres causing headaches and the deterioration of household plants.

George Eliot was playing on gas lighting's industrial associations in *The Mill on the Floss* (1860). Significantly, she sets 'stifling … glaring gas and hard flirtation' in opposition to the 'breath of poetry' of the purer glances and tones of the main characters. This linking of the hot, gaslit room with those involved in 'hard flirtation' suggests that the atmosphere in the room is polluted by both the gas and the unnatural behaviour of some of the occupants ([1860] 1991: 504).

In Dickens's *Hard Times* (1854), gas lighting and other household features in the homes of Bounderby and Gradgrind are portrayed primarily as industrial objects. Gradgrind's home is, for example, described in these terms:

> A lawn and garden and an infant avenue, all ruled straight like a botanical account book. Gas and ventilation, drainage and water-service, all of the primest quality. Iron clamps and girders, fireproof from top to bottom; mechanical lifts for the housemaids, with all their brushes and brooms; everything that the heart could desire. ([1854] 1995: 17)

This description suggests that these household objects are primarily industrial and anonymous rather than personal and domestic items. These domestic spaces are like factories rather than homes; unnatural and unhealthy settings for the raising of children.

Conclusion

When gas lighting was invented, it was, like any other new product, a blank slate on which Victorian culture could inscribe itself. As it moved from the streets into factories, theatres and shops it was invested with meanings and became a symbolic resource which writers could use to suggest the unnatural and deceptive qualities of domestic space or their occupants. This sense of the unnatural and deceptive was importantly conveyed to the reader by the incongruous transfer of equivocal public associations to domestic space. Meanings in domestic space and public space were not constructed in isolation but through constant interplay.

For contemporaries, the symbolism of gas lighting co-existed with the practical experience of it in public and domestic spaces. Both in practical and symbolic terms gas lighting was complex and of dubious appeal. It was difficult to use and its price and quality were hotly disputed. It was also a distinctive feature of London's commercial and entertainment spectacle which was both alluring and distasteful. A direct reflection of Victorian responses will always elude the historian, but this essay has attempted to present the framework in which these responses developed; a framework generated by the location of gas lighting in different types of space and by its effects on these spaces. A burnished metal or sparkling crystal gaselier, when placed in domestic space, was resonant with meaning, and it has to be considered as a cultural artefact of some complexity as well as a marker of technological development.

Notes

1 The price of gas and installation made it only affordable to the middle classes, until the 1890s when the 'penny in the slot' meter first became available. 'Gaselier' was the Victorian term for a gas chandelier.

2 Schivelbusch uses English household decoration guides and gas industry pamphlets, chiefly from the 1870s and 1880s, to argue that throughout the nineteenth century, the middle class considered gas lighting unsuitable in rooms for relaxing or entertaining. This is, however, problematic, since in the 1870s and 1880s, in contrast to earlier in the century, there were specific disadvantages in using gas. This was also the period when a critique of suburbia and lower-middle-class taste was generated.

3 The London press, both the national and the papers for the middle-class suburb of Hackney, was sampled, together with London Post Office directories and Hackney trade directories. All show a consistent and steep increase in manufacturers' advertisements for gas light fittings, apparatus and gas fitters from the 1840s to 1860s. Trade catalogues for light fittings were mainly available from the 1870s.

4 Court of the Common Council Minutes, 28 March 1872 (London Gas Museum Archive). The London Corporation and many parish authorities sponsored Parliamentary bills to try to obtain a better quality and cheaper gas for consumers. The London Corporation alone spent more than £29,000 from 1860 to 1880. Members of the public also organised many public meetings in local town halls.

5 An anonymous article entitled 'The bad consequences of lighting the streets' (*The New Times* 16 May 1819) lists seven reasons for rejecting gas lighting, the first being 'For Theological Reasons. Because it seems to be a violation of the order established by providence. According to this order, night is appointed for darkness, which is interrupted at stated times only by the light of the moon. We have no right to interfere, to pretend to correct the plan of the universe, and turn night into day.' See also Gas Light and Coke Company (n.d.) 12.

Bibliography

Accum, F. (1815), *A Practical Treatise on Gas Light*, London, Hayden.

All the Year Round, 16 March, 12 October 1861.

Altick, R. (1991), *The Presence of the Present: Topics of the Day in the Victorian Novel*, Columbus, Ohio State University.

Anon (1832), *Who's the Dupe or the Governor Outwitted – A Play Founded on Fact*, London Gas Museum Archive.

British Association of Gas Managers (1875) *Report of the Proceedings,* London Gas Museum Archive.

Burbidge, F. W. (1874), *Domestic Floriculture, Window Gardening and Floral Decorations*, Edinburgh, Blackwood.

Candidus (1817), *Observation of Gas Lights*, London, T. G. Underwood.

Dickens, C. (1995), *Sketches by Boz & Other Early Papers, 1833–9*, ed. M. Slater, London, Dent.

Dickens, C. [1848] (1982), *Dombey and Son*, Oxford, Oxford University Press.

Dickens, C. [1854] (1995), *Hard Times*, Harmondsworth, Penguin.

Dickens, C. [1865] (1994), *Our Mutual Friend*, London, Everyman.

Eastlake, C. L. [1869] (1878), *Hints on Household Taste*, London, Longman.

Edis, R. W. (1881), *Decoration and Furniture of Town Houses*, London, Macmillan.

Eliot, G. [1860[(1992), *The Mill on the Floss*, London, David Campbell.

English Woman's Domestic Magazine, 1874.

Examiner, 7 September 1817; 7 July 1880.

Ford, G. H. (1988), 'Light on darkness: gas, oil and tallow in Dickens's *Bleak House*', in S. I. Mintz, *From Smollett to James*, Charlottesville, University Press of Virginia.

Gas Light and Coke Company (n.d.), *History of the Gas Light and Coke Company*.

Hackney and Kingsland Gazette, 22 July 1874.

Illustrated London News, 27 November 1858. 11 November 1865, 16 July 1878.

Journal of the Institute of Gas Engineers, Commemorative Issue, July 1963.

Journal of the Royal Society of Arts, 1860, 1866, 1871.

King, G. (n.d.), *Advice to Gas Consumers on Gas Economy*, Birmingham, Martin Billing and Son.

Leeds City Art Galleries (1992), *Country House Lighting 1660–1890*, Leeds, Temple Newson.

Liberty, W. J. (1913), 'The centenary of gas lighting and its historical development', *The Illuminating Engineer*, 175–231.

Loftie, Mrs (1878), *The Dining Room*, London, Macmillan.

Messrs Spinney and Sons Gas Rent Book for Richmond 1838, London Gas Museum Archive.

Orrinsmith, Mrs (1878), *The Drawing Room*, London, R. Day and Sons and Macmillan.

Rubinstein, D. (1974), *Victorian Homes*, Newton Abbot, David and Charles.

Rutter, J. O. N. (1860), *On the Sale of Gas to Street Lamps: The Right to Lay Mains*, London, John Parker.

Rutter, J. O. N. (1865), *Advantages of Gas in Private Houses*, London, Virtue Bros.

Schivelbusch, W. (1988), *Disenchanted Night*, trans. A. Davies, Oxford, Berg.

The Times, 7 September 1817; 7 July 1880.

Timmins, S. [1866] (1967), *The Resources, Products and Industrial History of Birmingham and the Midland Hardware District*, London, Frank Cass and Co.

Trollope, A. [1857] (1980), *Barchester Towers*, Oxford, Oxford University Press.

Wainwright, C. (1979), 'The Garden Indoors', in *The Garden : A Celebration of One Thousand Years of British Gardening*, London, Mitchell Beazley.

Walsh, J. H. (1857), *A Manual of Domestic Economy: Suited to Families from £100 to £1000 a Year*, London, Routledge.

Winsor, F. (1807), 'Mr Nicholson's attack in his Philosophical Journal on Mr Winsor and the National Light and Heat Company with Mr Winsor's Defence', pamphlet reproduced in *History of the Gas Light and Coke Company 1812–1912,* 1913: 178.

Zola, E. [1886] (1992) *The Ladies Paradise*, Berkeley, University of California Press.

Tranquil havens? Critiquing the idea of home as the middle-class sanctuary

Moira Donald

What is a home? A possible answer to this apparently straightforward question might be: a physical structure which provides shelter and privacy for its inhabitants; a space within which the necessary bodily functions of sleeping, eating and reproducing can be executed by individuals living on their own, or more commonly in groups linked by ties of blood and mutual dependence. Is a home more than just the physical structure – the house or flat we call home? The English term 'home' suggests something of deeper significance – a moral or emotional resonance attached to the particular building we inhabit. But in other European languages the words 'house' and 'home' are the same, with a preposition added to the word 'house' to suggest the meaning of 'at home'.[1] But, of course, houses through history have fulfilled multifaceted functions beyond providing for the most basic family needs. If the focus of this volume had been the reading of domestic space in any earlier epoch, the essays contained within would certainly have included contributions on the function of the home in providing a locus (perhaps even the prime locus) for the productive labour of the group (the family or household) and the tools, materials and animals associated with that labour.

By the nineteenth century, however, homes in industrialising countries had, to some extent, lost the function of providing workspace in the sense of space for productive labour. A consequence of the so-called 'separation of home and work', as Davidoff and Hall (1987) have cogently argued, was the development of new gendered definitions of domesticity, in which the prime function of the home was to provide shelter; physical shelter in the traditional sense of a roof over one's head, but beyond that a private, almost spiritual shelter from the outside masculinised world of work. Research in recent years has shown that the extent to which work was separated from the home environment during the industrialisation process has been overestimated. Not only did a significant number of middle-class professions, such as the medical and legal professions, retain the tradition of setting aside part of the domestic space for the execution of professional duties, as Davidoff and Hall have shown, but also even in an urbanised society there were numerous working-class occupations (particularly female ones) which continued to be home-based into the nineteenth century and beyond (364–9). The latter point has been explored by Barbara Franzoi (1987) in her work on women's domestic industry in Britain and Germany.

Ironically, just at the very point in history when 'work' began to be defined as something done outside the home, the number of people employed within the home expanded to new heights. The nineteenth-century censuses inform us that a higher percentage of the population was employed in domestic service throughout the century than in factories, or indeed in any other sector of the economy. Domestic service was one of the major occupations in Victorian Britain. From 1851 to 1891 between 10 and 13 per cent of the officially occupied population of England and Wales was classified as servants. In 1871 and 1881, of a working population of around eleven million, approximately 1,400,000 people were employed in domestic service and the number was still rising by 1891.[2] When reading the nineteenth-century domestic space, therefore, it should not be forgotten that home was not the antonym of work. In this essay I want to develop the concept of the Victorian home as workplace by focusing not on the economically productive labour which, as Franzoi has shown, continued within many homes, but on the reproductive work of the home: the maintenance, cleaning and servicing of the domestic space. Judging only by those who were employed for wages to work in the domestic environment, it can be seen that the home was crucially a working environment. When one adds to these figures the millions of unwaged workers, the wives, daughters, aunts and nieces who also laboured daily in the home, it is evident just what a significant workplace the home was. Thus, the reading of the domestic space which I offer in this essay is in contrast to the more traditional male-oriented definition of the home as the counterpoint to the travails of the 'outside' world of work.

A further facet of taking an approach that interprets the domestic space as primarily workspace is the effect that this has on notions of the privacy of the domestic space. In this volume, Martin Hewitt has re-examined notions of lack of privacy within working-class domestic space, arguing that whilst this space was never the 'quintessence of privacy' to which Michelle Perrot suggests the middle-class home aspired, neither was it the classic slum, open to invasion by middle-class do-gooders. But one could argue that the ideal of middle-class privacy was as much a myth as the ideal of the tranquil haven. Indeed, I would go as far as to argue that the middle-class household was less private than its working-class counterpart.[3] In the wealthiest middle-class Victorian households the domestic arena would have been populated by children of various ages, scullery maids, a cook, a butler, a lady's maid, a nanny, the master and mistress of the house and often a resident relative from beyond the nuclear family. Beyond this, the house would have been entered daily by a much wider range of visitors than would be the norm today. Most social contact, and much business interaction, would have occurred within the domestic space. From the daily visits of shop boys with groceries, through afternoon calls amongst female acquaintances, to visits from the family doctor or the solicitor, to the regular dinner parties that were a feature of well-to-do Victorian society, there was typically a regular stream of visitors. Whilst the working-class householder could stand in the doorway to block the entry of the middle-class missionary, no such impedimentary tactics were available to the middle-class family. A servant answering the door would have had little social justification in refusing entrance to a person of higher social standing than themselves. In this sense, class difference is the key to privacy – or lack of it – in both working- and middle-class households. Just as middle-class visitors had no automatic right of entry to working-class homes, so it goes without saying that working-class visitors would have had no right of admission into middle-class homes.

However, to erect barriers of privacy within one's own social class was more problematic. While in theory the servant would announce the visitor and enquire if they might enter, in practice the impatient visitor need not wait for permission to be granted. In Jane Austen's work, for example, there are numerous incidents when female characters find themselves obliged to receive unwanted visitors in the domestic sanctum. A striking reversal of convention can be found in *Northanger Abbey* (1818), when the heroine, Catherine Morland, on having the exterior door opened for her by a servant, proceeds to rush up the stairs past the servant and, opening the door of the drawing-room, finds herself unannounced in the presence of Miss Tilney's family ([1818] 1995: 91-2). What makes this episode particularly interesting is that Catherine has not previously even been introduced to her friend's father, whose privacy she has thus unceremoniously flouted. While Catherine's behaviour is clearly out of the ordinary (the father is 'quite angry with the servant whose neglect had reduced her [Catherine] to open the door of the apartment herself'), nevertheless this scene gives the impression of the lack of privacy experienced by middle- to upper-class families in their own homes. Unlike the situation in working-class homes, this lack of privacy must have been constantly reinforced by the presence of resident servants, and indeed a desire for greater privacy has sometimes been cited as a contributory factor in the decline of residential servants in the middle decades of the twentieth century.

What sources are used to underpin my readings of the domestic space as workplace and non-private space? In my current research on houses and households in nineteenth-century Exeter I am developing a new approach of linking census material with physical evidence – the surviving housing stock. This work will help us to construct a more accurate picture of the home as workplace: in the analysis of the size of houses and the number of rooms, the number and ages of those resident and the number of servants employed to service the household. For present purposes I have drawn on the work of Davidoff and Hall, though recontextualising it to make a rather different argument from that put forward in their *Family Fortunes*, and I have used additional qualitative material from literary and autobiographical sources to illustrate my argument.

The middle-class Victorian home must surely rate as one of the most consciously contrived creations of domestic space in history. The affluent Victorian household ensured that its wealth and status were reflected in every aspect of its construction, furnishing and ornamentation. But the Victorian domestic space can be 'read' in many ways. Every individual who inhabited or entered that space would have interpreted it differently, depending on their own role within the space and within society in general. Wealthier middle-class households followed the upper-class paradigm of dividing the public rooms from the functional areas with a curtain or door (hence the title of a memoir by Lady Cynthia Asquith, 'In front of the green baize door' (Streatfeild, 1956)), and the former were carefully managed to convey to visitors a distinct impression of opulence, good taste and leisure. Evidence of this division can be seen in the interior architecture of even quite modest houses. Features such as the degree of ornamentation in the cornicing, the number of panels on interior doors and the presence or absence of picture rails are indicative of the status of the different rooms at the time the house was constructed. How, though, did the inhabitants of the ornate middle-class Victorian home negotiate the boundaries within it?

Within the middle-class house, space was divided into more or less private areas, as well as between 'upstairs' and 'downstairs' or 'front' and 'back', and only some of the inhabitants had the freedom to cross over these boundaries. There would also have been a strict allocation of space which children were allowed to inhabit. The Victorian nursery, fashionably imitated today in larger houses by the provision of a playroom, was, in reality, far removed from the room of late twentieth-century imagination. It was not created in recognition of children's need for space, but the opposite: it was designed to keep children out of adult space. For some Victorian children it was like a juvenile prison, yet it was not inhabited only by children, as Nanny would have spent most of her day there too, taking meals with young children, dressing and schooling them. There were also 'male' and 'female' spaces. The 'male' areas included the library or study and the dining-room after dinner. There was no exclusively 'female' terrain 'upstairs', with the exception of a dressing-room in larger houses) but the bedroom and drawing-room were the areas in which the women of the house could move most freely. The decoration of different areas also reflected their gendered use, with rooms assigned as male areas being frequently more richly and sombrely decorated and rooms primarily used by the women of the household being decorated in lighter colours. The domestic Victorian space, then, was elaborately segregated according to social status, age and gender.

Yet when individuals crossed boundaries, their reading of the same space would have been very different. The role of each person overlaid the physical divisions within the domestic space. The feelings of the maid who rose early in the morning to blacklead the grates in the upstairs rooms would have been very different from those of the male householder first entering the room to the welcome of a blazing fire. The silver which shone in the firelight may have been a source of pride to the master and mistress. To the maid who polished it the silver represented hours of elbow grease and perhaps more. It may have been symbolic of the great social and economic gulf which divided the inhabitants of the same domestic world. The middle-class Victorian home was by no means exclusively (nor even preponderantly) middle-class space. It was also a space inhabited by those lower down the social order who serviced it. Another aim of this essay is thus to draw attention to the obvious point, but one that is too easily forgotten, that the same space held different meanings for those whose lives were lived within it. The layout and dimensions of a late nineteenth-century, lower middle-class, semi-detached house (see figure 10) assist in conceptualising how the same

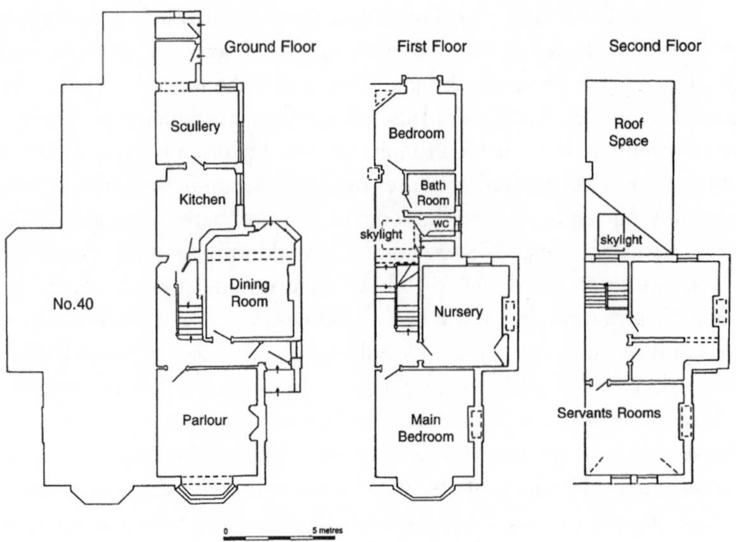

10 Plan, 41, Old Tiverton Road, Exeter, 1893.

domestic space might have been negotiated and experienced differently as a workplace.

When Davidoff and Hall first drew attention to the gendering of the domestic space in the nineteenth century they posited gender relations at the centre of the construction of class, arguing that the period 1750–1850 saw the development of a new phenomenon of separate spheres. The separate spheres model has been challenged, but nevertheless, Davidoff and Hall's work remains an extraordinary source in terms of its detailed reading of the domestic space. One of their intriguing characters, the Birmingham jeweller James Luckock, retired to a house he had built in the residential suburb of Edgbaston in 1820. Beside a trellis twined with creeping roses he placed a rustic seat bearing the inscription:

> I'll not repine though fate shut out,
> The gaudy World's tumultuous din
> He recks' not if the World without
> Who calm, enjoys the world within. (quoted in Davidoff and Hall, 1987: 371)

An active Unitarian, Luckock, in choosing his inscription, was no doubt referring in part to the inner peace of the soul, but there is also a conscious reference to the world of the home; Luckock's carefully created imitation mansion with whitewashed walls and carefully planted garden – a suburban paradise.

Another of Davidoff and Hall's key figures, the Birmingham Independent minister John Angell James, wrote:

> There are few terms in the English language … around which cluster so many blissful associations as that delight of every English heart, the word HOME. The elysium of love – the nursery of virtue – the garden of enjoyment – the temple of concord – the circle of all tender relationships – the playground of childhood – the dwelling of manhood – the retreat of age. (115)

Middle-class men, taking refuge in their homes from the world of business, competition and work, knew whose job it was to create this 'temple of concord'. As James goes on to say: 'this, – home – sweet home – is the sphere of wedded woman's mission'. The cost of creating this idealised domestic retreat was, of course, not to be counted. The increasing separation of home and work, the growth of middle-class suburbs and the gendered ideology of domesticity together created this myth of the home as refuge, as a peaceful sanctuary distant from the trials and tribulations of the workplace. But this powerful image served to deceive. For even those households which to the public gaze appeared to fulfil most nearly the middle-class Victorian paradigm were not quiet refuges but busy workplaces, the locus of back-breaking toil for many individuals working from the early hours of the morning to late at night. The realisation of the domestic ideal relied on the labours of servants directed by a mistress whose own labour had to made invisible.

The largely female workforce comprised not only the servants, but also the ladies of the house; the mistress herself and any resident female kin, including unmarried daughters, mothers, mothers-in-law and unmarried aunts. For women, the domestic space represented not so much a place of leisure as a place of work. In the nineteenth century the ideal of the leisured housewife was a goal to which those on the borders of the upper-working class and lower-middle class aspired, but leisure time was scarce even within the upper ranges of the middle class and the upper class.

As contemporary household manuals show, the running of a substantial household was not a leisure activity. Of all the female inhabitants of middle-class homes, the eligible unmarried daughters were most free of domestic responsibilities. However, even unmarried daughters would have contributed to the running of the household. Both the variation in the quantity and type of work demanded of the women within the middle-class family and the sensitivity of middle-class women to the need for that work to be concealed from outsiders are illustrated in contemporary novels of social observation. To return to the novels of Jane Austen, for example, there is little to indicate that her heroines do anything other than take walks, play music and gossip about their acquaintance. Close attention to the text reveals that there are few references to any of the chores of daily existence – indeed, the presence of servants and their contribution to the household are rarely mentioned. But the occasional comment throws light on the sensitivity of the issue of women's work within the wealthier classes. In *Pride and Prejudice* (1813), the visiting cleric, Mr Collins, offends his hostess, Mrs Bennet, when, in praising the dinner, he asks to which of his fair cousins' efforts the excellence of the cuisine is attributable. Mrs. Bennet assures him 'with some asperity that they were well able to keep a good cook and that her daughters had nothing to do in the kitchen' ([1813] 1985: 110). On another occasion Mrs Bennet is quick to take the opportunity to boast of her daughters' unsoiled hands. Her daughters' friend, Charlotte Lucas, the daughter of a recently knighted businessman, is sent for. Mrs Bennet informs the eligible Mr Bingley that Charlotte is needed at home for mince-pie-making and goes on to point out that: 'I always keep servants that can do their own work: my daughters are brought up differently' (89). These incidents reveal Mrs Bennet's desire to plead her daughters' idle existence in the interest of keeping up social appearances.

If some attempt was made in the higher stratum of society to give unmarried daughters an apparently leisured existence, nonetheless those daughters would have found married life and the running of their own households more work than play. This is clearly evident from such contemporary texts on household management as Ann Martin Taylor's guide *Practical Hints to Young Females on the Duties of a Wife, a Mother and a Mistress of a Family* (1815): 'The house only is well conducted … where there is a strict attention paid to order and regularity. To do everything in its proper time, to keep everything in its right place, and to use everything for its proper use is the *very essence* of good management' (27).

Insofar as household work has been examined historically, the focus has been on the work done by the servants, although surprisingly little has been written on any aspect of domestic labour. Yet the burdens of being the mistress of a middle-class establishment were considerable. Mistresses of substantial households had the responsibility of hiring, checking, keeping and firing employees, organising the overall management of the domestic space, supervising purchases of food and other household purchases, setting the timetable for seasonal chores, planning menus, overseeing the upbringing of children and carrying out social and charitable duties. Even at the higher levels of nineteenth-century society there could have been very little genuine leisure time available to women to indulge in those pursuits traditionally classed as feminine leisure activities. Indeed, even when women were supposedly not occupied they would generally have kept their hands busy with tasks such as sewing, while there was sufficient light.

The lower we go down the social scale within the middle class, the more blurred becomes the boundary between servants' work and the work of the 'lady of the house'. Let us take, for example, the experiences of Jane Carlyle, the wife of the historian Thomas Carlyle. We are still in the realms of the middle classes, but the Carlyle household was far from prosperous, particularly in the early years of their marriage during the 1830s. Jane Carlyle could only afford to keep one servant. Her diary and letters are full of the difficulties involved in running such a household, despite the fact that the marriage was childless. The Carlyles' house in Chelsea, although actually built in the reign of Queen Anne, had a typical Victorian layout, a nightmare for those working in it. It had eight rooms on four floors, with a small back extension. On the basement level there were two kitchens, the back kitchen being used as a washhouse. The back kitchen was stone-paved with a larder and coal cellar opening out from it, and a large, rarely used fireplace. The front kitchen had a stone sink, supplied by water pumped up from a well under the stone floor (a luxury), a kitchen range which had to be lit first thing every morning, a large dresser and a deal table. The range, already in the house when the Carlyles moved in, was a typical pre-Victorian open range with trivets, large black kettles in which water was boiled for all the household's needs (washing, cleaning and cooking), an oven for baking, a jack which hung in front of the fire for roasting and an iron contraption in the chimney which held a stewing pot. After the Carlyles had been nearly twenty years in the house they had installed a more up-to-date range with a boiler attached, from which a couple of gallons of hot water could be drawn from a tap attached to a cistern which had to be filled daily. Although below street level, the kitchen had two windows and was quite well lit on a sunny day. During long winter evenings, however, working in the kitchen must have been grim. As Thea Holme (1965), the author of a fascinating book on the Carlyles' home life has observed:

> To cook a meal by the light of the fire and one candle (Jane was careful with candles which cost tenpence a pound); to wash up without being able to see

> which was a stain and which the pattern on the plate, to pack away food in deep-set cupboards where it was difficult to make out what stood at the back of the shelf, to keep every corner swept clean of the stone-flagged floor, where stray crumbs attracted armies of black beetles and mice housed in the wainscot; all this must have presented problems to the conscientious servant. To clean and be clean, in perpetual twilight, by means of pump-water and kettles, required a high degree of patience, hardihood and industry. (10)

On the ground floor the house had a front and back parlour, divided by folding doors and a walk-in china cupboard. Both rooms had tables. Breakfast was taken in the back parlour which faced east, and the front parlour was used for dining. On the third and fourth floors were three bedrooms and Thomas Carlyle's library. For the first thirty years of their residence in this house the servant slept in the basement kitchen. The Carlyles did not always share the same bedroom, and in 1852 the room Jane used as her own was reduced by three feet to enlarge Thomas's library (Holme, 1965: 9). One could hardly expect a clearer demonstration of the relations between gender, status and the use of space in the middle-class Victorian home.

Much of the work in the Carlyles' house was done by a servant, but both Jane and her mother, who visited for long periods, also participated in menial work. Jane did not find it at all easy to find dependable servants. One-servant households were the least-liked option amongst servants. Being a maid-of-all-work was a position shunned by more experienced, trained workers. The Carlyles went through a succession of maids; in all, thirty-four individuals worked for them in the thirty-two years they occupied the house. In one letter Jane wrote: 'my goodness … why make bits of apologies for writing about the servants – as if 'the *servants*' were not a most important, a most fearful item in our female existence!' (Holme, 1965: 162). Jane went through agonies in her attempts to find reliable servants. Sometimes she was lucky and managed to find for a short time a servant who could manage all the main chores herself. At other times, the Carlyles found themselves without a servant or with a temporary stop-gap who could not cook or do all the tasks required of her. This sounds at first like laziness on Jane's part. But as we can see from a letter to her husband while he was away on a trip to Scotland, even when there was a maid in the house, Jane and her mother had their work cut out:

> 'Mother and I … have fallen naturally into a fair Division of labour, and we keep a very tidy house.' Sereetha [the maid] … 'attained the unhoped-for

> perfection' of getting up at half past six to light the fire and lay the breakfast. Jane herself rose at seven-thirty and made the coffee ... While Jane got the breakfast, Mrs Welsh made her own bed and tidied her room; and after the meal was over she followed Sereetha down to the basement, where, said her daughter, 'she jingles and scours, and from time to time scolds till all is right and tight there. I, above stairs, sweep the parlour, blacken the grate ... then mount aloft to make my own bed.' (Holme, 1965: 18)

As their financial position improved with Thomas Carlyle's growing reputation, Jane was eventually able to employ two servants on relatively good wages. They also had gas and water laid on, but she continued to be dogged by the problems of running the household until the end of her life (Holme, 1965: 147).

If running a middle-class home offered little respite to the 'mistress', however modest or grand the establishment, the Victorian house was even less of a welcoming prospect to the workforce employed within the confines of its walls. It was this 'invisible' workforce, those unsung heroines of the industrial revolution, the domestic servants – the polishers of the silver, the dusters of the pianos, mahogany dining-tables and tallboys, the washerwomen of the damask tablecloths and coarse linens, the blackeners of the hearths and the polishers of the brass doorknobs and fenders – who enabled the nineteenth-century middle classes to inhabit their suburban mansions, to consume and expand their consumption *ad infinitum*. The bulk of the domestic workforce was female, although many men also worked within the domestic space, loosely defined. In 1851 there were more than 750,000 women registered as servants on the census and this figure undoubtedly concealed others who were not listed as such (Cooper and Donald, 1995: 257–78). By the end of the century this figure had risen to well over a million. While the number of male indoor servants dropped (from about 75,000 in 1851 to fewer than 50,000 in 1901), a variety of other male domestic occupations mushroomed, showing some interesting changes in the use of domestic space throughout the century. The number of men employed as coachmen and grooms rose from 21,000 in 1851 to 75,000 in 1901. Also, by 1901 the number of men listed as chauffeurs stood at 23,000, which indicates not only that thousands of householders owned cars, but also that many houses had garages attached by the end of the century. Another change was the marked increased desirability of outside domestic space for leisure and food production. This can be seen in the number of men employed as gardeners, which shot up from a mere 4,500 in 1851 to nearly 88,000 in 1901 (Horn, 1990: 231–2).

What was the home like as a workplace? There is no one answer to this question: every situation was different. The size and location of the house, the character of the 'mistress', the size of the domestic staff, the extent of amenities such as wells, pumps and gas lighting, the cooking facilities, the number of hearths to be cleaned – all these factors and more dictated the nature of the job. The number of servants employed would depend on the age and status of the householder, the size of the family and the age of dependants. Whatever their individual circumstances, servants worked extremely long hours (unprotected by legislation) with little time off; the work was frequently heavy and dirty and undertaken in a situation where the employee was at the constant beck and call of the employer, with scarcely any privacy or legal protection.

The kitchen was the working hub of the household. Much of a servant's life was spent in a space which, in the average suburban Victorian home, was probably not much more than ten to twelve square metres. This space was often poorly ventilated and poorly lit, almost certainly too hot in summer, the air thick with coal dust; conditions were hardly better than in other contemporary occupations. The centrepiece of the nineteenth-century middle-class kitchen was the range. Originally an open coal-fired affair, as we have seen from the experience of the Carlyles cited above, this was gradually replaced through the century by a more efficient, closed system, fired first by coal, later by gas. Although this was a cooking device, its use necessitated other forms of domestic labour. There was the carrying of coal from cellar to kitchen (until piped gas arrived) and of course the coal dust and fumes entailed extensive cleaning. While the range with its oven and hotplates enabled the cook or housewife to undertake more complex cooking operations than were possible with the simple pot and spit used in more modest households, the range undoubtedly added to cleaning chores. The irony of so many of the improvements in domestic technology that the past century has seen is that improvement in one area all too often brings with it increased labour in another.[4] The range had many parts which needed to be cleaned, greased, blackleaded and polished. In addition, there was a large number of substantial pots and pans to clean; items which were used daily to create meals big enough for a household, where the numerous servants could more than double the number of mouths to be fed.

Much of the servants' time not spent in the kitchen would have been taken up in carrying water and trays up and down flights of stairs. It has been estimated that before the advent of piped water, daily consumption of water per head was somewhere in the region of six or seven gallons.

This amount was regarded as inadequate by reformers (who recommended a minimum of twelve gallons per head) but would nevertheless have necessitated many hours of water-carrying (Davidson, 1982: 14–15). Most middle-class homes had their own well and therefore the servants would not have had to make long journeys to fetch water. Less prestigious residences would not have had their own water supply until the early twentieth century. Country dwellings would have made use of a rainwater butt and wells were often shared between clusters of cottages. In towns, however, where many more people had to rely on the same supply, servants would have been accustomed to queue for hours to obtain water. It can safely be assumed that middle-class households consumed water in greater quantities than the recommended twelve gallons per head. Thus, even in a house with its own water supply, much of the day would have been spent in carrying water, both clean and foul, between the well or pump and between the kitchen and upper floors of a house. The worst job was to get rid of the foul water and although large households would have had a supply of fresh water by the mid-nineteenth century, in most places sewers were not constructed until later. Carrying water was such a feature of everyday life in the early nineteenth century that the German socialist August Bebel commented in a book published in 1878: 'If we had proposed to our wives fifty and sixty years ago to save their daughters and servants the trouble of fetching water by laying water-pipes, they would have declared that it was absurd and unnecessary and only taught daughters and servants idleness' ([1878] 1988: 116).

There can have been little opportunity for the promotion of idle habits as far as most servants were concerned. Their day would have started between 5.30 a.m. and 6.30 a.m. and lasted until late in the evening. Most households allowed no time to rest during the day. A day off a month was not uncommon, and of course meals were taken in the kitchen and sleeping quarters were either in the kitchen or in small, cold attic rooms. Given that domestic service was one of the major forms of employment in the nineteenth century, it is surprising that the subject of servants' lives and work has not been more widely studied by historians.[5] One widely cited contemporary source is a rarity: a diary written by a servant. The writer, Hannah Cullwick, kept the diary at the behest of her future husband, author A. J. Munby. The following excerpt is from 1860 when she was employed as a maid-of-all-work by a Kilburn upholsterer for whom she had worked for five years:

> Open'd the shutters and lighted the kitchen fire – shook my sooty things in the dusthole & emptied the soot there, swept & dusted the rooms & the hall, laid the cloth & got breakfast up – clean'd 2 pairs of boots, made the beds & emptied the slops, clear'd & wash'd the breakfast things up – clean'd the plate – clean'd the knives & got dinner up – clear'd away, clean'd the kitchen up – unpack'd a hamper – took two chickens to Mrs Brewer's and brought the message back – made a tart & pick'd & gutt'd two duck & roasted them – clean'd the steps & flags on my knees, blackleaded the scraper in the front of the house – clean'd the street flags too on my knees – had tea – clear'd away – wash'd up in the scullery – clean'd the pantry on my knees & scour'd the tables – scrubb'd the flags round the house and clean'd the window sills – got tea at 9 for the master & Mrs Warwick in my dirt but Ann [a fellow servant] carried it up – clean'd the privy & passage & scullery floor on my knees – wash'd the door & clean'd the sink down – put the supper ready for Ann to take up, for I was too dirty & tired to go up stairs. (quoted in Horn, 1990: 57-8)

The above reads as a litany of labour undertaken in the confines of the middle-class domestic space. Thus the façades of prosperous nineteenth-century homes enclosed interiors which were showcases for consumption, but they also hid unpleasant working conditions. A rather later but equally evocative description of the resonances such labour had for those who performed it is to be found in the autobiographical account by Jean Rennie, *Every Other Sunday* (1955). In this extract, Rennie recalls the time in 1946 when, as an office worker in a government ministry, she worked in the house close to Eaton Square where she had been a maid in the 1920s. The interior had seen some changes, but was basically 'identical in every way' to the one in which Rennie had worked as a kitchen maid:

> I cannot describe the feeling, a kind of ghostly shiver as I walked in the front door and up to my office, which had once been the drawing-room. There were still the remains of the white fireplace, one or two white doors, tall and wide, ornate ceilings. It was a physical pain in my heart – *not*, I must hasten to add, a nostalgic pain, to go down to the basement where we kept rows and rows of files. Here was the servants' hall, here was the butler's pantry … And this, this dark dungeon, with the long dresser and this great ugly stove, and the now rickety wooden table, worm-eaten, had been the kitchen where I, and others like me, had quite literally sweated away an existence that was accepted as 'that station in life'. (quoted in Burnett, 1975: 244)

The cultural ideal of the prosperous homes of the Victorian middle class as comfortable, well-furnished havens of tranquillity also needs reconsidering in relation to the masculine experience. For the middle-class male, the domestic space was probably not a place of labour; the fires were lit, clothes laid clean and ready and breakfast laid before he had to leave for work. During his absence the house was not a tranquil haven but a flurry of activity. However, he came home to find clothes ready to change into for dinner, children bathed and ready for bed and supper about to be served. The servants may have been exhausted, the 'mistress' may have had a tiresome and difficult day, but, as far as the 'master' was concerned, he was the only member of the household who had been at work all day. For him, and him only, the house represented the end of work, an opportunity for relaxation and enjoyment.

The model was an aristocratic one. In the higher echelons of nineteenth-century society where gentlemen did not go out to work but ran their estates from home, household work had to be kept as invisible as possible. In very large establishments, domestic life was carefully controlled. As Pamela Horn has shown, frequently there were strict rules not only about what part of the domestic space one could enter, but also at what time it was permissible to be there. In such establishments there could be little or no contact between 'the family' and the lower-ranking servants. Butlers and housekeepers were responsible for the management of other servants and were influential figures:

> regarded by the under-servants, shut away in their own quarters and never permitted to be seen in the front part of the house after the family and guests had left their bedrooms, almost as kings and queens. Only the head servants, body servants and those in attendance on the sitting rooms, or dining room, would be likely even to know their employers by sight. (Peel, 1934: 81–2, cited in Horn, 1990: 24)

According to Lady Cynthia Asquith, in a well-ordered household no maid was ever seen carrying a broom or duster. With the exception of the cleaning of the bedrooms, all housework had to be done before the family came downstairs, which meant that the servants had to get up very early to work. It was impossible to keep the 'upstairs' parts of the house clean without regular servicing, but that aspect of the domestic existence had to be kept invisible at all costs. As Lady Asquith concluded, both employers and employees 'knew their places and kept to them as planets in their orbits' (Asquith, in Streatfeild, 1956: 102, cited in Horn, 1990: 24–5). The metaphor is apt; the planets all occupy the same space, but they cross each others' paths without ever colliding.

The aristocratic dream of the smoothly functioning household with its invisible cogs and wheels was the model for the aspiring middle classes. Oddly though, at the lower levels of the middle class it was the labour of the housewife which had to be kept invisible, while the labour of the servant was displayed publicly to ensure status. In such households, far from staying out of sight, servants were displayed in the most public areas of the domestic space. In households employing only one maid, an important function of the servant was that of being seen answering the door to visitors. Some families even employed a girl once a week just to whiten the step and polish the doorknocker. The following quotation describes the Golders Green suburb in the 1920s, but it might equally apply to the smaller Victorian villa:

> Few of the houses were large enough to accommodate servants, but many families hired a maid, making sure that she was in attendance at least for the evening meal, which would be taken at the front of the house, with curtains drawn well back and lights blazing. (Jackson, cited in Barrett and Phillips, 1987: 25)

There was nothing uniquely British about the conspicuous display of servants or the invisibility of the housewife's labour. Sibylle Meyer, in an essay on the wives of civil servants in nineteenth-century Germany, reveals the lengths to which middle-class families would go to create the elaborate deception of leisured femininity. Families who could afford only one general servant were urged by household manuals to hire a temporary (male) servant for dinner parties. The housewife might have slaved away to create the meal that was served, she might have worked by hand the embroidered table linen, but she should employ someone to serve dinner for appearances' sake. As Meyer notes, the housewife must have suffered agonies on such occasions, fearing that the butler might commit a *faux pas* or, horror of horrors, might even be recognised as being the same person who had served the dinner in another household on some other occasion (Meyer, 1987: 159).

Visible or invisible, housewives and servants in their thousands were needed to service the middle-class homes of the Victorian period. The domestic space was not a peaceful sanctuary but a space in which people of different ages, sexes and social classes worked, cooperated and came into conflict on a daily basis. John Angell James's 1856 description of the domestic space cited earlier – 'there are few terms in the language … around which cluster so many blissful associations as that delight of every English heart, the word HOME' – reflected the cultural ideal. Half the population, at least, would have had some insight into the labour and effort which it took to create the apparently tranquil haven to which Victorian men like James dreamed of returning at the end of their day's work.

Notes

1 In German, *das Haus* (house), *zu Hause* (at home). The German word *das Heim* (home) is not used in the same way as 'home' in English. In Russian (transliterated), *dom* (house), *doma* (at home). In French, *la maison* (house), *notre maison* (our house or home), but the phrase 'at home' is best translated as *chez moi* (at my place). In Modern Greek (transliterated), *to spiti* (house or home).

2 These figures are taken from Edward Higgs, 1986: 419. Higgs believes that these figures, based on census returns, may be an overestimation due to classification problems. My view is that, if anything, the error lies in the opposite direction.

3 I use the term middle class to incorporate all who composed the middling section of society, above the rank of manual and low-grade clerical workers up to those bordering on the edges of the gentry, including managerial white-collar workers, professionals, clerics, businessmen and yeomen farmers.

4 Hence the title of the history of American household technology by R. S. Cowan, *More Work for Mother: The Ironies of Household Technology from the Open Hearth to the Microwave*, 1989.

5 Useful works include Higgs and Horn, 1990, and autobiographical accounts in Burnett, 1975, and Hellerstein et al., 1981, and Davidoff, 1974 should not be forgotten. From the same period there is also the useful comparative work by McBride, 1976.

Bibliography

Asquith, Lady C. (1956), 'In front of the green baize door', in N. Streatfeild (ed), *The Day Before Yesterday*, London, Collins.

Austen, J. [1813] (1985), *Pride and Prejudice*, ed. T. Tanner, Harmondsworth, Penguin.

Austen, J. [1818] (1995), *Northanger Abbey*, ed. M. Butler, Harmondsworth, Penguin.

Barrett, H. and Phillips, J. (1987), *Suburban Style: The British Home 1840–1960*, London, Macdonald.

Bebel, A. [1878] (1988), *Woman in the Past, Present and Future*, intro. M. Donald, London, Zwan.

Boris, E. (1994), 'The home as a workplace: "deconstructing dichotomies"', *International Review of Social History*, 39:3, 415–28.

Burnett, J. (1975), *Useful Toil: Autobiographies of Working People from the 1820s to the 1920s*, Newton Abbot, David and Charles.

Cooper, D. and Donald, M. (1995), 'Households and "hidden" kin in early nineteenth-century England: four case studies in suburban Exeter 1821–61', *Continuity and Change*, 10:2, 257–78.

Cowan, R. S. (1989), *More Work for Mother: The Ironies of Household Technology from the Open Hearth to the Microwave*, London, Free Association.

Cullwick, H. (1860) 'Hannah Cullwick's Diaries', Munby MSS, Cambridge, Trinity College, 14 July.

Davidoff, L. (1974), 'Mastered for life: servant and wife in Victorian and Edwardian England', *Journal of Social History*, 7, 406–28.

Davidoff, L. (1976), *A Day in the Life of a Victorian Domestic Servant*, London, Allen and Unwin.

Davidoff, L. and Hall, C. (1987), *Family Fortunes: Men and Women of the English Middle Class 1750–1850*, London, Hutchinson.

Davidson, C. (1982), *A Woman's Work is Never Done: A History of Housework in the British Isles 1650–1950*, London, Chatto and Windus.

Franzoi, B. (1987), '"... with the wolf always at the door ..." Women's work in domestic industry in Britain and Germany', in M. Boxer and J. Quataert (eds), *Connecting Spheres: Women in the Western World 1500 to the Present*, Oxford, Oxford University Press.

Hellerstein, E. O., Hume, L. P. and Offen, K. M. (eds) (1981), *Victorian Woman: A Documentary Account of Women's Lives in Nineteenth-Century England*, France and the United States, Brighton, Harvester.

Higgs, E. (1986), *Domestic Servants and Households in Rochdale 1851–71*, New York, Garland.

Holme, T. (1965), *The Carlyles at Home*, London, Oxford University Press.

Horn, P. (1990), *The Rise and Fall of the Domestic Servant*, Stroud, Sutton.

Jackson, A. (1973), *Semi-Detached London: Suburban Development, Life and Transport 1900–39*, London, Allen and Unwin.

James, J. A. [1852] (1856), *Female Piety or The Young Woman's Friend and Guide through Life to Immortality*, London.

McBride, T. (1976), *The Domestic Revolution: The Modernization of Domestic Service in England and France 1820–1920*, New York, Holmes and Meier.

McClintock, A. (1995), *Imperial Leather: Race, Gender and Sexuality in the Colonial Contest*, London, Routledge.

Meyer, S. (1987), 'The tiresome work of conspicuous leisure: on the domestic duties of wives of civil servants in the German Empire (1871–1918)', in M. Boxer and J. Quataert (eds), *Connecting Spheres: Women in the Western World from 1500 to the Present,* Oxford, Oxford University Press.

Peel, C. S. (1934), 'Homes and habitats', in G. M. Young (ed.), *Early Victorian England*, London, Oxford University Press.

Rennie, J. (1955), *Every Other Sunday: The Autobiography of a Kitchenmaid*, London, Arthur Barker.

Streatfeild, N. (ed.) (1956), *The Day Before Yesterday*, London, Collins.

Taylor, A. M. (1815), *Practical Hints to Young Females on the Duties of a Wife, a Mother and a Mistress of a Family*, London.

District visiting and the constitution of domestic space in the mid-nineteenth century

Martin Hewitt

Historiography

This essay seeks to take up Mary Poovey's challenge that 'when historians ... have ignored the role played by ideas about domesticity in the making of the working class, they have overlooked one of the pivotal points of social organisation and change' in the nineteenth century (1995: 130). It must be conceded that hitherto in treating working-class domesticity historians have generally been willing to rest satisfied with a series of truisms: that the nineteenth-century cult of domesticity involved not only highly gendered but also deeply class-specific forms of differentiation; that while the division of public from private spaces was fundamental to newly articulated middle-class cultures, for the working classes quite distinct forms of housing, family structure, work patterns and domestic economy all militated against the emergence of separate spheres; that the working classes did not absorb middle-class domesticity, but developed their own negotiated version of it (Davidoff and Hall, 1987; Perrot, [1987] 1990). Fleshing out this picture has proved difficult. Anna Clark's recent study of artisanal uses of the rhetoric of domesticity shows how the ideal could be reinterpreted and mobilised by the working classes, but still tells us little about its day-to-day realities (Clark, 1995). In fact, we are still surprisingly ignorant of the practicies of working-class domesticity. Most of what we think we do know derives from the highly ideologically charged accounts of middle-class social reformers.

In this context, domestic or district visiting provides a double opportunity: on the one hand, as a practice which clearly went to the heart of the way in which the domestic could be defined for the working classes; on the other, in the profusion of journals, accounts and recollections, as a set of texts which, while possessing their own linguistic codes and rhetorical strategies, nevertheless provide one of the few bodies of relatively unmediated depiction of the nature of the working-class home and its domesticity. The history of domestic visitation could be used to address many questions. The intention here is to focus on one of the most significant: the very mapping of the working-class domestic space, the constitution of the boundaries between the public and the private and of the terms on which passage between them was possible: the working-class sense of privacy.[1] Without doubt, the confrontation of the domestic visitor and the working classes was fundamental to the process by which such definitions were established on the ground.

To date, reference to the practice of domestic or district visiting has been used primarily to symbolise the lack of working-class privacy. Not only have historians emphasised the extent to which district visiting was central to middle-class efforts to achieve effective surveillance over the working-class home from the 1830s onwards (Seed, 1982), but they have also tended to go further, portraying the district visitor as omnipresent in working-class districts and hence working-class homes (Wohl, 1983; Prochaska, 1980; Brown, 1988; Lewis, 1986). Indeed, it is generally suggested that for many of the working class, 'there was no such thing as a strictly private life' (Mandler, 1990: 9–10).

Recently, the concept of 'social space', in part a transitional zone between the public and private, has been deployed to characterise much, if not all, of working-class living space, not just courts and alleys, but also domestic interiors (Mahood, 1995; Elliott, 1994). It would generally be accepted that, as the century progressed, there was 'a realignment of the relationship between what was private and what was public' in the working-class home: 'the threshold between the private and public spheres had been redrawn and made much less ambiguous' (Daunton, 1983: 215; Perrot, [1987] 1990). But these processes have been seen as largely confined to the period after 1870. In effect, it has been suggested that for much of the nineteenth century working-class domesticity was largely divorced from any sense of the private. However, although considerable attention has been given to tracing the institutional spread and profusion of visiting associations through the nineteenth century (Prochaska, 1990; D. Lewis, 1986; Luddy, 1995; Mahood, 1995; Humphreys, 1995) and David Vincent has begun, in 'Secrecy and the city, 1870–1939' (1995), to explore negotiations over privacy in the sense of control over information flows, very little attention has been given to the process of visiting itself (Summers, 1979) and to privacy in the sense of the interest in and ability of the working classes to define their homes as separate from public or communal space and to control access to them.

This essay seeks to argue that our picture of the weakness of the working-class sense of the private before the 1870s derives from an inadequate (although powerfully supported) reading of the literature of the middle-class engagement with the working-class home and an unsustainable elision between the two characteristics of privacy. The working classes were rarely able to establish the control over information about their daily lives achieved by the middle classes. But this does not mean they lacked a sense of the private, that the working classes were not able to construct their own domestic space.

Reading the working-class home as thoroughfare

It would be foolish to deny the power and pervasiveness of the conventional reading of mid-nineteenth-century working-class domestic space, or the fact that the literature of visiting did much to propagate and sustain it. The belief in the permeability of working-class domestic space comes through loudly in advice manuals and guides for visitors published from the 1830s to the 1860s. Indeed, such permeability was necessary to sustain the claim to systematic visiting of all households in a given district and hence the visitors' ability not only to revitalise inter-class relationships, but also to collect comprehensive religious and social statistics.

Admittedly, most included some general advice about approaching the working-class home in a gentle and conciliatory spirit. Visitors were urged to be 'humble, courteous and affectionate', to 'strive to enlist the kindly feelings of the inhabitants in favour of their purpose, by approaching them in a friendly and conciliatory manner' (Manchester and Salford Sanitary Association, n.d.) and 'to give their visits the appearance of those of a *friend*, rather than of an official'; they were advised to shake hands, make notes in private after leaving and ensure that they visited at convenient times (Plenderleath, 1858: 4–5). However, almost all such advice was couched in terms of how the visitor should behave *once in* the working-class home, and the advice that the literature of visiting proffers gives virtually no indication that there might be any difficulty in gaining entry. Instead, the picture presented is one of easy access. '[T]he London poor are accustomed to the notion of being visited and are more inclined to complain of being neglected than to look on the visitor as an intruder', opined Charles Bosanquet in 1874 in his *A Handy Book for Visitors of the Poor in London* (quoted in J. Lewis, 1986: 101). There might be occasional rebuffs, but these would merely be the passing result of drunkenness (almost certainly to be regretted on a subsequent visit), of ignorance, which could with a little delicacy easily be dispelled, or of sectarian bigotry, more difficult to overcome but also a special case, having no bearing on the willingness of the bulk of the working classes to allow access (Emra, 1839; Hilton, 1859; Surridge, 1871; *Home Mission Field*, July 1859).

The picture presented by this literature thus complements the wider interpretations of the working-class dwelling which Poovey has traced in the 1840s and 1850s. Just as the working classes were perceived as living in overcrowded conditions, with few of the furnishings or comforts which could make a house a home, so they had none of that sense of privacy which marked off the middle-class home as a haven from the world outside. When the issue of the working classes' sense of privacy was raised, it was only to regret that the poor had too little of a sense of privacy, so that 'it would be a blessed thing if the poor felt *more* instead of *less* of the sacredness of home' (Davies, 1855: 123). On the rare occasions when the danger of intrusion was mentioned, it was usually attached to concerns which did not directly relate to a sense of the working-class home as private space but rather to privacy in the sense of regulating access and information flows, that 'visits be [not] so frequent as to be intrusive, so long as to be inconvenient', or to an over-officious or prying manner adopted once inside (Ley, 1842: 11; Nixon, 1847). The suggestion that visitors risked trenching on some legitimate sense of working-class private space was exceptional.

I have found only a couple of direct references to doorstep conduct for visitors in visiting manuals themselves. The *District Visitor's Manual* (a compilation of district visiting advice literature published in 1840) proffers the highly ambiguous advice that calls should always be 'preceded by a tap on the door' (28–9) – which is not at all the same thing as saying that the visitor should then wait for an answer before entering. *The Female Visitor to the Poor* – semi-journal, semi-manual – makes the point that its heroine knocks and waits for entrance, 'for, stranger or friend, we would ever respect the right of the poor man in his cottage-castle'. It is noted that this is very much an unrealised ideal:

> I fear that the reason why some meet with a cold reception in the cottage ... is that they too much forget this distinction. They go into the homes of the poor as having a right to enter them, to make inquiries and to pass censures; and because they can bestow their silver and their gold, they feel they have a right to dictate and condemn. (Charlesworth, 1846: 194)

An only slightly more complex reading is available in the journals, autobiographical accounts and descriptions of visiting left by visitors.

Here there is often some sense of working-class policing of the domestic threshold. 'I scarcely know how to describe' the way, commented John Hunt, one London City Missionary, on commencing his visiting in 1858, he was:

> insulted, rebuffed, laughed at and treated with the coldest indifference. When I knocked at a door, up went an upstairs window and a head could be seen, demanding with some rudeness, 'What do you want?' At other times the front door was opened just ajar and no sooner was my errand known than the door slammed in my face. (1895: 27)

But such descriptions were usually rhetorical devices used to point up the success which visiting eventually brought. Hence, for Hunt, as for other visitors and missionaries, such early opposition was soon overcome, doors previously shut were opened, rejection gave way to enthusiastic welcome and the visitor's 'influence for good grew in a corresponding ratio with the people's knowledge of [them]'. Past failings might be acknowledged, but not present or future ones: although the cleric and the city missionary might have failed to reach everyone, Ellen Ranyard was confident that her new Bible-women 'will penetrate every home' (1859: 173). Very quickly, most accounts settled down to a picture in which welcome for the visitors was fulsome, while comments such as that of the Oxford Parochial District Visiting Society in 1833 that 'the visitors have been received with great civility and even cordiality' (12) rapidly became the staple of visiting literature.

There can be no doubt that the entrenched view of the working-class home as social (if not public) space was supported not just by the circulation of this kind of social commentary but also by its seepage into the broader literature of the mid-Victorian period. It would be an exaggeration to suggest that 'home missionary' fiction achieved the status of a genre in its own right. Nevertheless, in the hands of authors such as Mary Barber, Anna Charlesworth and Julia Wightman, it remained a recognisable form of writing (Barber, 1852, 1854, 1856, 1858; Charlesworth, 1846, 1858; Wightman, 1861, 1862; *Town and Forest*, 1860), peopled by earnest well-meaning visitors and grateful recipients of their attentions. At the same time, the visiting of the poor by the rich became a staple element of the social problem novel, standing at the apex of 'the idealization of domesticity and the popular revival of social and economic paternalism' which Catherine Gallagher has argued were at the heart of the form (1985: 115). In fact, characters such as Frances Trollope's Mary Brotherton (*Michael Armstrong, Factory Boy*, 1840),

Mary Elizabeth Braddon's Eliza Floyd (*Aurora Floyd,* 1863) and Elizabeth Gaskell's Margaret Hale (*North and South*, 1854–5) represent the district visitor not as a challenge to working-class domestic space but as a selfless and generous benefactor. Of course, there is a rival representation in the form of Dickens's Mrs Pardiggle (*Bleak House*, 1852–3) who, in contrast to the gentle and sensitive Margaret Hale, is officious and intrusive, assuming a right to enter the working-class house and to be heard out. Nevertheless, even if Mrs Pardiggle serves as a counterpoint to Dickens's heroine Esther Summerson (who feels 'uncomfortable', 'intrusive' and 'out of place' when joining Mrs Pardiggle in the brickmaker's cottage) and even if Margaret Hale is at pains not to force herself on Bessy Higgins, Dickens's and Gaskell's readings of the domestic space differ little from those in the wider literature. The parallels with autobiographical accounts and journals are also striking (Bayly, 1860: 222). As one writer to the *Church Guardian* in 1858 put it, Mrs Pardiggle, 'though a caricature, becomes a very unpleasant likeness to an original not uncommon' (17 October).

In his provocative book *The Foul and the Fragrant* (1986) Alain Corbin has argued that cage and den were the dominant ways in which the working-class home was figured in the social descriptions of the mid-nineteenth century. The writing, he argued, 'focused on the aspect of narrowness. The crampedness of the sleeping area, the depth of the yard, and the length of the alley created in the mind of the bourgeois (who normally had plenty of room) the impression of suffocation' (153). Yet the spatial elision which is so clearly expressed in this passage, in which room merges into yard and yard into alley, illuminates vividly the reasons why the figure of cage might equally be replaced by that of thoroughfare in characterising the dominant bourgeois construction of the working-class home.

As Poovey has pointed out, the emphasis given in the writings of Edwin Chadwick and Elizabeth Gaskell to the ways in which sewage and foul water seeped into the dwellings of the poor 'is a sign that, for Gaskell as for Chadwick, the homes of the poor can never be private in the sense that they cannot exclude the literal refuse from the streets' (1995: 144). Certainly, as Corbin demonstrates, in this writing, '[g]aining access to the poor man's stinking dwelling almost amounted to an underground expedition' (1986: 152). But the act of going underground, the moment of penetration, occurred on the entry into the working-class district or 'slum', or, at its most focused, in the move from street to court or alley, and not in the act of entering the home itself. Hence the passage from Miller's *Sketches of London*:

> We will enter these streets and peep into those dark, close, unhealthy, and forbidding-looking rooms. In these narrow alleys dusky twilight reigns throughout the sunny noon of day. We have to feel for the noisome staircases which open on either hand; and now we have found one, we will grope our way through this land of gloom and shadows. (*Scripture Readers' Journal*, 2, 1856–60: 21)

It is possible to go further and suggest that the working-class home was constructed not only with permeable walls but also without threshold and even without doors. For the middle classes, the door, of course, was crucial to the architecture and practice of privacy. As Philippa Tristram reminds us, English middle-class homes were unusual in that rooms were generally constructed with only one door, so that they did not connect and were more 'private' (1989: 244), while a whole complex of rituals of social etiquette was constructed around the outer door of the home. Yet in middle-class accounts of the working-class home the door tends to disappear; if it is mentioned at all it is only to note that it is ajar, that the house is thus open to scrutiny from the outside. One of the best fictional readings of this kind is to be found in Harriet Martineau's *Deerbrook* (1839). The novel is illuminating precisely because of the strength of its sense of the threshold, at least in the bourgeois context. Indeed, doors as social and physical obstacles reverberate through the entire text, which constructs a powerful picture of the rituals of the threshold, the meanings transmitted by different styles of knocking and the social roles which demand that the heroine, Margaret Ibbotson, is not seen answering the door herself. Yet, when it comes to Margaret's visit to the cholera-ravaged home of the working-class Platt family, the door and the threshold are once again rendered insubstantial and the novel's action moves in and out of the house without any sense that a social or spatial boundary is being crossed. Similarly, in Angus Reach's accounts of working-class Manchester for the *Morning Chronicle* around 1850, '[i]n most cases the doors of the houses stand hospitably open and young children cluster over the thresholds and swarm out upon the pavement' (quoted in Razzell and Wainwright, 1973: 167–8). Even as late as the 1870s Octavia Hill was suggesting that 'The front doors stood open night and day' (1875: 74).

In this context, Dickens's bricklayer's cottage has particular interest because it formed the subject of one of the original illustrations of *Bleak House* by Hablot Knight Browne and in this the conventional middle-class reading is given graphic embodiment (see figure 11). Three things are especially striking about this engraving: first, the multiplicity of uses

11 Hablot K. Browne, 'The Visit to the Brickmaker's', in Charles Dickens, *Bleak House* [1852–53] (1948).

of the room – cooking, washing, lounging and even drying clothes (the clothes line in particular hinting at the blurring of outdoor and indoor functions); second, the two working-class figures immediately beyond the outer door, both watching and discussing events within, which reinforcing the transparency of the threshold and the openness of the domestic space to surveillance; third, the way in which the domestic interior is framed by the two open doors (the interior door may well represent a pantry cupboard, but it could as easily represent a rear entrance; whatever, it is an *open* door and establishes the room as open-ended, as passage, as thoroughfare). This kind of imagery, which can be found replicated in, for example, the internal and external illustrations to Mary Barber's *Castle Rag* (1858) and *Sunshine* (1854), contrasts starkly with the more enclosed representations typical of the idealised agricultural labourer's cottage (Payne, 1998).

In this sense, it might be argued that the practice of domestic visiting and its literature marked a fascinating inversion of the ideology of the separate spheres, in that while the model middle-class home was constructed as refuge and haven, as a place purified by its sealing off from the public world, the working-class home was considered as pollutant in moral as well as sanitary terms, opened out to the public world of the slum into which it was so readily aggregated.

Reading the working-class house as home

The degree to which such attitudes became entrenched in mid-Victorian culture is perhaps illustrated by the case of one unfortunate Manchester man who was arrested in 1865 after a fracas caused by the police's attempt to move him on. Found outside the door of a working-class home in the early hours of the morning, his explanation that he had knocked and was waiting for someone to come down and let him in was apparently simply too farfetched to be accepted (*Manchester City News*, 29 July 1865). As a result, the open or absent door has become part of the conventional picture of the working-class 'slums', complete with working men and women sitting on doorsteps, standing in doorways, gossiping and participating in community life. Nevertheless, by rereading the accounts of district visitors it is possible to produce an alternative and perhaps more convincing reading of these texts which suggests a much more complex picture. From this, a stronger, although admittedly sometimes fragile and contingent, sense of working-class privacy emerges.

In the conventional narrative of district visiting activity the initial obstacles presented to visitors and missionaries are dwelt upon as a necessary element in the justification of the improvement they were claimed to have effected, so that the available sample is firmly skewed in favour of those instances where some kind of ultimate success could be boasted. However, there is little reason to doubt that visitors often achieved access only after a lengthy process of attrition. George Wilson, the London City Mission missionary in Westminster in the 1840s, accepted that he had 'for a long time been denied access and treated with contempt, the door shut in his face, and hard names and foul language used' (*London City Mission Magazine*, 5, 1846: 101). A missionary in Kennington in 1856, while congratulating himself that after nine months of labour he was finding more houses accessible, nevertheless had to confess that 'there still remain very many where I cannot get access' (*London City Mission Magazine* 21, 1856: 100).

Visitors were generally chary of comprehensive descriptions beyond vague expressions of optimism. But reading their accounts carefully suggests the fragility of the confidence expressed. To claim that 'domiciliary visitation is by many thankfully received' (*County Towns Mission Maga-*

zine 5, 1862: 94) was to acknowledge that by many (and perhaps most) it was not. If necessary, it would be relatively easy to accumulate a multitude of comments along the lines of the complaint of the 'many rebuffs' noted by a visitor in Paddington in 1844 (*London City Mission Magazine,* 1844: 40). The very justification of initiatives such as Ranyard's Biblewomen was the inability of other visitors to reach the whole of the working classes. Even Ranyard, in less guarded moments, was prepared to accept that doorstep rebuffs were quite common, hence her praise for the Jewish quarter of Spitalfields, even though she could often not get entry, because at least 'in no instance have I received an uncivil reception, nor had the door slammed in my face, without an answer, as is too frequently the case elsewhere' (1859: 108–9).

Although, as has been suggested, the doorstep transaction was often invisible in visitors' accounts, the sheer amount of this material which survives means that by piecing together the scattered references it is possible to construct a picture of what we might describe as doorstep etiquette, of the rituals of access to the working-class house. There was, unfortunately, no single practice; doorstep etiquette appears to have depended rather on a series of variables: the nature of the accommodation, the social position of its inhabitants, the character of the district (rural or urban) and broader geographies of region. In tenements or large houses sublet by floors or rooms, the hall and stairways were usually treated as public space (although there were clearly many exceptions to this practice). However, the internal doors would normally be closed, as would the external doors of single-family dwellings. It was unusual for these doors to be locked during either day or night, but by no means unheard of and certainly more likely as one moved up the social scale. Likewise, there were different patterns of response to a knock at the door. In some cases it is clear that a visitor would be called in upon knocking; in some cases occupants would call out an enquiry as to what the visitor wanted without going to or opening the door. The predominant pattern (and again this is increasingly the norm the greater the claim to respectability) seems to have been for occupants to respond to a knock by answering the door (and for the visitor to wait for the knock to be answered).

That it was conventional to answer the door should alert us to the extent to which the threshold of the working-class home was policed, notwithstanding the assumption of many visitors that it was only good manners that they be invited in. A range of strategies was used to control access, many of which involved using the door to prevent entry. Doors were sometimes locked against the visitor; where doors had no locks, it was not unusual in some districts for the door handles themselves to be removed. Frequently, missionaries had to hold conversations through unopened doors or were greeted by a head leaning out of a window enquiring as to their business before sending them off. Children were employed in perhaps unconscious aping of the rituals with which the middle-class domestic space was policed, answering the door and putting off unwanted visitors: according to one account, 'I scarcely ever find the door open in any part of [my district]; and after being kept waiting for some time, a child is frequently sent to open it, and when I ask for her mother, she is "too busy to see the person with the tracts"' (*London City Mission Magazine*, 1856: 99). Where occupants were willing to open the door, this was often clearly done with extreme care, a few inches being deemed sufficient. Although this provided visitors with an opportunity to engage in conversation and perhaps persuade the occupant to invite them in, it also marked an assumption that care needed to be taken when opening the door to an unexpected knock. Time and again, whether the door was opened only a few inches or more fully, it would be firmly, if not violently, slammed once the nature of the visitor had been ascertained. And, perhaps most telling of all, even when willing to converse with the missionary many working-class occupants were prepared to do this only on the doorstep. They did not invite the visitors or missionaries in.

As a result, visitors had often to resort to guile in order to gain entry: not just taking every opportunity to accost recalcitrants in the street but deliberately preying on children in the hope that they would provide internal pressure; knocking authoritatively and then slipping straight in when the door was opened; responding to an enquiry as to who was knocking by announcing themselves 'a friend', and slipping even the most reluctant a tract in the hope that, when returning on the pretext of collecting it, they would be invited in while it was located. It is apparent from their accounts that the practice of the visitors in entering the working-class home without waiting to be invited was often not so much an assumption that their visit would be welcomed as a deliberate effort to forestall attempts to keep them out. Hence, when recounting his visits to a fortune-teller, one missionary recalled that he 'usually receives my visits and earnest admonitions, in good temper; the truth is, however, I generally *walk in* and make at once for the *interior* of his miserable dwelling, believing that if I waited at the door he would refuse to be seen by me' (*Children's Missionary Magazine*, 1, 1851: 55).

This evidence presents an alternative picture, in which the working-class threshold was not invisible but was often carefully policed. In most cases we can only presume the motivations which lay behind such rejections, especially as they seem to have existed in tension with a general attitude of openness and hospitality among the working classes. Certainly, the Irish home missionary Patrick O'Brien noted that he had no difficulty in obtaining access to working-class homes as long as he maintained the character of a fellow worker. The difficulty came when he tried to shift conversation round to more spiritual matters – once his position was known, he was likely to be quickly thrown out (O'Brien, 1856). In similar vein, visitors in Manchester in the 1830s noted that the first visit through their district was much easier than the second, when their intention was known, and refusal of entry much more common (*Manchester and Salford City Mission Report,* 1840: 12).

If visitors were marked off by dress from the classes they were visiting, there seems to have been a general expectation that at the very least they would give a clear explanation of their purpose on entering. The way in which several manuals emphasised that visitors should make it clear that they were emissaries of the parish priest or district visiting society implies that some degree of 'authority' had to be claimed in order to legitimise their presence at the door or in the home. In some cases, the argument is more explicitly made that it was precisely the advantage of regular visitation, with the opportunity which it presented to establish some kind of personal and friendly relations with the families visited, that it could overcome any sense of intrusion and invasion of privacy (Oxford Parochial Visiting Society, 1834).

The tenor of the visitors' accounts would certainly suggest that the combined influences of deference and familiarity (if not friendship) did help in negotiating entry to the working-class domestic space. Instances occur with surprising frequency in which visitors or missionaries were able to gain access to and remain in homes where they were clearly not wanted but from which the occupants seemed unwilling to eject them. It appears to have been much more common for unwilling occupants to try to avoid visitors by fleeing the room than to try to eject them. Where flight was impossible, resignation often reigned. This frame of mind is summed up by the account of a female visitor in Luton, who recalled an incident in which, asking a housewife found at the door of her dwelling for a tract left on a former visit, 'She got up and went into the house to fetch it, whither I followed and shut the door, which, as soon as she observed, she sat down with the air of one who feels they must be resigned to their fate' (*County Towns Mission Record*, 1, 1853–5: 95). According to one missionary at Dartford, 'There is no open hostility. The people generally receive me, but there is a callous indifference which is often far more difficult to encounter and overcome' (*County Towns Mission Magazine*, 5, 1862: 112). In the case of homeworkers, this was often manifested by a pointed refusal to stop work to listen to what missionaries or scripture readers had to say. As suggested by Dickens's exchange between Mrs Pardiggle, who promises 'I shall come to you again, in your regular order' and the bricklayer, who responds, '"So long as you go now" … folding his arms and shutting his eyes with an oath, "you may do wot you like"!' (Dickens, 1852–3: 108), this kind of acquiescence tells us more about the relative social power of the parties in the exchange than about the weakness of working-class privacy.

Not that there were not innumerable examples of missionaries who had entered dwellings being driven out, often with considerable violence. Accounts talk of visitors being threatened with axes, pots or any household utensils to hand, of having dirty water or worse emptied on them as they climbed stairs, of being met with a volley of oaths and curses and of being physically bundled out of the door if they had the temerity to stand their ground. Even among the sick and dying, the unannounced intrusion of a visitor could spark a furious dismissal: 'A man confined to his bed and dangerously ill … raised himself up in a passion and told me to be gone immediately out of his house and not dare to appear here again', reported a Manchester missionary in 1838 (*Manchester and Salford City Mission Report*, 1838: 21).

Quotations like this imply that some significance was being placed on the inviolability of the domestic space, without providing any concrete evidence that the working classes were prepared to articulate an ideology of domestic privacy. Nevertheless, at times and albeit infrequently, something which looks more solidly like working-class versions of the ideologies of domestic privacy does surface. 'I am in my own house, and an Englishman's house is his castle. Nobody sent for you, and I am not obliged to answer your questions', one missionary was quickly informed in 1846 when he refused to take the hint and retire gracefully, being bundled bodily out of the house (*London City Mission Magazine*, 1846: 73). Similarly, the early Bible-women, who had hoped to train further women by taking them with them on their rounds, found that 'The people, expecting a quiet visit from the good woman in whom they had begun to place confidence, resented … any perpetual introduction of strange faces and asked, "if they were going to be made a puppet show of"' (Ranyard, 1859: 52–3). Perhaps surprisingly, the element of privacy in the sense of controlling information which is hinted at here appears scarcely at all before the 1860s, although by that decade there are scattered allusions to hostility to visitors on the basis, as a missionary from the Isle of Wight reported in 1865, that they were 'a sort of religious policemen' (*County Towns Mission Magazine*, 1865: 124). '"It is no use your coming here"', a Reading visitor was told in the same year, '"all that you want is to pry into other people's business, just to see how we live and what we have in the house"' (114).

Reframing the visiting process

Can these comments be reconciled with the dominant picture presented initially or is there nothing more here than two partial readings, each complete with its own selective quotation? That reconciliation is possible becomes more readily apparent once it is recognised that it is not just the rhetoric of the doorstep which needs to be reread but the whole constructed picture of domestic visiting.[2]

In the first place it must be acknowledged that, for all the profusion of visiting associations, it is doubtful whether (with the possible exception of working-class London) anything approaching sustained comprehensive coverage was achieved in the mid-nineteenth-century urban context. In many cases large expanses of the most notorious working-class housing were abandoned. Even within those districts where visitors and missionaries were active, for all the rhetoric of universalism, most district visiting was a highly selective process. Few, if any, voluntary visiting associations expected their volunteers to visit households which had not made clear their willingness to receive visits: usually a cleric, scripture-reader or stipendiary visitor was sent round before them to weed out those households likely to be uncooperative. Hence the Manchester and Salford District Provident Society employed a paid visitor, one of whose duties was, when a new visitor was assigned to a district, to do the rounds of that district, explaining that a regular visitor was to follow and ensuring 'that no objectionable houses [were] among the number assigned' (1842–3: 11). While the manuals stressed systematic visiting, the recollections of voluntary visitors often imply quite the reverse (Wightman, 1861, 1862).

Even paid visitors appear to have distinguished between 'visitable' and 'unvisitable' houses, and although it is difficult to identify on what basis this decision was made, it was certainly more than just a division between those who made an outright refusal of admission and those who did not. Hence the comment of one Manchester City Missionary that 'I have called at the door of every dwelling on the district [*sic*] and have only in a few cases been positively refused admittance; but there is a considerable number (I cannot yet say how many) that may be marked off as unvisitable' (*Manchester and Salford City Mission Magazine*, November 1854: 153). Indications vary as to the proportion of houses in any district which might present sufficient obstacles to be left unvisited even by professional visitors; in general, the figure might be somewhere between 10 and 20 per cent of all households, but it could be as high as 50 per cent (*London City Mission Magazine*, May 1840: 12) and voluntary visiting would normally have been considerably more selective.

Moreover, although in the language of visiting a careful distinction was made between a 'call' (when, although the door was opened, it was quickly closed again or, when admission was granted but for some reason – for example, the family was eating – no conversation of any substance took place) and a 'visit' (defined by having allowed the visitor to engage in some kind of religious or improving conversation), it is clear that the term 'visit' did not necessarily imply that admission was granted. The 'Hints for a Missionary Entering Upon His District' circulated by the County Towns Mission Society in 1853 made this explicit, noting that 'A good visit may be had as one stands at a door, when further admittance is refused' (*County Towns Mission Record*, 1, 1853–5: 110).

As a result, it is clear that a great deal of visiting was highly selective and that the rhetoric of universal visitation was sustained by a sleight of hand which focused on the visitation of houses already identified as 'visitable', a concept which in itself did not necessarily imply access. Likewise, the visitors' journals give a crucially selective account of their engagement with domestic space, the initial hostility faced on taking up a new district being replaced by a general ready acceptance of their visits because for the most part those households where they would not be welcome had been filtered out of their routine. Hence the fact that, in established visitors' accounts, instances of opposition often derive from encounters occasioned when a visited family has moved and been replaced, without the knowledge of the visitor, by a less amenable householder.

There is a further complication. On the one hand, measures of the proportion of houses which home missionaries or district visitors deemed 'unvisitable', and even individual cases of exclusion, do not easily translate into unambiguous evidence of the degree to which the working classes were able and willing to assert their privacy (for example, a Catholic who fiercely resisted the attentions of an Anglican scripture reader might have no sense of his or her right to exclude a Catholic priest or nun). On the other hand, the degree of willingness or resignation with which visitors were received might relate less to an individual's attitudes to privacy than to their particular material circumstances. We cannot simply condemn all visiting as alien, hostile and intrusive; in the absence of comprehensive welfare provision it could also be a vital resource, and there is considerable evidence that the working classes adopted a highly pragmatic and instrumental stance towards middle-class visiting.

For a minority, visiting clearly functioned in ways akin to the initial aspirations of the middle classes: it provided them with access to religious ministrations pitched at their intellectual and cultural level or the consolations of vicarious respectability which could be extracted from deferential intercourse with social superiors. For most, the attentions of the visitors were accepted much more discreetly. Visitors were a useful resource in times of sickness and death, providing the kind of house calls which even conscientious ministers could rarely sustain. Significantly, close reading of visitors' journals suggests that, increasingly, as the century progressed, visitors, subjected to a greater demand from the neighbourhoods they visited, diverged from the ideal of house-to-house visiting to concentrate on ministering to the sick and dying. In some cases visitors were used as part of the culture of controversy which infused much mid-century religious life, in others as a congenial sounding-board for general complaints and neighbourhood gossip (Leigh, 1864). Above all, many working-class households could not afford (or were unwilling) to repudiate visitors outright, because they were a fundamental channel of charitable relief and a vital source of character reference in support of applications to other bodies. The advice literature of visiting is saturated with judgements of the need to separate the visiting and relief-giving functions: the establishment of effective relationships, it was argued, could not be achieved where one party looked to the other to provide material aid. Yet all the evidence demonstrates that visitors found this impossible. Without some supply of blankets, food-tickets, hospital recommendations or money, access to the working-class home, as the visitors themselves recognised, would have been much more difficult. '[T]hat sympathy is not much valued', commented Wesleyan Minister James Kendall, 'which can pray and weep and leave no sixpence to buy a bit of bread' (1852: 11). Even the city missionaries, whose rules stringently enforced the prohibition of a direct provision of relief, were active in getting infirmary recommendations and introductions to other charities.

Given the precariousness of living for the mid-nineteenth-century working classes, together with the absence of an effective safety-net in times of sickness or unemployment, the pressures to submit to the regular but usually relatively infrequent ministrations of the district visitor must have been immense. In these circumstances, the resistance which it is possible to perceive through a careful reading of the accounts of district visiting, partial and patchy as it is, bears eloquent testimony to the deep-seatedness of the working-class sense of domestic privacy.

Conclusion

The work of Mary Poovey, with which this essay began, can be placed in the larger context of those works, at the head of which stands Henri Lefebvre's *The Production of Space* (1991), which have examined the ways in which the modern capitalist state and the processes of modernity homogenise space, flatten out difference and destroy barriers to the domination of the bourgeoisie. It is easy to see the possible significance of district visiting in this process: in the years before the expansion of the direct intervention in the working-class home by state agents which emerged after 1870, the kinds of voluntary endeavour which have been examined here formed the vanguard of attempts to break down the spatial obstacles and geographic resistances which stood in the way of that domination.

Yet, as detailed here, the history of district visiting also confirms another of the central emphases of Lefebvre's work – that social space is produced neither by the physical boundaries that might appear to enclose or define it nor by the ways in which spaces are conceptualised, written and read. Rather, it is produced in the mediations of these two by the practices which gave space social meaning and form. By moving beyond the constructions of working-class domestic space in mid-Victorian fiction, social commentary and advice literature to an examination of the practices through which the working-class home was constituted, it is possible to recover a hitherto neglected aspect of working-class culture. The working-class home was never 'the quintessence of privacy' to which Michelle Perrot suggests the middle-class home aspired ([1987] 1990: 347) but nor was it the undifferentiated segment of the wider 'slum' which is often forced to stand for it in middle-class accounts. If, as Gaston Bachelard has argued, '[a] house constitutes a body of images that give mankind proofs and illusions of stability' ([1958] 1994: 17), then it is perhaps not surprising that, faced with overwhelming evidence of an unstable working class, social observers were led to deny the physical existence of a working-class domestic space.

But in this, social observers were misled and have misled those who would rely on them uncritically. Undoubtedly, more needs to be done than has been possible here to uncover the dynamics of working-class domesticity. Closer enquiry might reveal more about the different meanings attached to male and female visiting, might furnish a fuller picture of distinctions between urban and rural practices and might fill out the divergences allowed by different forms of housing and within different sections of the working class. Nevertheless, the overall picture seems clear enough. If the mid-century working class had understandably attenuated notions of domesticity and recognised that in small crowded dwellings they could have little control of the flow of information about their daily lives, they did nonetheless have a clear, if pragmatically implemented, notion of their own domestic space.

Notes

1 The relationship between 'domestic' and 'private' is close, but it is not one of equivalence. As David Vincent (1995) has pointed out, the notion of privacy has two distinct aspects: the first involves claims not to be badgered – among other things to control access to the home; the second involves claims to limit the supply and flow of personal information.

2 Many of the arguments considered in the rest of this section are presented in much greater detail in my article 'The travails of domestic visiting: Manchester 1830–1870', *Historical Research* 71, 175 (June 1998), 196–227.

Bibliography

Bachelard, G. [1958] (1994), *The Poetics of Space*, trans. M. Jolas, Boston, Beacon.

Barber, M. A. S. (1852), *The Hearths of the Poor: or True English Stories for Real English Life*, London, J. Nisbet.

Barber, M. A. S. (1854), *Sunshine: or Believing and Rejoicing: A Series of Home and Foreign Missionary Sketches*, London J. Nisbet.

Barber, M. A. S. (1856), *The Poor Folk at Home; and What can we Do for them?*, London, J. Nisbet

Barber, M. A. S. (1858), *Castle Rag and its Dependencies: or The Sins and Sorrows of the Poor*, London, J. Nisbet.

Bayly, M. (1860), *Ragged Homes and How to Mend Them*, London, James Nisbet.

Brown, C. G. (1988), 'Did urbanization secularize Britain?', *Urban History Year Book*, 15, 1–14.

Charlesworth, A. (1846), *The Female Visitor to the Poor, or Records of Female Parochial Visiting, by a clergyman's daughter*, London, Seeley, Burnside and Seeley.

Charlesworth, A. (1858), *A Book for the Cottage, or the History of Mary and her Family*, London, Seeleys.

Children's Missionary Magazine, 1851–55.

Church Guardian, 1858.

Clark, A. (1995), *The Struggle for the Breeches: Gender and the Making of the British Working Class*, Berkeley, University of California Press.

Corbin, A. (1986), *The Foul and the Fragrant: Odor and the French Social Imagination*, Leamington Spa, Berg.

County Towns Mission Magazine, 1862–67.

County Towns Mission Record, 1852–53.

Daunton, M. J. (1983), 'Public place and private space: the Victorian city and the working-class household', in D. Fraser and A. Sutcliffe, *The Pursuit of Urban History*, London, Edward Arnold.

Davidoff, L. and Hall, C. (1987), *Family Fortunes: Men and Women of the English Middle Class, 1780–1850*, London, Hutchinson.

Davies, Rev. J. L. (1855), 'District visiting', in *Lectures to Ladies on Practical Subjects,* London, Macmillan.

Dickens, C. [1852–53] (1948), *Bleak House*, Oxford, Oxford Illustrated Dickens.

District Visitor's Manual (1840), London, J. W. Parker.

Elliott, D. W. (1994), 'The female visitor and the marriage of classes in Gaskell's North and South', *Nineteenth-Century Literature*, 49:1, 21–49.

Emra, L. (1839), *Things Old and New, or Recollections by a District Visitor*, London, Hamilton, Adams and Co.

Gallagher, C. (1985), *The Industrial Reformation of English Fiction, 1832–67*, Chicago, University of Chicago Press.

Gaskell, E. [1854–55] (1970), *North and South*, Harmondsworth, Penguin.

Hill, O. (1875), *Homes of the London Poor*, London, Macmillan.

Hilton, A. D. (1859), *Aid to Parochial Visiting, or a manual for keeping a record concerning each parishioner, for the use of clergymen and district visitors*, London, John and Charles Mozley.

Hints on District Visiting Societies: A Plan for their Formation and Suggestions to Visitors (1836), London, Longman, Rees, Orme, Brown, Green and Longman.

Home Mission Field, 1859–70.

Humphreys, R. (1995), *Sin, Organised Charity and the Poor Law in Victorian England*, London, Macmillan.

Hunt, J. (1895), *Pioneer Work in the Great City: The Autobiography of a London City Missionary,* London, S. W. Partridge.

Kendall, J. (1852), *Remarks on Pastoral Visiting among the Wesleyans*, London, Partridge and Oakley.

Lefebvre, H. (1991), *The Production of Space*, trans. D. Nicholson-Smith, Oxford, Blackwell.

Leigh, G. (1864), *Gertrude Leigh; or The District Visitor*, London, Christian Knowledge Society.

Lewis, D. M. (1986), *Lighten Their Darkness: The Evangelical Mission to Working-Class London, 1828–1860,* Westport, Greenwood Press.

Lewis, J. (1986), 'The working-class wife and mother and state intervention, 1870–1918', in J. Lewis (ed.), *Labour and Love: Women's Experience of Home and Family*, Oxford, Basil Blackwell.

Ley, Revd J. (Curate St Aldates, Oxford) (1842), *The Duty of a Lay Visitor of the Poor, practically considered in a letter to a friend*, Oxford, J. H. Parker.

London City Mission Magazine, 1840–65.

Luddy, M. (1995), *Women and Philanthropy in Nineteenth-Century Ireland*, Cambridge, Cambrige University Press.

Mahood, L. (1995), *Policing Gender, Class and Family in Britain, 1800–1945*, London, University College London Press.

Manchester and Salford City Mission (1838–67), *Annual Report*.

Manchester and Salford City Mission Magazine, 1854–61.

Manchester and Salford District Provident Society (1834–67), *Annual Report*.

Manchester and Salford Sanitary Association, *Hints on District Visiting*, n.d.

Mandler, P., (ed.) (1990), *The Poor on Relief in the Nineteenth-Century Metropolis*, Philadelphia, University of Philadelphia Press.

Martineau, H. [1839] (1983), *Deerbrook*, London, Virago.

Nixon, E. J. (1847), *A Manual of District Visiting: With Hints and Directions to Visitors, being an address to the members of the Edge Hill District Visiting Society*, London.

O'Brien, P. (1856), *Patrick O'Brien, or The Power of Truth*, London, Wertheim and Macintosh.

Oxford Parochial District Visiting Society (1833–34), *Annual Report*.

Payne, C. (1998), 'Rural virtues for urban consumption: cottage scenes in early Victorian painting', *Journal of Victorian Culture* 3:1 (Spring 1998), 45–68.

Perrot, M. [1987] (1990), *History of Private Life IV: From the Fires of Revolution to the Great War,* London, Harvard University Press.

Plenderleath, W. C. (1858), *The Parish Priest's Visiting List, with a few remarks on Parochial Visiting,* London, Joseph Masters.

Poovey, M. (1995), *Making a Social Body: British Cultural Formation 1830-1864*, Chicago, University of Chicago Press.

Prochaska F. K. (1980), *Women and Philanthropy in Nineteenth-Century England*, Oxford, Oxford University Press.

Ranyard, E. (1859), *The Missing Link, or Bible-women in the Homes of the London Poor,* London, James Nisbet.

Razzell, P. E. and Wainwright, G. W. (eds) (1973), *The Victorian Working Class: Letters to the Morning Chronicle*, London, Cass.

Scripture Readers' Journal, 2, 1856–60.

Seed, J. (1982), 'Unitarianism, political economy and the antinomies of liberal culture in Manchester, 1830–1850', *Social History*, 7:1, 1–26.

Summers, A. (1979), '"A home from home"; women's philanthropic work in the nineteenth century', in S. Burman (ed.), *Fit Work for Women*, London, Croom Helm.

Surridge, H. A. D. (1871), *A Manual of Hints to Visiting Friends of the Poor*, London, James Nesbit.

Town and Forest (1860), London, Richard Bentley.

Town and Village Mission Record, 1852–53.

Tristram, P. (1989), *Living Space in Fact and Fiction*, London, Routledge.
Vincent, D. (1995), 'Secrecy and the city, 1870–1939', *Urban History*, 22:3, 365–83.
Wightman, J. B. (1861), *Helen Dundas, or the Pastor's Wife*, London, James Nisbet.
Wightman, J. B. (1862), *Haste to the Rescue, or work while it is day*, London, James Nisbet.
Wohl, A. S. (1983), *Endangered Lives: Public Health in Victorian Britain*, London, Dent.

Gendered space: housing, privacy and domesticity in the nineteenth-century United States

S. J. Kleinberg

'Truly her home is a woman's world.'
Harriet Hanson Robinson, *Diary*, 24 April 1867

Space reflects and structures social organisation. Once 'bounded and shaped' it exerts its own influence, establishing social maps with which people of different ages, classes, sexes and races navigate (Ardener, 1981: 11). In the nineteenth century, domestic space delineated social and economic hierarchies. A society which divided social space into the interior world of the home (for married women and children) and the exterior world of work (for men and some single women) separated the responsibilities of the sexes at the same time that it defined their geographical ranges. It also condemned those who transgressed these boundaries for not fulfilling their expected social roles.

This essay examines nineteenth-century constructs of space, the variations in class and racial delineations of the female environment and the way in which an initially middle-class paradigm (the separation of spheres) became incorporated into both the legal system and domestic architecture. Rapid economic and social change shaped cultural perceptions as an increasingly heterogeneous population and the noxious side effects of densely populated urban settings (noise, filth and disease) fostered a desire for privacy and the perception that the home should be a refuge from the city.

American homes signified their inhabitants' well-being and became an 'acceptable form of material indulgence' in the nineteenth century (Clark, 1986: 59). For Americans of all classes, the house symbolised stability and prosperity, so that a bigger dwelling place and a more lavish use of space indicated higher status. As middle-class incomes increased and the urban environment deteriorated, architecture manifested gender roles by separating the sexes within the home. While domestic novelists segregated the sexes by depicting the home as a sanctuary from the outside world, architectural periodicals, style magazines and fiction all defined distinct domestic spaces for affluent women.

The classes ascribed different meanings to their homes, reflecting their distinct understandings of women's roles and of their abilities to achieve their domestic ideals. Immigrants, unskilled workers and racial minorities continued to use their dwellings as places of work and defined women as economic contributors to the household long after the middle and skilled working classes had turned their homes into places to escape from work. As the nineteenth century progressed, the well-to-do dedicated their homes to domesticity, consumption and reproduction rather than to domestic manufacturing or income production. They regarded women's activities within the home as a vocation and labour of love, rather than toil (Boydston, 1990). These fundamental distinctions mirrored class variations in women's economic roles, but all classes considered the home as indicative of social and economic standing.

Charlotte Smith, president of the short-lived Women's National Industrial League and editor of *The Working Woman* (1887), lamented the fate of working women whose 'unfurnished and scant lodging' indicated their poverty (1). Other authors portrayed downward mobility through the smaller quarters forced upon families who descended the occupational hierarchy. The loss of respectability could be measured by giving up domestic help, then moving from a house to a flat, 'a flat without a parlor. Hannah Bumpus regarded a parlor as necessary to a respectable family as a wedding ring to a virtuous woman' (Churchill, 1917: 6).

Edith Wharton also measured success and failure through domestic space. In *The House of Mirth* (1905) Lily Bart's social descent takes her into smaller and more degraded architectural spaces. She moves from a house on Fifth Avenue to a small private hotel, a boarding house and, in an indication of having fallen completely out of her caste, to a conversation in a kitchen with a woman of the labouring class. At the other end of the ethnic/occupational spectrum, immigrant novelist Anzia Yezierska warned against placing too much emphasis on domestic refinements. Hanneh Hayyeh in *Hungry Hearts* (1920) scrimps and scrapes for years to have 'a white painted kitchen', the symbol of domestic peace and order in the uptown mansion where she cleans. Once her rapacious landlord discovers her improvements he raises her rent and then throws her out onto the street (66). Her domestic ambition results in homelessness because, as a tenant, she has no real control over her dwelling place.

Affluent women ran no such risks in their interior decoration. They ornamented the space purchased by men, as Thorstein Veblen observed in his *Theory of the Leisure Class* (1899), displaying their husbands' wealth as they embellished their homes with increasingly elaborate swirls of cloth and carved furniture. Larger, highly decorated and well-furnished homes replaced simple dwellings, while purchased objects ousted home- and handmade ones (G. Wright, 1980). Even frugal women got caught up in this whirl of consumption. Harriet Hanson Robinson remarked in her diary after the American Civil War, 'too much, we must not spend so much', when she discovered her household expenses had more than doubled as her husband's salary rose (Bushman, 1981: 108).

Middle-class urban women had a crucial role in the definition and redefinition of domestic space. From the 1830s onward the cult of true womanhood caught the imaginations of women in eastern towns and cities. Described by Barbara Welter as hostages in the home, true women made their dwellings into cheerful places so that 'brothers, husbands and sons would not go elsewhere in search of a good time' (1966: 151). The home became the sacred space in a society confronting the less desirable aspects of commercialisation and industrialisation, including heightened materialism. Women were to provide a refuge from the outside world where men could rest and relax from their daily toil.

As industrialisation transposed women's manufacturing functions from home to marketplace, urban women who could afford to purchase items such as cloth, bread, cheese, butter, milk, meat, shoes and bed linen stopped making them at home. They transferred energies from home-manufacturing to child-rearing and providing a comfortable, soothing environment for husbands. They substituted domesticity for productivity, turning the home into an emotional rather than an economic space. Domestic advisers informed women that making one's home into 'a loving place of rest and joy and comfort for those who are dear to her' was every true woman's first wish (Welter, 1966: 155).

Well-to-do women's homes evolved from a hive of productivity into a sacred space whose inhabitants needed protection from the outside world. Sarah Josepha Hale, editor of the influential *Godey's Lady's Book* and prolific author, defined woman's empire as the world of the home, contrasting it with an evil outside world in her poem 'Empire of Woman' ([1845] 1989: 114–16):

> The Outward World, for rugged Toil design'd
> Where Evil from true Good the crown hath riven,
> Has been to Man's dominion ever given;
> But Woman's empire, holier, more refin'd
> Moulds, moves and sways the fall'n but God-breath'd mind.

This vision suggested a retreat from the unpleasantness, competition and confusion of the city and employment and specifically located women within the domestic environment.

The popularity of *Godey's Lady's Book* and other mid-century women's magazines suggests that advice passed from mother to daughter had little salience in an era of rapid technological innovation. Instead, women turned to magazines and household manuals for guidance. Catharine Beecher and Harriet Beecher Stowe's *The American Women's Home* (1869) discussed interior decoration, architecture and female attire. They glorified housework to educated women, admonishing them to make their own clothes and do their own housework. Their followers believed that the home was truly a woman's world, symbolising stability and prosperity (Bushman, 1981).

Domestic novels such as Louisa May Alcott's *Little Women* (1868) depict the home as the centre of women's existence, with the urban, industrial world kept at a distance. Instead of going into the mills to work alongside foreign-born women, the March girls earn money through poorly paid domestic pursuits. Their home is a sanctuary, despite the family's straitened circumstances (Elbert, 1987).

Although impoverished, the March family home is a place of safety and retreat which they own. The other epic work of mid-nineteenth-century domestic American fiction, Harriet Beecher Stowe's *Uncle Tom's Cabin or Life Among the Lowly* (1852), showed the hollowness of domestic ideals for enslaved African-Americans. Slave-owners violated bondspeople's homes through financial mismanagement, cruelty and sexual appetites. Stowe condemned slavery because it destroyed the home life of slaves and, by implication, that of their owners. Slavery traduced the boundaries between the domestic and commercial, 'bringing the confusion of the marketplace into the kitchen, the center of the family shelter', according to cultural critic Gillian Brown (1990: 16). Stowe used the all-pervasive rhetoric of motherhood and sentimental domesticity to bridge the racial divide. She imbued her African-American characters with contemporary virtues, including piety and maternal love. Stowe's writing exemplified her sister Catharine's advice to exert influence through the domestic circle by applying female virtues to the most contentious national issues of the day (Sklar, 1973).

The appeal of domesticity and the desire for privacy in the home was by no means limited to the literary middle classes. Women of different social and racial backgrounds aspired to a home of their own; what changed over the course of the nineteenth century was the ability to achieve those aims and the willingness to use women's domestic labour or gainful employment to accomplish them. Harriet Jacobs concluded *Incidents in the Life of a Slave Girl* (1861) by telling the reader that her 'story ends with freedom; not in the usual way, with marriage. I and my children are now free! ... The dream of my life is not yet realised. I do not sit with my children in a home of my own. I still long for a hearthstone of my own, however humble' ([1861] 1987: 210).

Jacobs, like Stowe, used the term 'home' to refer to far more than a roof over one's head. As literary historian Claudia Tate observes in *Domestic Allegories of Political Desire* (1992), freedom for Jacobs had a domestic dimension which male abolitionists never considered. Freedom gave former bondswomen the right to be mothers in charge of their own homes and families. Jacobs desired not so much a room of her own, a place to be private from her family, as a home of her own, a space which whites could not transgress.

Most former slaves lived in the rural south, engaged in market-oriented agricultural labour with little ability to withdraw from economic productivity even if they so desired (Jones, 1985). In the world of white rural domesticity, epitomised by Laura Ingalls Wilder's *Little House* books, domesticity, production and reproduction also remain integrated. Writers of the western experience, notably Willa Cather, show women inhabiting rough sod houses that blend into the landscape. In such a context women may transcend domesticity by working on the land. Yet both Ingalls Wilder and Cather also capture the potential claustrophobia of the rural residence, as harsh winters trap women and men in the home, sometimes without enough to eat.

The articulation of domestic space as private had less salience in white rural areas where families shared a small dwelling space and had less need to keep strangers away. The very small homes of frontier settlements permitted little gendering of domestic space. All family members shared the one or two rooms, even though Pa roamed farther than Ma, setting traps and exchanging labour with other farmers. As rural families became more settled, they added rooms to their houses, separating living and cooking space, giving privacy to family members but also isolating women in the kitchen. Commercial agriculture and larger homes fostered geographical divisions in men's and women's space (Bush, 1982). Despite this separation, women's and men's work overlapped in rural America, as labour shortages and the pressures of harvest and planting meant that women as well as men did field labour, especially on smaller farms and in the South, where African-American women persisted in field work well into the twentieth century.

Throughout the century, rural women used their homes to produce food and make money selling their eggs and butter, but middle-class women's use of their homes to bring cash into the household declined. At mid-century, women from diverse social backgrounds took in boarders to augment family incomes and achieve home-ownership. Emily Norcross Dickinson (the poet's mother) had lodgers in the 1830s although she came from an affluent family. A typical middle-class household at mid-century might contain several boarders, with the housewife's labour making a considerable contribution to the family income and enabling children to stay on longer in school (Ryan, 1981). In 1880, about one-quarter of Pittsburgh's boarders lodged with middle-class families, but by 1900 few did so, a pattern replicated in other large cities across the nation (Kleinberg, 1989).

Several factors contributed to the decline of boarding among the middle and upper classes at the century's end. As they moved to the suburbs, they were physically more remote from the shops, factories and offices which employed large numbers of single people. Even those who resided in or near urban centres rejected taking in boarders to supplement the male breadwinner's income. The growing emphasis on domestic privacy and the home as a refuge from the city and its people led middle-class women to close their doors to strangers.

As Edith Wharton observed, 'privacy is one of the first requisites of civilised life' (Wharton and Codman, 1897: 22). This desire to be insulated from urban chaos prompted new architectural forms. Leading architects built houses which deliberately sheltered the well-to-do from passers-by and the urban scene. Henry Hobson Richardson pioneered houses which reflected this quest for privacy. The house he designed for the Glessner family in Chicago presented tiny slit windows, fortress fashion, to the dangerous street corner, while enjoying a private garden hidden behind high walls. Such homes conformed to affluent people's belief in the importance of distancing themselves from disturbances (Boris, 1988).

The middle class manipulated and formed its environment as a bulwark against the city. Homes were positioned to avoid stressful situations resulting from too much contact with neighbours, noise or noxious odours, while low-load environments were created in which they exercised control over incoming stimuli (Mehrabian, 1976). Lawns, fences and distance from the urban core minimised intrusions, allowing the middle-class housewife to exercise control over her domain, safe from threats posed by outsiders. Instead of being situated directly on the street, suburban homes had a front garden and large strip of lawn as green insulation from the threatening outside world. Massive velvet curtains, draped over sheer gauze or lace curtains, prevented the outside from encroaching. Ethel Spencer in *The Spencers of Amberson Avenue* (1983), her memoir of her childhood at the turn of the century, recalls that heavy velvet curtains hushed noise from the street and ensured acoustical and visual privacy.

Middle- and upper-class homes subdivided domestic space into male and female areas. Women inhabited the drawing-room, while men had the library, the billiard room and smoking-room (Chase, 1996). Women servants had the kitchen as their headquarters, although they moved throughout the house in order to clean it. This class/gender division of domestic space encapsulated the distance between worlds. Domestic activities were relegated to one set of spaces shared by women of all classes; middle-class women inhabited a limited social space with men. Space usage thus exemplified hierarchies of gender, with male spaces such as the library being preserved from female intrusions.

Charlotte Perkins Gilman explores the distribution of domestic space, underscoring its gendered dynamics. She observes that 'father, being the economic base of the whole structure, has the most power' and the most space. He obtained seclusion for himself in his den or study or garden, while the mother, 'poor invaded soul – finds even the bathroom door no bar to hammering little hands' ([1902] 1972: 39–40). Mothers were at the mercy of their children, visitors, tradesmen and servants. In Gilman's view, privacy was a myth, at least as far as women were concerned, although it remained a cherished value.

The middle-class quest for privacy and control over the environment resulted in a profusion of rooms, each with its own function. These separated family members from each other and kept visitors to clearly defined public spaces. Individual bedrooms gave each family member a further measure of isolation within the household. House-plan books stressed the seclusion of the living quarters from the rest of the house. When a visitor entered the house, the authors of *The Honest House* noted approvingly, 'he sees little except the room in which he finds himself. He does not penetrate at once into the privacy of the house' (Goodnow and Adams, 1914: 134). The stranger should be carefully controlled, restricted to strictly defined public spaces and prevented from penetrating the family's personal space.

Middle-class families not only closed their doors to boarders and restricted access to visitors, they also became less willing to accept outsiders into their homes as servants. A declining number of domestics lived with, or as part of, the family in bourgeois homes. In *Little Women* (1868), the maid (native-born, white and from the same milieu as her employers) considers herself to be part of the family. All female members of the household undertake domestic tasks. Such easy camaraderie had all but disappeared from middle-class homes at the turn of the century (Salmon, 1897). Servants were relegated to attics, kitchens and pantries, where adult members of the family rarely stayed for long. Homes built for affluent Americans in the late nineteenth and early twentieth centuries frequently contained a secondary staircase for servants to climb. Rising from the kitchen or rear hallway, these narrow stairs minimised cross-class contacts despite residence under the same roof.

Employers wished to keep African-American and immigrant women servants at a distance, as Harriet Beecher Stowe's advice to middle-class women to do their own work indicated. Stowe urged women to avoid becoming 'the slave of a coarse vulgar Irishwoman' (1864: 758) by undertaking their own cleaning and cooking. Nearly forty years later Charlotte Perkins Gilman complained that privacy was impossible if one employed live-in help. They were 'strangers by birth, by class, by race, by education – as utterly alien as it is possible to conceive'. It was impossible to talk of privacy once servants had been introduced ([1902] 1972: 42).

Employers made little effort to look after the physical comforts of their staff. Although most middle-class homes had indoor plumbing by the turn of the century, their owners kept these conveniences for themselves. Affluent Pittsburgher Ethel Spencer recalled that servants lived in abysmal conditions in wealthy homes at the turn of the century. Servants had washstands in their rooms and a slop jar on the floor, since they were forbidden to use the family's facilities. 'Maids had to fetch water from a housemaid's closet on the second floor. Their toilet was in a dark hole under the cellar stairs and there was no bathtub for them anywhere. If they bathed at all, it must have been in the laundry tubs.' She believed there was nothing unusual about these arrangements; her house offered as much (or as little) comfort to servants as most others (1983: 27). The

Spencers' servants lived on the top floor. In other households domestics bedded down in the kitchen itself or in a room next to it. They were physically separated from the family, glimpsing a world they could only aspire to but never inhabit (Goodnow and Adams, 1914: 136).

By the turn of the century some social commentators depicted domesticity as claustrophobic and a threat to women's autonomy and sanity. No story questions women's relation to domestic space more acutely than Charlotte Perkins Gilman's 'The Yellow Wallpaper' (1891). Confined to an upstairs room with bars on the windows and peeling flamboyant yellow wallpaper, the narrator is forced to endure a rest cure by her doting family following the birth of her son. The wallpaper, with its blotches and stains, accentuates her post-partum depression, as do the threats to send her to Dr S. Weir Mitchell, an anti-feminist physician who prescribed inactivity as the cure for neurasthenic women (Parker, 1972). The domestic space oppresses the narrator in an era when middle-class women participated in an expanding range of activities outside the home.

Advancing domestic technology and smaller families facilitated this activism and made it feasible for middle-class women to dispense with live-in household help altogether. The proportion of business-class women employing domestic help declined sharply in the early twentieth century. Yet these women also spent slightly less time engaged in housework than their mothers (Lynd and Lynd, [1929] 1956). Home economists, mass-market women's magazines and manufacturers of processed foods and household technology urged women to take advantage of the new goods appearing on the market, to substitute canned and processed foods for fresh ones and to complete the transition from producer to consumer. They enlisted both science and emotion in their drive to sell modern methods and materials to American women (Cowan, 1983). Such innovations enabled middle-class women to expand their horizons beyond their own households, although the domestic paradigm remained central to social activism at the end of the nineteenth and beginning of the twentieth century as maternalism became the basis of female activism (Skocpol, 1992; Gordon, 1994; Sklar, 1995b).

The better-off members of the working class subscribed to the prevailing domestic ideology, even if they had arguably lower levels of social activism (Skocpol, 1992). Working-class newspapers proclaimed that most women's 'lives are spent at home and amid household cares'. Such papers hoped to help female readers make their homes 'pleasant and comfortable' through their household hints columns and stories featuring honest, home-owning working families (*People's Monthly*, 1871: 3). 'Our own home' figured as the 'pride of the father, the perpetual comfort of the wife and mother, the salvation of the boys, and the great instructor and elevator of the girls of the family' (*People's Monthly*, 1872: 126).

For affluent workers the home indicated the dominant gender paradigms of the era, embodying male earning prowess and female domesticity as well as facilitating the inculcation of these virtues in the next generation. In the 1880s the Chicago *Labor Enquirer* reiterated the skilled workers' vision of the home in words redolent of the genteel apostles of domesticity. A home of their own would keep 'tired men from the saloons, protect children from the streets and place women in their constitutional sphere of home making' (*Labor Enquirer*, 1887: 1). Some commentators noted that female domesticity freed men of all classes for recreation outside the home. Husbands frequently went 'out to join the men', while their wives stayed at home to mind the children (Streightoff, 1911: 138).

The aristocracy of labour and the middle classes had similar attitudes towards domesticity in the late nineteenth century, but the poorer members of society still used their dwellings as places of work and defined women as economic contributors to the household. Housing conditions and expectations diverged more widely than ever by this time. Middle- and upper-class homes had become emotional and social centres, but poorer ones still contained economic production. Working-class, especially immigrant, women used their domestic labour to augment husbands' and children's wages through the early decades of the twentieth century, with large numbers of African-American women doing field labour and domestic work. They engaged in the hard physical labour that middle-class women had rejected for themselves as surely as they stopped baking their own bread (Lynd and Lynd, [1929] 1956).

Middle-class and skilled workers' families lived in a world where one room fulfilled one function; they had more rooms than people in the house. 'Four people in twelve rooms', exclaims Mike of the family where his fiancée Mary works as a maid in *Out of This Furnace* (1941) a novel of immigrant life in the steel mill districts of Western Pennsylvania. Dorta, with whom he boards, has 'eleven in four, in three if you don't count the kitchen' (Bell, [1941] 1976: 132). Although population densities varied between cities, most industrial workers lived in cramped conditions, with new immigrants faring very badly indeed. The house in the suburbs of Pittsburgh described by Thomas Bell had, in fact, six residents (two of them servants) and thus averaged 0.5 people to a room. In large cities in 1894, working families averaged about 1.5 people per room, a greater population density than earlier in the century (Wright, 1894: 584–94). Larger middle-class dwellings devoted most of their space to living and sleeping quarters and less to family service functions (Kleinberg, 1989).

Out of This Furnace depicts Mary Dobrejak's health deteriorating under the combined strain of 'six boarders, three children and a husband to look after, meals to cook, clothes to wash. Her hours were from four-thirty in the morning to nine at night, seven days a week' (132). Left a widow after a steel mill accident, Mary struggles to feed and wash for her boarders and family. She eventually contracts tuberculosis and is placed in a sanatorium, never to return to her own home. For other immigrant women the home remained a dwelling- and workplace where they could monetise their labour through converting the domestic space into an economic one (Bodnar et al., 1982).

As the gulf between the affluent and impoverished widened during the late nineteenth century, ownership levels declined in city centres and increased on the suburban periphery. Home-ownership correlated inversely with crowding. Land prices rose in city centres, encouraging subdivision of existing units and accelerating middle-class flight to the suburbs.

Rising standards of living facilitated house purchases for the middle class and upper reaches of the working class. In 1890, about 38 per cent of all Americans owned their own homes, rising to 47 per cent by 1900. The middle class, where husbands earned incomes of $1,500 (for example, an insurance company clerk) to $4,000 (a lawyer), could afford a modest house on the suburban fringe of most large cities. Artisans and skilled workers with incomes of $500–$800 might also purchase a home, but would need assistance from wage-earning children and a frugal wife. Unskilled workers, those living on $1.65 a day or about $450–$500 a year (assuming full-time employment and no slack periods), could only afford a home with the assistance of multiple wage earners (More, 1907; Wood, 1919; Clark, 1986). Between 10 and 20 per cent of the urban working class owned homes in the 1890s and there were virtually no homeowners in the immigrant districts of Manhattan (Wright, 1890; United States Bureau of the Census, 1902: 2).

Even where land costs were lower, home-ownership entailed enormous sacrifices from all members of poor working-class families, thrusting the burden of wage earning onto women and children at a time when social reformers expressed great concern about the presence of both groups in the labour force. Home-ownership exacted a high price from families subsisting on incomes of less than $20 per week. In order to keep up payments on a tumble-down house 'back of the yards', Slavic immigrants in Upton Sinclair's *The Jungle* (1906) send their ten- and eleven-year-old sons to work. 'There was no reason why their family should starve when tens of thousands of children no older were earning their own livings' (123). The final degradation is Ona's submission to her boss's sexual harassment. 'He told me he would have me turned off. He told me he would – we would all of us lose our places.' She tries to explain to her husband, 'I only did it … to save us. It was our only chance' (151). Ona sacrifices herself for the home, giving up her purity in order to pay the mortgage.

Home-ownership, observed social surveyor Edith Abbott, 'entailed an effort to secure property and future welfare at the cost of present health, comfort, and decent living' (1936: 37). Chicago social workers found undernourished children and overworked mothers heavily represented among the ranks of homeowners. Chicago school system records from the 1920s indicate that nearly two-fifths of the children withdrawn from school came from families who were buying a home of their own (37–9). As the careworn mother in *The Dwelling-Place of Light* (1917) tries to explain to daughters ashamed of their small rented flat, 'I guess if your father and I had put both you girls in the mills and crowded into one room and cooked in a corner and lived on onions and macaroni and put four boarders each in the other rooms, I guess we could have had a house, too' (Churchill, 1917: 7). Home-ownership came at a heavy price for the poorer members of the working class. It would have required both mother and daughters to become economically active and to convert domestic space into economic space.

Reacting to an expanding immigrant population and rising population densities, many Americans sought rules and laws to regulate what they perceived as a chaotic environment in the nineteenth century. Lawmakers attempted to remove money-making activities from the home physically, in order to protect the domestic space, married women and children from contamination. By the turn of the century, when middle-class women no longer converted domestic labour into money-making, law-makers condemned women who continued the older pattern of working in the home through taking in boarders, handcraft production or tenement manufacturing (Boris, 1994).

Social reformers believed conscientious mothers could not combine maternity and boarding-house keeping. 'The proper care of children does not leave the average mother much time to do the extra work necessary for boarders or lodgers', stated one social investigator (Hall, 1933: 36). Cramped spaces in working-class homes made it difficult to separate children from strangers. Social surveyor Margaret Byington deplored the impact of lodgers on family living standards ([1910] 1974). She believed it intolerable that families living in one or two rooms boarded single men. Since everyone congregated in the kitchen, which doubled as a sleeping room, it was impossible to segregate the sexes properly.

Yet poor mothers still needed to use their homes to earn money. In the early twentieth century, charity officials disapproved of this use of domestic space. The Pennsylvania *Mothers' Assistance Manual* warned that widows were 'often depressed and tired, physically below normal. The presence of a man in the same house, with a full pay envelope, may offer an overwhelming temptation' (Commonwealth of Pennsylvania, 1927: 14). Worried that dependent widows would breach social conventions, state charity officials prohibited them from taking in unrelated male boarders. Such disapproval displayed the extent to which the home and the women and children within it were believed to need protection from outsiders (Ladd-Taylor, 1994). The home became the preserve of the nuclear family, and widows relied increasingly upon their own extra-household labour for support. Where they could not make ends meet they turned to myriad charities and the state for assistance, but few took in boarders after the first decade of the twentieth century (Kleinberg, 1996a).

Working-class rooms accommodated many functions. Particularly among poorer households and those who took in boarders, the kitchen became the 'kitchen/eating/sitting-room'. It integrated rather than segregated men, women, children, boarders and family members. The entire household clustered in it, rather than it being the preserve of servants or the woman of the household. It was filled in winter with people seeking the only warmth in the house. In the summer it was steamy and hot from cooking, washing and ironing, a place from which men and children escaped, to work, to the saloon or to the streets and alleyways, but from which mothers had no escape. Working-class homes lacked the spatial separation which enabled the middle class to create soothing environments and private worlds. Doors and windows remained open to the streets, so that everyone saw, heard and smelled what went on in their neighbours' homes.

Social surveyors considered this lack of privacy to be one of the chief curses of the tenement. Where boarders mingled with the family, where washing took place down the hall or in the yard, it was 'idle to speak of privacy' (Riis, [1890] 1957: 119). Indeed, family quarrels became public property under such circumstances. Although the middle class kept its domestic problems within the family circle, the working-class family in distress was not closed off from the eyes and ears of the neighbourhood. Instead, crowded conditions, shared facilities and open windows meant that neighbours knew the intimate details of each other's lives.

Divorce records highlight class-distinctive uses of space. While the middle class relied primarily on relatives for testimony in Baltimore's divorces between 1850 and 1915, labourers and artisans called upon nearby residents. Working-class families gave aid and comfort in times of family crisis, but the neighbours observed the events, the comings and goings and the arguments. They could 'hear what occurred upstairs from the downstairs room'. They saw husbands sporting other women around the neighbourhood while the wives stayed home. They watched the wives take up residence with other men, frequently close to the marital home. They looked through uncurtained windows when a woman entertained men other than her husband in the family home. By implication, they observed the relations between husband and wife as well (Baltimore County Circuit Court, 1899).

One consequence of crowding in working-class neighbourhoods was that the residents of those districts lacked a clearly articulated view of space. There was much less segregation of public and private activities than among the middle class. The testimony in divorce trials was more explicit in working-class cases than in middle-class ones. Activities took place where there was room, not in a room especially designated for them. Because the working class, of necessity, lived so much of its life out of doors and in public places such as saloons, its activities were more likely to be observed by others, either neighbours or the social reformist observers of the poor.

People varied in the manner in which they dealt with this information. Some 'did not want to get involved in family affairs' and spoke up only after one party had moved out (Baltimore County Circuit Court, Equity Papers A, 1899, Box 247). Non-involvement diffused some of the tensions inherent in crowded working-class districts. People trained themselves not to intercede, not to act on what they observed. One woman testified that she saw a man repeatedly strike his wife. She disapproved of this behaviour but would not interfere in relations between spouses; she certainly did not call the police. Another working-class witness described how a labourer abused his wife by beating her so badly 'that the attention of the neighbors were [*sic*] attracted by her screams and outcries'. He, too, remained aloof from the violence. Neighbours testified in court, but rarely became directly involved in family affairs. They believed there was little they could do to help the individual out of an intolerable domestic situation except publicly state what they had observed if called to testify in a court of law (Gordon, 1989).

The Baltimore divorce records indicate working-class neighbours were privy to much personal information, including how well people cared for their children, their spouses and their homes. They knew who remained faithful to their marriage vows, whose baby arrived too soon after the wedding and who demanded his dinner the instant he came home from work and was abusive if he did not get it. Since one had to be a two-year resident of the city before filing a petition for divorce, the records are biased in favour of the more settled members of the working class, but in this context these were not anonymous Americans (Hareven, 1971). These divorce records show that fewer members of the working class could purchase solitude, especially as the century ended and housing densities rose, but they tried to insulate themselves from their neighbours by not getting involved in their domestic quarrels. In poor neighbourhoods privacy came not from heavy curtains or spacious dwellings, but from not listening to quarrels or not acting upon what one witnessed (Kleinberg, 1989).

These discrete interpretations of the use of the home and women's role within it, as well as the ability to purchase the ideal home, brought the classes into conflict in an increasingly heterogeneous world. The middle class sought to impose its vision of domestic order upon an urbanised proletariat separated by growing economic, social, geographical and cultural differences from the well-to-do (Kleinberg, 1996b). Various types of legislation – public health regulations, the control and elimination of industrial home work, zoning and the supervision of charity recipients' home life – all signified a willingness to use the state as a tool to implement a particular vision of domestic order and gendered use of space (Abramovitz, 1988). By the turn of the century, social reformers strongly believed that the home must be reserved for the family and completely separated from income production.

Middle-class reformers linked their opposition to industrial home work with their social understandings of home, family, motherhood and child welfare. Bringing work into the home, as Eileen Boris indicates in *Home to Work* (1994), her analysis of sweated labour, subverted the prevailing ideology of the home as sacred space. At the end of the nineteenth and beginning of the twentieth century the primarily female National Consumers' League campaigned vigorously to have industrial work in the home regulated or outlawed. The League deplored the poor, unsanitary conditions under which cigar, artificial flower- and garment-makers, pecan-shellers, pin-carders and jewellery-assemblers operated and the long hours the workers had to devote to their tasks. Such work traduced the separation of spheres devoutly desired by middle-class women and the reservation of the home for solely domestic functions.

Elizabeth Beardsley Butler, investigating women's work in the Pittsburgh District in 1907, lamented the circumstances which forced women to sew jeans and neglect their household duties. One woman toiled from early morning until late at night with no time to clean the floors. Her children were 'ragged, ignorant, uncared for'. Florence Kelley, an investigator for the National Consumers' League in 1910, condemned the home work system which forced women to neglect their homes and children while they laboured under 'the twofold strain of home maker and wage earner' (Butler, 1909: 137). Reformers complained that sweated labour (and, indeed, married women's working outside the home) violated the gender norms while placing an intolerable burden on the women who attempted to fulfil two conflicting roles.

Sweated labour also imperilled the middle-class woman's household. The transmission of disease by washerwomen preoccupied public health officials at the turn of the century. One lamented that he had seen washing 'on the sick bed of a tuberculosis patient. From these homes Negroes come into our homes and, as our servants, are in the most intimate contact with us' (Lee, 1904: 208). In order to protect the homes of the middle class, some reformers advocated the supervision of working-class homes. The physician in charge of the Atlanta Children's Dispensary of the Woman's Board of City Missions condemned the widespread practice of African-American women earning money by taking in laundry. He recommended the inspection of washerwomen's homes so they would not spread germs from their infected homes to their white customers. Another Southern physician claimed that 'disease among the Negroes is a danger to the entire population', since disease was rife in 'the dirty Negro sections of our cities' (Visanska, 1908: 582). Reformers also wished to oversee the domestic environment of widowed mothers receiving state pensions to help bring up their children. State and city boards of charity inspected recipients' homes to ensure they were clean and fitting places to bring up children, occasionally terminating assistance to families in improper environments (Kleinberg, 1996a). Nonconformity in one's domestic arrangements could cost a family dear.

The solution to these violations of space was to regulate and segregate the homes of the transgressors. Increasingly in the early twentieth century, legislation regulated what homes could be used for. Zoning and tenement house regulations prohibited the manufacture of articles in domestic settings and removed industry and business from residential neighbourhoods. Middle-class reformers brought their concepts of privacy, spaciousness and gendered space to the urban core through their settlement houses, housing reform acts and social service agencies. Settlement houses explicitly set out to teach immigrant and working-class women the appropriate and correct care of their homes (Sklar, 1995b).

By the beginning of the twentieth century public opinion, as manifested in welfare and housing legislation, asserted the reservation of domestic space for non-economic purposes. Many middle-class women participated in activities outside the home, but still regarded the home as a sacred space in which no work could take place. The labour of married women in the home should be for love, not income production. The gendered use of space thus mirrored the separation of home and workplace to which the industrial revolution gave rise. Although working-class women could not entirely emulate middle-class women's devotion to emotional domesticity, that model of domesticity became the norm in American society.

Bibliography

Abbott, E. (1936), *The Tenements of Chicago, 1908–1935*, Chicago, University of Chicago Press.

Abramovitz, M. (1988), *Regulating the Lives of Women: Social Welfare Policy from Colonial Times to the Present*, Boston, South End Press.

Alcott, L. M. (1868), *Little Women*, Boston, Roberts Bros.

Ardener, S. (1981), 'Ground rules and social maps for women', in S. Ardener, *Women and Space: Ground Rules and Social Maps*, London, Croom Helm.

Baltimore County Circuit Court, Equity Papers A and B, MdHR 602-002-031 and 602-002-032 (1850–1915), Annapolis, Maryland Hall of Records.

Baltimore Supervisor of City Charities (1929), 'Specimen Letter Confirming Mothers' Relief Grant', 29 October 1929, Baltimore City Archives.

Beecher, C. and Stowe, H. B. (1869), *The American Woman's Home, or Principles of Domestic Science*, New York, J. B. Ford and Co.

Bell, T. [1941](1976), *Out of This Furnace*, Pittsburgh, University of Pittsburgh Press.

Bodnar, J., Simon, R. and Weber, M. (1982), *Lives of Their Own: Blacks, Italians and Poles in Pittsburgh, 1900–1960*, Urbana, University of Illinois Press.

Boris, E. (1988), *Art and Labor: Ruskin, Morris and the Craftsman Ideal in America*,

Philadelphia, Temple University Press.

Boris, E. (1994), *Home to Work: Motherhood and the Politics of Industrial Homework in the United States*, Cambridge, Cambridge University Press.

Boydston, J. (1990), *Home and Work: Housework, Wages and the Ideology of Labor in the Early Republic*, New York and Oxford, Oxford University Press.

Brown, G. (1990), *Domestic Individualism: Imagining Self in Nineteenth-Century America*, Berkeley, University of California Press.

Bush, C. G. (1982), 'The barn is his, the house is mine: agricultural technology and sex roles', in George H. Daniels and Mark H. Rose (eds), *Agricultural Technology and Sex Roles*, Beverly Hills, California, CA, Sage.

Bushman C. L. (1981), *'A Good Poor Man's Wife' Being a Chronicle of Harriet Hanson Robinson and Her Family in Nineteenth-Century New England*, Hanover and London, New England University Press.

Butler, E. (1909), *Women and the Trades*, New York, Charities Publication Committee.

Byington, M. [1910](1974), *Homestead: The Households of a Milltown*, Pittsburgh, University Centre for International Studies.

Chase, V. (1996), 'Edith Wharton, *The Decoration of Houses* and gender in turn-of-the-century America', in D. E. Coleman and C. Henderson (eds), *Architecture and Feminism*, New York, Princeton Architectural Press.

Churchill, W. (1917), *The Dwelling-Place of Light*, New York, Macmillan.

Clark, C. E., Jr (1986), *The American Family Home 1800–1960*, Chapel Hill, University of North Carolina Press.

Commonwealth of Pennsylvania (1927), *Manual of the Mothers' Assistance Fund,* Harrisburg, J. L. L. Kuhn.

Cowan, R. S. (1983), *More Work for Mother: The Ironies of Household Technology from Open Hearth to Microwave*, New York, Basic Books.

Elbert, S. (1987), *A Hunger for Home: Louisa May Alcott's Place in American Culture*, New Brunswick, NJ, Rutgers University Press.

Gilman, C. P. [1902] (1972), *The Home: Its Work and Influence*, Urbana, University of Illinois Press.

Goodnow, R. R. and Adams, R. (1914), *The Honest House*, New York, Century Company.

Gordon, L. (1989), *Heroes of their Own Lives: The Politics and History of Family Violence*, London, Virago.

Gordon, L. (1994), *Pitied but Not Entitled*, New York, Free Press.

Hale, S. J. [1845] (1989), 'Empire of Woman', in M. B. Norton (ed.), *Major Problems in American Women's History*, 1989, Lexington, MA, D. C. Heath.

Hall, E. L. (1933), *Mother's Assistance in Philadelphia: Actual and Potential Costs: A Study of 1010 Families*, Hanover, NH, University of New Hampshire Press.

Hareven, T. (1971), *Anonymous Americans*, Englewood Cliffs, NJ, Prentice Hall.

Jacobs, H. [1861](1987), *Incidents in the Life of a Slave Girl*, ed. J. F. Yellin, Cambridge, MA, Harvard University Press.

Jones, J. (1985), *Labor of Love, Labor of Sorrow: Black Women, Work and the Family from Slavery to the Present*, New York, Basic Books.

Kleinberg, S. J. (1989), *The Shadow of the Mills: Working-Class Families in Pittsburgh*, Pittsburgh, University of Pittsburgh Press.

Kleinberg, S. J. (1996a), 'The economic origins of the welfare state 1870–1939', in H. Bak, F. van Holthoon and H. Krabbendam (eds), *Social and Secure? Politics and the Culture of the Welfare State: A Comparative Inquiry*, Amsterdam, V. U. Press.

Kleinberg, S. J. (1996b), 'Seeking the meaning of life: the family in the Pittsburgh Survey', in M. Greenwald and M. Anderson (eds), *The Pittsburgh Survey Revisited*, Pittsburgh, University of Pittsburgh Press.

Labor Enquirer (1897), 1:18.

Ladd-Taylor, M. (1994), *Mother-Work: Women, Child Welfare and the State 1890–1930*, Urbana, University of Illinois Press.

Lee, R. (1904), 'Negro health', *American Hospital Association Conference Proceedings*, Jacksonville, Florida, 30 November–4 December 1904, 207–9.

Lynd, R. and Lynd H. M. [1929](1956), *Middletown: A Study in Modern American Culture,* New York, Harcourt, Brace and World.

Mehrabian, A. (1976), *Public Places and Private Spaces*, New York, Basic Books.

More, L.B. (1907), *Wage-Earner's Budgets: A Study of Standards and Cost of Living in New York City*, New York, Henry Holt and Company.

Parker, G. (1972), *The Oven Birds: American Women on Womanhood 1820–1920*, New York, Anchor Doubleday.

People's Monthly (1871), 1:1.

People's Monthly (1872), 1:8.

Riis, J. A. [1890](1957), *How the Other Half Lives*, New York, Hill and Wang.

Ryan, M. P. (1981), *The Cradle of the Middle Class: The Family in Oneida County, New York, 1780-1865*, Cambridge, Cambridge University Press.

Salmon, L. (1897), *Domestic Service*, New York, Macmillan.

Sinclair, U. (1906), *The Jungle*, New York, Doubleday.

Sklar, K. K. (1973), *Catharine Beecher: A Study in American Domesticity*, New Haven, Yale University Press.

Sklar, K. K. (1995a), *Florence Kelley*, New Haven, Yale University Press.

Sklar, K. K. (1995b), 'Two political cultures in the progressive era: the national consumers' league and the American Association for Labor Legislation', in L. Kerber, A. Kessler-Harris and K. K. Sklar, *U.S. History as Women's History: New Feminist Essays*, Chapel Hill, University of North Carolina Press.

Skocpol, T. (1992), *Protecting Soldiers and Mothers*, Cambridge, MA, Harvard University Press.

Smith, C. (1887), 'How women are treated', *The Working Woman*, 1:23, 15 October.

Spencer, E. (1983), *The Spencers of Amberson Avenue*, Pittsburgh, University of Pittsburgh Press.

Stowe, H. B. (1864), 'Home and Hearth Papers 6', *Atlantic Monthly*, 13, 754–761.

Streightoff, F. H. (1911), *The Standard of Living among the Industrial People of America*, Boston, Houghton Mifflin.

Tate, C. (1992), *Domestic Allegories of Political Desire: The Black Heroine's Text at the Turn of the Century*, Oxford, Oxford University Press.

United States Bureau of the Census (1902), *Census of Population*, 2, Washington, DC, Government Printing Office.

Veblen, T. (1899), *Theory of the Leisure Class*, New York, Macmillan.

Visanska, S. A. (1908), 'How to prevent the spread of contagious diseases', *Atlanta Journal-Record of Medicine*, 1, 582.

Welter, B. (1966), 'The cult of true womanhood', *American Quarterly*, 18, 151–74.
Wharton, E. (1905), *House of Mirth*, New York, Scribners.
Wharton, E. and Codman, O. (1897), *The Decoration of Houses*, New York, Scribners.
Wilder, L. I. (1958), *On the Banks of Plum Creek*, London, Methuen.
Wood, E. E. (1919), *The Housing of the Unskilled Wage Earner: America's Next Problem*, New York, Macmillan Company.
Wright, C. D. (1894), *Seventh Special Report of the Commissioner of Labor: The Slums of Great Cities: New York, Baltimore, Chicago and Philadelphia*, Washington, DC, Government Printing.
Wright, G. (1980), *Moralism and the Model Home: Domestic Architecture and Cultural Conflict in Chicago 1873–1913*, Chicago, University of Chicago Press.
Yezierska, A. (1920), *Hungry Hearts*, Boston, Houghton Mifflin.

Theatre and the private sphere in the fiction of Louisa May Alcott

Alan Louis Ackerman, Jr

> There is no form of amusement more generally popular at the present day than that of private theatricals and although at first sight it may appear strange that people should take great delight in seeing their friends play at acting, when with less trouble they could see the real thing done by trained actors, it is actually not difficult to find an explanation for the enjoyment which attaches to these performances.
>
> (A *Practical Guide to Amateur Theatricals*, 1881)

In the second half of the nineteenth century, both in Europe and America, middle-class families came increasingly to recognise their own theatricality. The 'genteel performance' of middle-class social relationships, as Karen Halttunen has persuasively shown, became increasingly self-conscious in the 1850s and 1860s. Nowhere, Halttunen argues, 'was the new direction of middle class culture more evident than in the vogue of private theatricals that swept the parlors of America' (1982: 153). Private theatricals dramatised what was otherwise a widely accepted metaphor; a new, domesticated version of the *theatrum mundi*. 'The primary theatre of private life in the nineteenth century', writes French historian Michelle Perrot, 'was the family.' The family, Perrot claims, 'established the characters and roles, the practices and rites, the intrigues and conflicts, typical of the private sphere' (1990: 97).

However, if the language of theatricality was increasingly employed to describe and understand the private sphere, it was also a language with serious limitations. Specifically, it was a language confined by the epistemological boundaries of melodrama and farce. Both in the parlour and in the commercial theatre, ethical ambiguities were simplified and characterological nuances erased. For example, in his 1866 *Amateur's Handbook and Guide to Home or Drawing-Room Theatricals*, Tony Denier strongly advocates a 'natural' style of acting but, paradoxically, he also limits the range of such acting to the 'types of humanity' (10). And, in a similarly restricted view of dramatic character, the playwright Bronson Howard insists as one of his 'axioms' of the theatre that 'the death, in an ordinary play [not a tragedy], of a woman who is not pure ... is inevitable' ([1886] 1914: 30). While parlour theatricals and popular melodramas commonly depicted domestic scenes (one famous example being George Aiken's 1852 dramatisation of *Uncle Tom's Cabin*), it would be years before Americans would accept the domestic realism of Ibsen or, in general, dramatic portrayals of women's social and sexual desires in contemporary private life without being scandalised.

Mid-nineteenth-century audiences applauded the innovative appearance of the stage as an enclosed room and the representation of private, middle-class life among 'real' objects. They did not favour the exploration of complex moral and psychological truths within those walls. William Dean Howells, one of Ibsen's great defenders in America, remarked in 1899, 'The latest performance of Ibsen's *Ghosts* has been followed by quite as loud and long an outburst of wounded delicacy in public and private criticism as the earliest [performance] provoked. Now, as then, the play has been found immoral, pathological and revolting (quoted in Murphy, 1992: 101). James A. Herne's *Margaret Fleming* (1890), an unsentimental exploration of a woman's character, set principally in the living-room in Margaret's home, was a critical success but a popular failure when first produced.

However, despite setbacks for playwrights in the commercial theatre and limitations on actors in the private sphere, there were unrecognised venues in which dramatic realism began to penetrate the domestic ethos. In this essay, I investigate representations of theatre in the fiction of Louisa May Alcott. In various stories and novels written between 1854 and 1886, Alcott reconfigures inherited notions of theatre and theatricality to represent a complex vision of the relationship between theatricality and domestic life. In these texts, an incipient form of dramatic realism appears when plays are staged in domestic space. Alcott has two basic and often interlocking strategies for showing a relationship between theatre and the private sphere. The first is to convert the home or some part of the home into a theatrical space ... often, literally, into a theatre. And the second is to represent the private life of a professional actress. Independently, these strategies may not appear particularly original but, where they operate together, Alcott's work illustrates how fictional representations of theatre, or meta-private-theatricals, can produce unsentimental glimpses of domestic life.

In a number of ways, Alcott's work indicates a continuation and a reassessment of Jane Austen's representation of theatre in *Mansfield Park* (1814). Although the anti-theatricalism of *Mansfield Park* no longer seemed relevant in the elaborately theatrical culture of late nineteenth-century America, Austen's representation of theatre was well known if widely misinterpreted. Ironically, guidebooks for amateur actors, such as O. A. Roorbach's *A Practical Guide to Amateur Theatricals* (1881), cite Austen approvingly in order to lend their works authority. It is useful, therefore, to consider briefly how Austen did, in fact, construct the domestic theatre of her novel.

Theatre is posed as a direct threat to a particularised notion of domestic space. 'What signifies a theatre? ' asks Austen's young, brilliant and superficial Henry Crawford. 'Any room in this house might suffice' ([1814] 1966: 149). Crawford has no formal experience of acting, he longs to give it a try and, it turns out, he has a natural gift. His opposite, of course, is the quiet and passive Fanny Price and his attempt to woo and marry her becomes the central crisis of the novel; their relationship is virtually an allegory of the tension between forces of change and those of conservatism.

The integrity of the family is the central theme of *Mansfield Park* and every locus of action outside of Mansfield Park is characterised by dysfunctional families. The most exceptionable character in the theatricals episode is the one person who has no family bonds whatsoever. It is the outsider, the Honourable John Yates, who introduces the notion of theatre or 'the infection' into Mansfield Park to begin with and who eventually elopes with the younger daughter Julia. Opposition to theatre is strongly and repeatedly asserted, principally by Sir Thomas Bertram's younger son Edmund. Ironically, Edmund's eventual participation in the theatricals results from his anxiety to protect the privacy of the house. He is finally prevailed upon to take a role when the rest of the players threaten to invite an outsider to take the one male part yet to be filled or, in other words, to violate the family circle. To the unimpeachable Fanny, Edmund tries to explain his inconsistency:

> Perhaps you are not so much aware as I am, of the mischief that may, of the unpleasantness that must, arise from a young man's being received in this manner … domesticated among us … authorized to come at all hours … and placed suddenly on a footing which must do away with all restraints. To think only of the license which every rehearsal must tend to create. (175)

If the theatre must be private, Edmund determines, it must be completely private. The danger is in the blurring of the public and the private. Therefore, Edmund sets out, by participating, to exclude all strangers and thus attempts to be the means of 'restraining the publicity of the business'.

Mansfield Park is a profound commentary both on the family and on various intrusive, destabilising forces of the nineteenth century which threaten it. The density and sophistication of Austen's ironies may lead the reader to question the essential distinctness of the two social spheres, the theatrical world of John Yates on the one hand and the quiet home epitomised by the passive Fanny on the other. But the superficial resolution of the theatricals episode, the suppression of theatre by Sir Thomas, and Fanny's apparent vindication must also lead the reader to view the theatre as subversive of family interests.

In Alcott's *Little Women* (1868), as in *Mansfield Park*, the absent father is a precondition for theatricals in the home. The discussion of the absent father which frames private theatricals in both novels emphasises paradoxically both the self-sufficiency and the vulnerability of the domestic sphere. The March family's 'Operatic Tragedy' is, however, more purely private than the Bertrams' 'Lovers' Vows'. The four March sisters are the only actors; they both invent the drama and play every role. Moreover, even when playing theatrical roles, their extradramatic personalities and their specific roles in the family are affirmed. Jo is always Jo, rebellious daughter and headstrong sister. The theatricals allow her to 'act out' but ultimately emphasise her basic conformity to familial expectations. Her sister Meg makes this clear when she writes:

> Jo, of course, played the villains, ghosts, bandits and disdainful queens; for her tragedy-loving soul delighted in lurid parts, and no drama was perfect in her eyes without a touch of the demonic or supernatural. Meg loved the sentimental roles, the tender maiden with the airy robes and flowing locks, who made impossible sacrifices for ideal lovers, or the cavalier, singing soft serenades and performing lofty acts of gallantry and prowess. Amy was the fairy sprite, while Beth enacted the page or messenger when the scene required their aid. (Alcott, 1893: 8)

The roles assumed by the sisters reinforce notions of family, for they confirm the sisters' identities in the family independent of the play. Thus, in *Little Women* theatricals seem to have a moral orientation directly opposed to that of theatricals in *Mansfield Park*. Unlike the situation at Mansfield Park, the interest in private theatricals in the March home re-emphasises 'the idealization of the family as an institution that could restrain the forces of conflict and diversity in American society' (Halttunen, 1984: 234).

However, in Alcott's fiction, where the line between public and private is less clearly defined, moral complacency about the theatre and theatricality becomes more problematic. Like Austen, Alcott represents theatre with a strongly moralistic tone but Alcott's representations are also often caught in a web of contradictions; the good actress, for example, cannot easily be a 'good woman' too. For Alcott, theatre challenges notions of the separateness of private and public, of female and male social spheres and the ideological systems that the separate spheres entail. There are many interesting examples of theatre in Alcott's fiction where the borders of home are more permeable than they are in *Little Women*. And the paradox of the good actress and good woman is a pervasive problem both in Alcott's domestic-tutelary novels and in her sensation fiction.[1]

Insofar as theatre is a central metaphor in Alcott's work, it must be understood in its relation to an historical theatre and range of dramatic practice. As a metatheatrical device, the play-within-a-play (or within-a-novel) brings into focus particular dramaturgical assumptions. If a theatrical production implicitly privileges character over plot, for example, this bias will be reflected with a special clarity in a play-within-a-play. And, while the play-within-a-play may also reflect on a kind of plot (for example, it may parody melodramatic action or the form of a well-made play), representations of theatre in the novel tend to highlight the problem of 'character'. In Alcott's fiction, metatheatricality indicates, most importantly, something about character. In this sense especially, Alcott's fictional representations of theatre clearly reflect dramaturgical assumptions of her day: between 1860 and 1880 an increasing concern about the nature of dramatic character is represented both in new kinds of drama and in new productions of old works.

An important feature of dramas written in the third quarter of the nineteenth century for private or drawing-room entertainment is the defamiliarisation of the domestic ethos. By transforming their parlours into theatres, middle-class performers self-consciously played with the conventions of everyday life. Of the countless parlour theatricals published and produced in Alcott's day, *Mr John Smith* (1868), by Sarah Annie Frost, is a particularly good example of a play that defamiliarises the domestic ethos. The drama opens with Mr John Smith still shaking the snow from his clothes after a train ride from New York City and a long hike through a disorienting blizzard. The transition from the cold 'outside' world to that of the warm and supposedly safe drawing-room will ultimately prove to be highly ironic. Mr Smith mistakenly believes that he has arrived at the home of his eccentric old friend, Dr Harris. In fact, Smith has stumbled into a party of amateur actors and actresses preparing for their first performance. It is, moreover, no ordinary performance, for it is not to be of a single drama but, since all the guests wish to be stars, a patchwork of tragedies and comedies, ranging from *Macbeth* to *School for Scandal*. As characters enter and exit, in costume, posing, reciting, acting, they incorporate Smith into the scenes, assuming that he is aware that it is all theatre. In comparison with actors in a play-within-a-play, characters such as John Smith, who are outside the represented drama, are *theatrically unhistrionic*.

John Smith, of course, is totally confused; he assumes that he has come to a lunatic asylum or that he is witnessing some bizarre new experiment of his unusual friend, the doctor. In this setting, theatre and 'reality' merge seamlessly. One character calls to another, 'Macbeth, Ophelia wants you!' (Frost, 1868: 26). To Smith, Ophelia seems a poor young lady who has gone insane, Macduff a dangerous psychopath. An extensive familiarity with dramaturgical methods (for example, the stride of Forrest or the 'style' of Macready) is assumed by all of the characters except John Smith, who insists in the end, 'I was never in a theatre, sir, in my life and know nothing about it!' (37). Smith may fail to see the implications of his own confusion, but for the audience members who sit in a parlour which merges with the one in the play, Smith's despair humorously makes fresh the familiar forms of domestic intercourse.

Moreover, it is not only John Smith who is confused by these actors; they are also mistaken about who he is. They are expecting another Mr John Smith from New York and welcome this John Smith as a familiar member of their group, complicit in all the same assumptions. But their John Smith is a professional actor affiliated with a theatre in the city, who has promised to write their prologue, interludes and epilogue and to act as prompter. 'Such a remarkable name!' exclaims Lily Jones when she learns of the mistake in the end (36). The central problem from which all other comic possibilities follow, therefore, as the title character's generic name suggests, is to mistake a private citizen for a professional actor. Here the professional theatre has come, or is wrongly supposed to have come, into the private home. On the one hand, there is an implication that the private sphere is irremediably theatricalised. But, at the same time, the recalcitrance of John Smith indicates a theatrical space outside of 'theatricality'.

Whether or not Alcott knew *Mr John Smith*, she undoubtedly knew plays like it. And she was able to employ such epistemological comedy in complex and socially incisive ways. In particular, Alcott uses the *mise en abyme* to show how scepticism about character in a theatrical society could rebound most seriously to the disadvantage of women who did not have a clear allegiance to the public or the private sphere. For these women, the actress was an important paradigm.

Behind a Mask; or, a Woman's Power (1866), Alcott's last and, arguably, her best sensation story, inverts the premise of *Mr John Smith*. The theatrical Jean Muir enters the home of the affluent and untheatrical Coventry family. Despite soliciting a governess for younger sister Bella, the family is extremely reluctant to receive a stranger in their home. Jean Muir, a close cousin of Becky Sharp, is, among other things, a former actress. She is also recovering from a dangerous fever contracted, naturally, in France. And, like the Honourable John Yates, the intruder who brought the theatrical infection to Mansfield Park, Jean Muir has no serious family attachments.

Miss Muir's first scene with the Coventry family involves many theatrical moments (such as an unexpected fainting spell while playing the piano) and the family members themselves understand the scene as theatre: '"Scene first, very well done", whispered Gerald to his cousin.' Overhearing this remark, Jean looks over her shoulder with a 'gesture like Rachel' and replies in a penetrating voice, 'Thanks, the last scene shall be still better' ([1866] 1988: 101).[2] But it is only in her room, when 'the curtain is down' and Jean literally disrobes, that Alcott allows us a peek at the 'real' Jean Muir:

> The metamorphosis was wonderful, but the disguise was more in the expression she assumed than in any art of costume or false adornment. Now she was alone, and her mobile features settled into their natural expression, weary, hard, and bitter. (106)

Jean is an excellent actress but, the story seems to suggest, a bad and very dangerous woman. 'Theatricality', as Nina Auerbach notes, 'is such a rich and fearful word in Victorian culture that it is most accurately defined … in relation to what it is not. Sincerity is sanctified and it is not sincere' (1990: 4). Moreover, this form of private theatricality has distinctly gendered overtones. Whereas theatricality in public spaces is often a metaphor for a kind of masculine self-promotion, private theatricality tends to have connotations of feminine promiscuity, a view clearly articulated by Schopenhauer in his notoriously misogynist statement, 'On Women':

> In the girl nature has had in view what could in theatrical terms be called a stage-effect: it has provided her with super-abundant beauty and charm for

> a few years at the expense of the whole remainder of her life, so that during these years she may so capture the imagination of a man that he is carried away into undertaking to support her honourably in some form or other for the rest of her life, a step he would hardly seem to take for purely rational considerations. (1851: 81)

Such is the most serious danger of theatricality in private life, the ability of insincere women to subvert masculine self-interest. The Coventry family is defenceless against Jean. By virtue of her theatrical powers, she soon becomes the life of the house, a favourite of the servants and the object of every man's desire.

In *Behind a Mask*, Alcott seeks to create in the actress a heroine who is both financially and personally secure but who can also share a domestic space with other intimates. In chapter five, 'How the Girl Did It', a blithe company of young people assembles to stage a series of *tableaux vivants* in Sir John Coventry's saloon. Jean Muir, of course, is the focus of each *tableau*, the most successful of which is a picture of two lovers that she performs with brother Gerald. This *tableau* is successful not principally because of its effect upon the audience but because of its effect upon Gerald:

> It lasted but a moment; yet in that moment Coventry experienced another new sensation. Many women had smiled on him, but he had remained heart-whole, cool, and careless, quite unconscious of the power which a woman possesses and knows how to use, for the weal or woe of man. Now, as he knelt there with a soft arm about him, a slender waist yielding to his touch, and a maiden heart throbbing against his cheek, for the first time in his life he felt the indescribable spell of womanhood, and looked the ardent lover to perfection. (Alcott, [1866] 1988:149)

The irony, of course, is that Gerald's first experience of 'real' womanhood takes place in an explicitly theatrical scene. Encouraged by the audience's enthusiastic response, the lovers perform another *tableau* even more moving than the first. Gerald is under the little woman's power and they glide away together to a 'secluded little nook, half boudoir, half conservatory' in order to enact what Jean later refers to as 'strictly private theatricals, in which Monsieur and myself were the only actors' (198). There they achieve a deeper level of intimacy, or so it seems to Gerald. 'We are acting our parts in reality now', Jean sighs beneath his velvet cloak. But the tension between the inner 'Coventry' world and the extrafamilial world symbolised by the professional actress intensifies as Jean comes closer to winning the heart of each member of the nuclear family.

Ultimately, Jean aims to marry into the family. While Gerald falls deeper into love, however, the threat of information about Jean's past looms on the horizon; she is forced to work for the match nearest at hand, marriage with the elderly Sir John. As Judith Fetterley comments, 'The job requires extraordinary self-discipline and self-control. Jean must continually act as if she is not acting and pretend that she is not pretending; she must never let the ultimate mask of "real self" slip' (1983: 7). Jean seeks to provoke Sir John into a proposal without overstepping 'the bounds of maiden modesty' (Alcott, [1866] 1988: 177). When she does, in fact, achieve her match, provoking the gentle Sir John to propose (this event being the 'last scene [that is] better than the first'), 'the blessed sense of safety which came to her filled Jean Muir with such intense satisfaction that tears of real feeling stood in her eyes and the glad assent she gave was the truest word that had passed her lips for months' (181). At this point, one may feel licensed to view Jean Muir with more sympathy than earlier sections of the novella have invited. Her end (a happy marriage) to some degree belies the means (theatricality). The fact that Jean Muir's first basic ambition was to have a home of her own is, finally, the greatest argument on her behalf. And her wedding to Sir John is the climax to which the novella builds insistently: 'When the ring was fairly on, a smile broke over her face. When Sir John kissed and called her his "little wife", she shed a tear or two of sincere happiness' (192). We are never permitted to forget, moreover, that financial necessity is one of the most pressing factors compelling Jean to her theatrical devices.

As in *Mr John Smith*, the meeting of the self-consciously theatrical and the unconsciously theatrical defamiliarises or exposes conventions of social behaviour that, because they occur in private, are supposedly more 'natural' than those of public life. Through Jean's letters to a friend, for example, Alcott invites us to take an unsentimental view both of Jean's character and of the family unit in explicitly theatrical terms. 'Bah!' Jean writes, 'How I hate sentiment! I drank your health from your own little flask and went to bed to dream that I was playing Lady Tartuffe … as I am' (196). Jean's construction of all that has happened since her coming to the home indicates the detachment of a character who knows the value of being a member of a family but one who has not idealised the institution. Because her appreciation of the family is not a romantic one, Jean renders family life in vivid colours, exposing its corruptions. But implicit in all of her mockery is a basic acceptance of the importance of the family and the rules of family life. She actually seeks to punish those members of the family who do not appreciate what they have, who do not, in other words, respect each other or the family as a unit:

> I laugh at the farce and enjoy it, for I only wait till the prize I desire is fairly mine, to turn and reject this lover who has proved himself false to brother, mistress, and his own conscience. For my sake he cast off the beautiful woman who truly loved him; he forgot his promise to his brother; and put by his pride to beg of me the worn-out heart that is not worth a good man's love. (199)

The story represents Jean Muir's rejection of sentimental complacency while also emphasising her need of a family unit in order to survive. Once she hears what Jean has written, Mrs Coventry clasps her daughter 'as if Jean Muir would burst in to annihilate the whole family' (199). The story's great point, however, is that annihilation of the family is the last thing that Jean wants. She wants the family to survive and she wants to be part of it. In the end, she (now Lady Coventry) and Sir John enter the family circle, literally and figuratively. 'For [Sir John's] sake forgive me', she says, entering the parlour. 'And let there be peace between us' (201).

Jean Muir's position in the Coventry household is characterised by two basic conditions: first, her cynical detachment and, second, her profound dependence. The tension generated by this paradoxical relation to the home is vital to understanding both Alcott's theatrical fiction and the rise of domestic realism in American theatre history. In the 1860s and 1870s a profound change was taking place on the American stage and it is in the context of that change that Alcott's fiction should be read. It is worth noting that Alcott, an avid theatre-goer throughout her life, was deeply impressed by one or two productions in particular. Principally, in Edwin Booth's *Hamlet*, Alcott felt that she had seen 'my ideal done at last' (Cheney, 1890: 102). *Hamlet* was her favourite play and Edwin Booth her favourite actor. Booth's *Hamlet* strongly emphasised character over plot, reversing the priorities of melodramatic productions a generation earlier. Booth's famous 1870 production especially dramatised relations among the family members and to this end a new and highly sensitive staging of the play-within-the-play was achieved.[3]

Booth's interpretation of *Hamlet* marked a radical departure from that of the waning school of American acting epitomised by Edwin Forrest whose robust and athletic Dane was a far cry from Booth's gentlemanly and even effeminate hero. In the play-within-the-play scene, wrote one reviewer, Forrest had 'more the air of some huge gypsy, watching with roguish glance an opportunity to rob the hen-roost, than a highly intellectual analyser of nature trying to decry on the human countenance the evidence of guilt' (Shattuck, 1969: 14). In short, the interest that Forrest's Hamlet takes in the play-within-the-play privileges plot over character. For Booth, on the other hand, this scene is a crucial indicator of Hamlet's basic weakness and intellectuality. First of all, in Booth's staging the emphasis has shifted from the play staged for the royal family to the royal family members themselves. In the 'traditional' staging, 'The Mousetrap' had been presented up-stage centre, with the family split (Hamlet and Ophelia on one side and Claudius and Gertrude on the other), looking back toward the play. In Booth's 'modern' staging, Hamlet and Ophelia are up-stage centre, Claudius and Gertrude stage right and the play itself occupies the weakest space of action, stage left. The family has become the focus of interest, with Hamlet at the centre, while Claudius and Gertrude assume a chiasmic relation to the Player King and Queen. The subversive content of 'The Mousetrap' is thus dramatised in the relations between the family members as the emphasis on the players is downplayed and the contrast between Hamlet and Claudius heightened.

Booth's Hamlet displays a 'fine mixture of deference and irony' toward the Queen his mother, in the play-within-a-play scene. His filial affection for both father and mother excited the praise of many critics. 'He is inexpressibly gentle', wrote William Winter. 'He has honored father and mother with that beautiful filial affection which is rooted in the soul and which shows the angel in the man' (Shattuck: 95). Booth was at the heart of a new cultural sensibility, one in which intellectual refinement was combined crucially with the sanctity of private life. Booth was reviewed by one friendly critic as:

> the first Hamlet for many a day who, in the closet scene, does not consider it necessary to rave and rant at the Queen like a drunken pot-boy … he is the first Hamlet for many a day whose conduct in the same scene would not justify the interference of third parties, on the supposition that he intended to commit assault and battery upon his mother … he is the first Prince of Denmark for many a year who has dared, in this same scene, to conduct himself like a gentleman, and not a blackguard. (*New York Tribune*, 27 November 1861: 42)

Here was an actor who knew how to treat his mother. And the reviewer singles out the closet scene as the one, *par excellence*, in which to differentiate Booth from the Forrest school. In Booth's *Hamlet*, a complex and subtle characterisation is theatrically realised in a domestic space, a son alone with his mother in her room. For Alcott, the representation of close yet troubled family relationships in the theatre must have been especially provocative for, in her own life, theatre had recently seemed a release from emotionally trying family responsibilities. Three years before Alcott first saw Booth's *Hamlet*, in 1855, the Alcott family had moved to Walpole, New Hampshire. There Louisa and her sister Anna quickly became involved in the Walpole Amateur Dramatic Company. The Company, which performed in the Walpole Town Hall, with music by the Walpole Serenade Band, confined itself primarily to comedies of the 1840s and 1850s. In these comedies, Louisa tended to play middle-aged, unmarried women, such as the loud-mouthed Widow Pottle in J. R. Planché's *The Jacobite* (1848). In the public house she owns, Widow Pottle, as her daughter's lover laments, 'abuses the privilege of her sex' (9). As the comic relief, Louisa's characters satirise the ideal of the quiet domestic abode but never fundamentally challenge it. Anna, who was also a gifted actress, tended to play the young beauties destined for domestic happiness. Louisa noted: 'Anna was the star, her acting being really very fine. I did "Mrs. Malaprop [in Sheridan's *The Rivals*]", "Widow Pottle" and the old ladies' (Cheney, 1890: 82).[4]

At this time Alcott also began to have more exposure to the professional theatre. Fanny Kemble came to Walpole where Alcott met her in 1855 and over the course of the year Alcott began, with the help of her uncle Dr Charles Windship, to attempt to place her own plays with Thomas Barry, manager of the Boston Theatre. In 1857 the family moved back to Concord where the Concord Stock Company became a vital escape for Alcott from a home in which her younger sister Elizabeth was dying of the effects of scarlet fever. In Concord, as in Walpole, Alcott played widows and character roles, while her sister played ingénues, lovers and young brides. While Louisa attempted to advance her theatre career, however, the Alcott family was experiencing its most significant strain. In her journal, Alcott explicitly articulates an important dichotomy between home and theatre while also indicating their deep relationship in her experience: 'I lead two lives. One seems gay with plays, etc. the other very sad … in Betty's room; for though she wishes us to act and loves to see us get ready, the shadow is there and Mother and I see it' (Cheney, 1890: 96). The next two entries focus almost entirely on two subjects; theatre and her sister's decline:

> December … Some fine plays for charity.
>
> January, 1858 … Lizzie much worse; Dr G. says there is no hope … and we tried to bear it bravely for her sake. We gave up plays; Father came

> home; and Anna took up the housekeeping, so that Mother and I could devote ourselves to her. Sad, quiet days in her room. (96–7)

On 14 March Lizzie died quietly in the middle of the night. In June, Alcott, who had been given a free pass to the Boston theatre by Barry, went to see Charlotte Cushman and 'had a stage-struck fit'. Her dreams seemed nearly realised when Barry agreed to give her a professional break in the role of Widow Pottle. 'It was all a secret and I had hopes of trying a new life; the old one being so changed now, I felt as if I must find interest in something absorbing' (98). Unfortunately however, Barry, who was to play the male lead, broke his leg and the plan fell through. Louisa's disappointment in the journal is revealing:

> I had to give it up; and when it was known, the dear, respectable relations were horrified at the idea. I'll try again by-and-by and see if I have the gift. Perhaps it is acting, and not writing, I'm meant for. Nature must have a vent somehow … Worked off my stage fit in writing a story, and felt better; also a moral tale. (99)

The horror of her parents at the idea of Louisa as actress, her resolution to be an actress nonetheless, her sense of acting and writing as related modes of giving vent to nature and her catharsis in the end through writing a good moral tale, all indicate a dynamic, tense and also murky relation between theatre and the home in Alcott's imagination, as well as the deep tension between acting and writing, public and private modes of creativity.

Alcott's moral tale, 'Marion Earle; or Only an Actress', which emerged from these events in 1858, is a story which earnestly seeks to establish a productive and even a sacred relationship between the actress and the domestic woman.[5] In the first scene of the story, which itself is constructed in a series of melodramatic set pieces, Marion appears on the stage in a comedy. In her dramatic role, Marion 'put by her cares and was the gay and brilliant creature that she seemed'. However, soon after leaving the stage with a jest on her lips, a cry is heard backstage. The play continues 'but it now received the divided attention of those who had been absorbed before'. When she returns to the stage, Marion struggles unsuccessfully to play her comic role, for she has learned backstage, in the middle of the performance, that her little sister May is dead.

> When, after a long pause, Marion appeared, a quick murmur arose, for in her face there might be read a tale of suffering that brought tears of pity into womanly eyes, and changed the comedy to a tragedy … Apparently unconscious of the sympathising faces looking into hers, or the consoling whispers

> of her fellow players, Marion went on, mechanically performing every action of her part like one in a dream, except that now and then there flitted across her face a look of intense and eager longing, and her eyes seemed to look in vain for some means of escape; but the stern patience of a martyr seemed to bear her up, and she played on, a shadow in the scene whose brightness she had lately been … With the same painful faithfulness, she tried to sing [her concluding song], her voice faltered and failed … her heart was too full.

No longer in her theatrical role, Marion turns to the audience members: 'Kind friends, pardon me … I cannot sing … for my little May is dead!' This ingenuous appeal is, paradoxically, the most dramatic utterance of the evening. It is, indeed, a *coup de théâtre*. Women weep and men silently throw flowers at the actress's feet. In one respect, this story clearly projects Louisa May Alcott's personal fantasy, an attempt both to reimagine and to affirm her own dual life of the previous year, when she had been, on the one hand, the actress away from home and, on the other, the nurse to her dying sister Lizzie. In this story the sincerity of the private woman validates the performance of the public figure. Marion Earle is an actress as 'virtuous and cultivated' as 'faithful wives, good mothers and true-hearted women'.

And yet, like other virtuous actresses in Alcott's fiction, Marion is not destined to survive the story. In the end, her goodness is her downfall. Her former lover, Robert Leicester, sick with a 'contagious fever', comes to her home where she happens to be sheltering his abandoned wife and child. After nursing Robert back to health and assuring herself that the nuclear family has been reunited, the saintly actress departs but, of course, she has been infected with the illness which soon kills her. Marion's death represents a moral crisis, for it is apparent that private life is not conducive to the art of the actress. In fact, despite Marion's talents as both actress and nurturing woman, theatre in this story represents a challenge to the domestic and the feminine. In Alcott's early work, theatre implicitly challenges the 'natural' characteristics of the sexes; it subverts dichotomies of passive–active, interior–exterior, female–male (Perrot, 1990: 100). The domestic actress therefore represents a moral crisis of the utmost importance.

The paradox embodied by the virtuous (and, by definition, domestic) actress was much on Alcott's mind in the 1850s. The play she aimed to produce in 1858, during her sister's decline, was 'The Rival Prima Donnas', a dramatisation of only her second published story (1854) of the same title. 'The Rival Prima Donnas' tells the story of two women, the 'fair' and 'blameless' Beatrice, who has resigned her position as first lady of the opera in order to make a quiet home, and the up-and-coming 'young debutante' Theresa. The opening scene establishes the split architecturally, with Beatrice in the curtained box and Theresa on the stage. Beatrice, in the middle of the performance, vanishes even from the private box and reappears at home with painter and fiancé, Claude. It is an emblematic transition. 'Have I not tried the world and found its flattering homage false?' asks Beatrice of her intended:

> Have I not sought for happiness in wealth and fame and sought in vain until I found it in your love? What then do I leave but all I am most weary of, and what do I gain but all I prize and cherish most on the earth? The painter's home I will make beautiful with the useless wealth I have won, and the painter's heart I will make happy by all the blessings a woman's love can give! Then do not fear for me, what *can* I lose in leaving a careless world for a husband and a home? ([1854] 1990: 12)

This vision of domestic happiness, however, will soon be frustrated and Beatrice's goodness trampled: 'As she spoke she laid her proud head trustingly upon his breast, little dreaming of the bitter disappointment her fond words brought to the false heart where all her hope and faith were placed.' At midnight Claude departs for a rendezvous with Theresa. The moral polarity of good Beatrice and evil Theresa seems clearly represented when, to the slightly remorseful Claude, Theresa explicitly articulates his choice:

> If Beatrice be still so dear to you, I fear there is no place in your heart for me, therefore choose now between us, for I will have no rival in your love. If Beatrice be dearest, then go and share with her the *quiet home* she longs for and in her calm affection may you find the happiness you seek, but if your many vows be true and Theresa most beloved, then come and tread with me the path that lies before us, share with me the wealth and fame I go to win, and in the *gay brilliant world* find all that makes love pleasant and happiness in my fond faithful love, both are before you, therefore choose and let all doubts be ended here forever. (15; my emphasis)

Naturally, Claude, who is confessedly playing a part himself and, thus, is deeply bound to the world of acting, chooses Theresa. Beatrice, the 'deceived, deserted woman', comes to the theatre one last time. And, although hiding behind the drooping curtains of her box, she is, Alcott insists, equally as capable of acting the role represented by Theresa on the stage 'with a truth and power that would have thrilled the hearts which beat so quickly now' (19). Instead, when Theresa takes her bows,

Beatrice throws down an iron crown concealed in roses which kills her rival and leads, ultimately, to her own insanity.

Although the title of 'The Rival Prima Donnas' seems to privilege the professional and public rivalry of the two women, it is clearly the private and the domestic aspect of the story that is most important. The story's opening explicitly establishes Beatrice's 'generosity' and total lack of jealousy regarding Theresa's ascendance on the stage. In fact, after the first act, Beatrice's appreciation of her rival's professional success is most conspicuous 'as forgetful of all but the trembling singer before her she clapped her white hands and cast the flowers from her own bosom at her wondering rival's feet' (11). Moreover, Beatrice loses none of her ability as a performer, as the narrator emphasises at the climax. Beatrice simply chooses a different sphere of action, the private as opposed to the public. However, although the story invites us to favour Beatrice over Theresa, to privilege private over public, it may be wiser to recognise a play between these bipolarities that is not clearly resolved. After all, the most wicked act of the story, murder, is committed in the end by Beatrice, not Theresa. Theresa, moreover, is never despicable; on the contrary, the story manifests a profound appreciation for artistic talent, of which Theresa clearly has plenty. Beatrice may once have been virtuous, but she is disappointed in the end; this is not the tale of goodness rewarded that we expect from melodrama. And Alcott's own enjoyment of playing villains and witches may also provide some context in which to reconsider the 'moral' of this tale.

Read in the light of stories such as 'Marion Earle' and 'The Rival Prima Donnas', *Behind a Mask*, written ten years later, clearly represents an advance for the actress turned domestic, for Jean, though tainted, not only lives but she also wins a husband. Ultimately, of course, she must reject the handsome Gerald to marry old Sir John, a choice that has much in common with Jo March's rejection of the dashing Laurie and marriage to the avuncular Professor Bhaer. The older men validate the quiet harmony of the domestic sphere, bringing only minor sexual and 'romantic' tension. But, unlike Marion and Beatrice, Jean does manage to negotiate the treacherous terrain between the world of professional theatre and the domestic sphere without losing either her life or her mind. She may never be completely absolved of the sin of theatricality and she clearly remains a problematic heroine but, in her ability to move from the world of theatre to the world of the home, Jean, more successfully than either Marion or Beatrice, represents brief glimpses of realism through the self-consciously theatrical.

After representing actresses in fiction throughout her career, Alcott seems to resolve the good actress/good woman paradox in her last and most sentimental novel, *Jo's Boys* (1886). Miss Cameron, a character apparently modelled on Fanny Kemble, fulfils not a sensational but a tutelary function.[6] She faces the same struggle to maintain her privacy that the now famous writer, Mrs Jo, does. She is a public figure, who has retreated to a private space both to refresh herself and to work on her art. This fact alone indicates a new notion of the theatre: the space of the actress's real creativity is no longer the stage but the privacy of her own home. At Rocky Nook, where the Laurences (Amy and Laurie) have a house:

> Miss Cameron, the great actress, had hired one of the villas and retired thither to rest and 'create' a new part for next season. She saw no one but a friend or two, had a private beach and was invisible except during her daily drive, or when the opera glasses of curious gazers were fixed on a blue figure disporting itself in the sea. The Laurences knew her, but respected her privacy. (1886: 130)

Little Josie Brooke, however, who is staying with her aunt and uncle, pines to meet the great woman, who both 'thrills thousands by her art' and wins friends by her virtue. Miss Cameron is a model of refinement and cultivation. The notion that one must *cultivate* a 'good heart' is a basic lesson of the maternal-tutelary mode and, ultimately, cultivation becomes the bridge between actress and woman. The virtuous actress, previously understood as a contradiction, is reimagined through the concept of 'culture'.

As a virtuous actress, moreover, Miss Cameron is doubly validated and she in turn seems to validate both of the spheres (public and private) in which she moves: 'The stage needs just such women to purify and elevate the profession which should teach as well as amuse' (130). Consequently, Alcott privileges Miss Cameron to become Josie's mentor. The actress is given access to the private world of Plumfield, which is literally turned into a theatre before her eyes in the private theatricals produced by Mrs Jo and company. Unlike the *tableaux vivants* in *Behind a Mask*, private theatricals at Plumfield require that all participants understand their 'reality' in the same way. Theatricality in *Jo's Boys* implies not insincerity, as it did in *Behind a Mask,* but the 'truth' that happiness is in the cultivated private sphere.

Generally Miss Cameron advises young girls like Josie to be 'good wives and happy mothers in quiet homes' (139). Theatre and the 'quiet home' remain essentially two separate worlds and those who inhabit them are of two 'classes'. However, 'culture' is now a form of mediation, a quality necessary to fit a girl for either world and to allow a woman to move between them both:

> I can give you no better advice than to go on loving and studying our great master [Shakespeare] ... It is an education in itself, and a lifetime is not long enough to teach you all his secrets. But there is much to do before you can hope to echo his words ... Now you will be disappointed, for instead of telling you to come and study with me, or go and act in some second-rate theatre at once, I advise you to go back to school and finish your education. That is the first step, for all accomplishments are needed and a single talent makes a very imperfect character. Cultivate mind and body, heart and soul, and make yourself an intelligent, graceful, beautiful, and healthy girl. (140–1)

In Miss Cameron's advice, Josie recognises the counsel of her own family. Josie's Aunt Amy feels 'that whether her niece was an actress or not she *must* be a gentlewoman' (129). Her family emphasises education (they run a school) as well as a new form of theatre ... a fundamentally domestic theatre. Uncle Laurie and Aunt Jo in fact 'plan plays about true and lovely things ... simple domestic scenes that touch people's hearts and make them laugh and cry and feel better.' Her uncle tells her that she must not think of doing tragedy and Miss Cameron agrees that the girl is not ready for 'high art', which includes freezing the blood and firing the imagination (142).

However, if, in *Jo's Boys*, the professional theatre seems to capitulate to a sentimental domestic vision – and chapter fourteen, 'Plays at Plumfield', is literally a dramatisation of that capitulation – there are also signs of faint and indirect resistance, a sense that the domestic ethos may touch the heart but it also entails a loss of fun. In fact, the 'blood-and-thunder' melodramas favoured by Jo, as a girl in *Little Women*, exert their presence to the very end when the narrator remarks:

> It is a strong temptation to the weary historian to close the present tale with an earthquake which should engulf Plumfield and its environs so deeply in the bowels of the earth that no youthful Schliemann could ever find a vestige of it. But as that somewhat melodramatic conclusion might shock my gentle readers, I will refrain. (315)

Though the narrator does not employ the explosive conventions of the melodramatic theatre and instead quietly lets 'the curtain fall forever on the March family', one is left with the sense that haunting the edges of the happy home is a kind of theatre that is incongruous with domestic bliss. Moreover, though Miss Cameron seems to resolve the good actress/good woman dichotomy, Alcott offers details throughout the novel that undermine this apparent resolution.

Alcott's use of theatre to reinforce the sanctity of the home in the domestic novels of the March family appears especially ironic in light of repeated references to *Macbeth*. *Macbeth* establishes an important link between Jo March, Miss Cameron and Josie Brooke. At the beginning of *Little Women* Jo exclaims:

> I do think *The Witch's Curse, an Operatic Tragedy* is rather a nice thing, but I'd like to try *Macbeth*, if we only had a trapdoor for Banquo. I always wanted to do the killing part. 'Is that a dagger I see before me?' muttered Jo, rolling her eyes and clutching at the air, as she had seen a famous tragedian do. (8)

The events of *Little Women* occur in the late 1840s, when Jo is about fifteen. The famous tragedian to whom she refers is Edwin Forrest, the greatest American Macbeth of his generation and the dramaturgy she evokes, therefore, is not the rising domestic realism but the melodrama of an earlier period. Moreover, her reference specifically to Forrest is significant because Forrest's *Macbeth* was at the heart of a major public controversy which culminated in 1849 in the Astor Place Riot. That riot, which cost more than twenty lives, epitomised the destructive power of the 'public' at the theatre.[7]

At one time or another Jo March, Miss Cameron and Josie Brooke all display an enthusiasm for *Macbeth*, a play with an extraordinarily dark vision of the family, of women generally and of mothers particularly. Peculiarly, when Nat and Daisy are reunited at the end of *Jo's Boys*, Josie 'danced round them like Macbeth's three witches in one' (314). The repeated references to *Macbeth* in Alcott's domestic writing may seem singularly incongruous. In *Macbeth*, no home is safe. Of the two female characters, one imagines herself dashing out her newborn's brains and the other is unable to protect her children or herself from assassins hired by Macbeth himself. In *Macbeth*, there is a deep animus against the very concept of motherhood.

In *Jo's Boys*, at the crucial moment when Josie begins acting in Miss Cameron's parlour without knowing that Miss Cameron is in the room, she is mouthing Lady Macbeth's last speech. It is a moment and a speech that connects Josie to a long history of great actresses and to theatre history generally and it is a moment that fore-ordains her ultimate career choice. Standing alone in Miss Cameron's parlour, waiting for the great actress to appear, Josie forgets herself and, gazing at the portraits of other great actresses, begins 'to imitate Mrs Siddons as Lady Macbeth':

> Looking up at the engraving … she held her nosegay like the candle in the sleepwalking scene, and knit her youthful brows distressfully while murmuring the speech of the haunted queen. So busy was she that Miss Cameron watched her for several minutes unseen, then startled her by sweeping in with the words upon her lips, the look upon her face, which made that one of her greatest scenes. (136)

Lady Macbeth's last speech ('The Thane of Fife had a wife; where is she now?') is the initial point of artistic contact for protégée and mentor, as if this play, which represents the death of families, is the starting point for a career in theatre. Miss Cameron, as Josie recalls, had lost a lover years ago and 'since had lived only for art' (137). There remains, in other words, an important sense in which family and theatre are mutually exclusive.

In *Jo's Boys*, however, Josie's theatrical triumph comes not as Lady Macbeth but as a character much like herself, in a play written not by Shakespeare but by Aunt Jo. Karen Halttunen argues convincingly that 'Josie Brooke helps fulfil Miss Cameron's dream to purify American theatre by carrying family theatre onto the public stage' (Halttunen, 1984: 249). The play at Plumfield itself is about a simple country family nearly destroyed, as Halttunen puts it, 'by contact with the evil world outside the home'. It is a play about the sanctity of private life, performed for a private audience. And the professional actress, Miss Cameron, who is included in the select group attending, enters into the illusion as thoroughly as the most naive theatregoer does. Above all, it is a play about and for mothers. 'I wanted to show that the mother was the heroine as soon as possible', comments the playwright, Aunt Jo (Alcott, 1886: 208). And yet, despite the play's excessive sentimentality, the performance does aim unconsciously at a certain kind of realism. In this chapter, Alcott represents the drama of domestic sentiment through a quasi-naturalistic mode of acting. Actors are most successful when they just act natural. For example, 'Josie's unaffected start when she sees her [mother, Meg, who also plays her stage mother] and the cry, "Why there's mother!" was such a hearty little bit of nature, it hardly needed the impatient tripping over her train as she ran into the arms that seemed now to be her nearest refuge' (211). But, while Josie is theatrically unhistrionic, the play has no psychological content. It is, as a melodrama, entirely plot driven. Dramaturgically the play at Plumfield is deeply conflicted. Dramatic realism begins in the home, in the family, among people with whom one is intimate and familiar and the most perfect theatrical illusion is that which does not appear to be theatre at all. But, at the same time, the play at Plumfield represents a retreat from issues that theatre raises elsewhere in Alcott's work. As a whole, *Jo's Boys* clearly, even insistently, marks both the compelling force and the limitations of sentimental theatre. 'Having endeavored to suit everyone by many weddings, few deaths, and as much prosperity as the eternal fitness of things will allow', the narrator cynically remarks in the end, 'let the music stop, the lights die out, and the curtain fall forever on the March family' (316).

In 1879, Ibsen wrote a radical new play called *A Doll's House*, in which the female protagonist, a housewife named Nora, comes to realise that what she thought had been domestic felicity had been a fantasy, a performance. The epiphany that her entire life has been an act moves the play to a new kind of theatre. In a conclusion that stunned Victorian audiences first in Europe and, fifteen years later, in America, Nora articulates her wish for a marriage that is 'real'; then she slams the door, irrevocably, behind her. This single act moved the drama into a new kind of moral space. In this play, Ibsen rejects complacency about the theatricality of social life, but he also eschews the sort of sentimental unmasking which aims, reductively, to distinguish the sincere from the depraved. This form of dramatic realism indicates a space of moral ambiguity where the exuberantly theatrical meets the theatrically unhistrionic.

Although Alcott manifests no awareness at the end of her life of the domestic realism beginning to appear on European stages, she does show, in a variety of works and genres, that the theatre of private life is full of contradictory demands. Some of the most prominent of Alcott's recent critics … Karen Halttunen, Nina Auerbach and Richard Brodhead … have emphasised that, in various forms, the tension in Alcott's fiction between a richly fulfilling private sphere and a dangerous and exciting (not to mention remunerative) public sphere generates the vital energy of her fiction. As this essay has demonstrated, despite the self-conscious theatricality of the private sphere in late nineteenth-century America, Alcott's actresses ultimately fail to bridge the gap between domesticity and theatre. Their attempts lead to death, insanity or at least to the stigma of moral corruption. Alcott's own life and career, both somewhat constricted by domestic obligations, further contribute an element of pathos to the unresolvable tensions she represents in her work. Private theatricals in Alcott's work indicate, most importantly, the limits of old dramaturgical modes for representing a complete, morally complex, domestic space. And yet, Alcott implies, theatre of some kind is an inescapable aspect of existence. 'It is impossible', she admits simply, in *Jo's Boys*, 'for the humble historian of the March family to write a story without theatricals in it' (203).

Notes

1 See, for example, Alcott's novel *Work* (1873), in which protagonist and short-term actress Christe Devon asks herself, 'If three years of this life have made me this, what shall I be in ten? A fine actress perhaps, but how good a woman?' (43).

2 Rachel (1820–1858), the greatest French tragic actress of the nineteenth century, performed with her own troupe in New York between August 1855 and January 1856. Her greatest roles were in the classical repertoire, but Rachel was also known for being an inspired natural performer. See Banham, 1988.

3 Shattuck (1969) is the primary source for my discussion of Booth's *Hamlet*. The most extraordinary document in Shattuck's book is a massive recording, by a twenty-one-year-old fan named Charles Clarke, of Booth's performance of Hamlet in 1870 in Booth's Theatre in New York. All further references to Booth's *Hamlet* are taken from documents cited in Shattuck's extensive work.

4 In Richard Brinsley Sheridan's *The Rivals* (1775), Mrs Malaprop incompetently defends the institution of the family, in which, as she sees it, conjugal love plays very little part.

5 Quotations from 'Marion Earle' taken from the microfilm. I am indebted to Christine R. Bailey of the Pennsylvania State University Libraries rare books collection for a copy of the microfilm of Alcott's story from the *New York Atlas* (12 September 1858). I became aware of this recently discovered story through Madeleine Stern's article (1992).

6 Fanny Kemble (1809–1893) was an English actress who first came to America in 1832. In 1834, in Philadelphia, Kemble married Pierce Butler, whom she later learned to be a slaveowner. This issue, among others, induced Kemble to leave her husband in 1845. They were divorced in 1848. Later that year she played Lady Macbeth to Macready's Macbeth. Kemble was also the niece of Sarah Siddons (arguably the greatest tragic actress of the English stage) whose portrait Miss Cameron has upon her wall. For the last twenty-six years of her life, Kemble gave 'public' drawing-room readings of Shakespeare, which were famous throughout America. Significantly, Miss Cameron's principal piece of advice for Josie is to study Shakespeare.

7 Fanny Kemble, Alcott's model for Miss Cameron, had played Lady Macbeth opposite William Charles Macready, the other actor at the centre of the Astor Place Riot. For more on the Astor Place Riot, see Levine, 1988: 64–8; McConachie, 1992: 147–52 and Grimsted, 1968: 68–75.

Bibliography

A Practical Guide to Private Theatricals (1881), New York, O. A. Roorbach.

Adelman, J. (1987), '"Born of woman": fantasies of maternal power in *Macbeth*', in M. Garber (ed.), *Cannibals, Witches and Divorce: Estranging the Renaissance* (English

Institute Essays), Baltimore, Johns Hopkins University Press.

Alcott, L. M. [1854] (1990) 'The Rival Prima Donnas', in M. Stern, D. Shealy and J. Myerson (eds), *Louisa May Alcott: Selected Fiction* , Boston, Little, Brown and Company.

Alcott, L. M. (1858), 'Marion Earle; or, Only an Actress!', *New York Atlas*, 12 September.

Alcott, L. M. [1866](1988), *Behind a Mask*, in E. Showalter (ed.), *Alternative Alcott*, New Brunswick, Rutgers University Press.

Alcott, L. M. [1868](1983), *Little Women*, New York, Signet Classic.

Alcott, L. M. [1873](1994), *Work: A Story of Experience*, ed. J. Kasson, New York, Penguin.

Alcott, L. M. (1886), *Jo's Boys and How They Turned Out*, Boston, Little, Brown and Company.

Alcott, L. M. (1893), *Comic Tragedies Written by 'Jo' and 'Meg' and Acted by the 'Little Women',* Boston, Roberts Brothers.

Auerbach, N. (1978), *Communities of Women: An Idea in Fiction*, Cambridge, MA, Harvard University Press.

Auerbach, N. (1990), *Private Theatricals: The Lives of the Victorians,* Cambridge, MA, Harvard University Press.

Austen, J. [1814](1966), *Mansfield Park*, ed. T. Tanner, New York, Penguin.

Banham, M., (ed.) (1988), *The Cambridge Guide to World Theatre*, New York, Cambridge University Press.

Cheney, E. (ed.) (1890), *Louisa May Alcott: Her Life, Letters, and Journals*, Boston, Roberts Brothers.

Denier, T. (1866), *The Amateur's Hand-Book and Guide to Home or Drawing Room Theatricals: How to Get Them Up and How to Act in Them*, New York, Samuel French.

Fetterley, J. (1983), 'Impersonating "Little Women": the radicalism of Alcott's *Behind a Mask*', *Women's Studies,* 10, 1–14.

Frost, S. A. (1868), *Mr John Smith, Amateur Theatricals and Fairy-Tale Dramas: A Collection of Original Plays, Expressly Designed for Drawing-Room Performance,* New York, Dick and Fitzgerald.

Grimsted, D. (1968), *Melodrama Unveiled: American Theatre and Culture 1800–1850*, Berkeley, University of California Press.

Halttunen, K. (1982), *Confidence Men and Painted Women: A Study of Middle-Class Culture in America 1830–1870*, New Haven, Yale University Press.

Halttunen, K. (1984), 'The domestic drama of Louisa May Alcott', *Feminist Studies*, 10:2, 233–54.

Howard, B. [1886](1914), *Autobiography of a Play,* New York, Dramatic Museum of Columbia University.

Levine, L. (1988), *Highbrow/Lowbrow: The Emergence of Cultural Hierarchy in America*, Cambridge, MA, Harvard University Press.

McConachie, B. (1992), *Melodramatic Formations: American Theatre and Society 1820–1870*, Iowa City, University of Iowa Press.

Murphy, B. (ed.) (1992), *A Realist in the American Theatre: Selected Drama Criticism of William Dean Howells,* Athens, Ohio, Ohio University Press. *New York Tribune*, 27 November 1861.

Perrot, M. (ed.) (1990), *A History of Private Life 4: From the Fires of Revolution to the Great War*, trans. A. Goldhammer, Cambridge, MA, Harvard University Press.

Planché, J. R. (1848), *The Jacobite: A Comic Drama in Two Acts*, New York, Douglas.

Rump, E. (ed.) (1988), *The School for Scandal and Other Plays*, New York, Penguin.

Schopenhauer, A. (1851), 'On Women', in *Essays and Aphorisms* (1970), trans. R. J. Hollingdale, London, Penguin.

Shattuck, C. (1969), *The Hamlet of Edwin Booth*, Urbana, University of Illinois Press.

Stern, M. (1992), 'An early Alcott sensation story: "Marion Earle; or, Only an Actress!"', *Nineteenth-Century Literature*, 47:1, 91–8.

The architecture of manners: Henry James, Edith Wharton and The Mount

Sarah Luria

When he visited the largest private house in the country – George Vanderbilt's Biltmore – in February 1905, Henry James was dumbstruck. He wrote to his friend Edith Wharton from the 'strange, colossal heart-breaking house' in Asheville, North Carolina, that 'the desolation and discomfort of the ... whole scene are, in spite of the mitigating millions everywhere expressed, indescribable' (Dwight, 1994). James went on:

> I can't go into it – it's too much of a 'subject': I mean one's sense of the extraordinary impenitent madness (of millions) which led to the erection in this vast niggery wilderness, of so gigantic and elaborate a monument to all that *isn't* socially possible there. It's, *in effect*, like a gorgeous practical joke – but at one's own expense, after all, if one has to live in solitude in these league-long marble halls, and sit in alternate Gothic and Palladian cathedrals, as it were – where now only the temperature stalks about – with the 'regrets,' sighing along the wind, of those who have declined. (133–4)

By James's fanciful analysis, it would seem that it is precisely because of the 'mitigating millions everywhere expressed' that Biltmore is 'indescribable'. The size and volubility of the estate overpowers any more subtle expression and leads instead to an eerie silence. James points specifically to just why this is so. If we follow his path of associations and recall his fascination with colloquial metaphor, we see that his claim that he 'can't go into' his subject has an easily overlooked, quite concrete, meaning: James can't go into the subject of Biltmore because the house has literally no interior for him to go into. James ties the size of the subject (too big for the space of a letter) to the size of the house itself ('gigantic'), implying that the house has no proper interior – its 'league-long' halls are home only to the weather, the 'temperature' and the 'wind.' In *The American Scene* (1907), James's account of his return tour through this country after a twenty-five year absence, James explicitly makes this charge against the new houses of the rich: 'The custom rages like a conspiracy for nipping the interior in the bud, for denying its right to exist, for ignoring and defeating it in every possible way' ([1907] 1946: 167). The chilly drafts of Biltmore extinguish 'social possibilities' and stifle expression. No one wants to travel a thousand miles to sit in a big cold house in the Smoky Mountains and so there is little to report, except for the 'big subject' which is, of course, that there is so little to report.

While she could stomach far more extravagance than James could, Edith Wharton would have easily recognised these structural flaws behind Biltmore's indescribability.[1] Wharton had co-authored a book on interior decoration, *The Decoration of Houses* (1897), in which she detailed just why so little of interest seemed to happen in the fashionable rooms of the well-to-do. Instead of coy rooms where one could sit by the fire and write a letter or have an intimate chat, a raw craving for public approval ruled modern design. Houses were brutally opened up: their grand front entrances and large windows exposed them to public view. Significantly, Wharton notes, the writing-table, once a central fixture in the family drawing-room, had been replaced by 'that modern futility, the silver-table'. As a result, 'the writing-table is either banished or put in some dark corner, where it is little wonder that the ink dries unused and a vase of flowers grows in the middle of the blotting-pad' (Wharton and Codman, [1897] 1978: 21). In ceasing to be homes, houses had all but evicted the literary side of life. They gave up depth and narratibility for the sake of publicising wealth. 'Oh, yes; we were awfully dear, for what we are and for what we do', the mansions along the New Jersey shore boasted pathetically to James (James, [1907] 1946: 8).

In this essay I analyse the extraordinary degree to which James and Wharton believed that physical conditions, established by both architecture and place, could enable or thwart the literary side of life – everything from 'the play of social relation', as James called it, to the writing of novels ([1907] 1946: 167). In a negative sense, to be sure, the palaces and extravagant lifestyles of the Gilded Age provided literary material. After attending a party in Newport at Breakers, another Vanderbilt family estate, Wharton wrote to a friend, 'the Vanderbilt entertainment was just what you say – but for a novelist gathering documents for an American novel, it was all the more valuable, alas!' (Dwight, 1994: 97). Paradoxically, then, it is precisely that Biltmore lacks interiority that makes it such a 'big subject' – one James and Wharton 'go into' in countless ways through their novels and writings. From these architectural critiques, however, also emerges a positive plan for a truly literary house that could not only heighten social intercourse but also provide the perfect space in which to write.

Wharton and James believed that the home embodied and enforced a social, moral and economic order. Through their literary architecture they sought to redress two dominant domestic models of the Gilded Age – the agoraphobic Victorian town-houses of the old leisure class and the brazenly open mansions of the new Wall Street plutocracy. James and Wharton centred their domestic plan around an innermost room, a space of reflection and writing. The rest of the house served to provide a sequence of increasingly private spaces which led to and protected this sacred chamber. Wharton and James reproduced this climactic floor plan in their architectural criticism, their novels and, most concretely, at The Mount, the summer villa Wharton designed for herself in Lenox, Massachusetts (see figure 12).[2] I shall argue that, unlike the town-house's excessive restraint or the mansion's excessive consumption, the literary architecture of Wharton and James formulated a subtle social economics of restrained consumption. The chain of rooms both encouraged and deferred consumption by guardedly inviting the visitor to keep moving deeper into the house. Ultimately, however, the rooms led to restraint – to a space where one imagined but resisted the actual possession of one's innermost desires. They led, in other words, to the writing of fiction

12 The Mount today, terrace side/east elevation. Photograph: Steve Ziglar.

rather than the transgressing of social laws. The possibility of owning one's desires is traded for the more virtuous sublimation of those desires into an endless stream of possible stories for publication. In this way, the literary architecture of Wharton and James reconciled the breach between modern business and Victorian manners by combining positive features of both; their design renewed a tantalising commerce between public and private life, while nevertheless preserving a sacred innermost chamber.

That these two novelists of manners should have taken such a keen interest in domestic architecture has intrigued architectural and literary historians alike.[3] Amy Kaplan and Judith Fryer, in particular, have argued that Wharton's architectural expertise enabled her to redesign domestic space so that it released, rather than buried, her full creative powers.[4] Although they establish a link between domestic architecture and Wharton's identity as an author, both Fryer and Kaplan argue that Wharton's literary powers flourish mainly outside the home. Wharton's determination to join the male-dominated literary marketplace, Kaplan argues, 'pit[s] professional authorship against domesticity' and 'posits a creative realm outside of and antagonistic to the domestic domain' (1988: 70, 74). Fryer suggests that Wharton's creativity was most free in the 'secret garden' in which Wharton said she wrote. Ironically, this imaginary of walled-in, outdoor space, Fryer concludes, is in conflict with the architecture Wharton so admired: 'Secret garden … implies secret, blooming passion of a forbidden or illicit sort,' a 'mind-body fusion that [Wharton] negates in the rigidly controlled structures of her houses, gardens and novels of manners' (1986: 173). In the end, both Fryer and Kaplan suggest that the interest of Wharton's architecture lies mainly in its role as an 'apprenticeship', a 'metaphor' or an analogy for her novels.[5]

In contrast, I contend that Wharton's domesticity is inseparable from her work. The house is essential because it physically realises the aesthetic of deferred and ultimately renounced gratification so prominent in Wharton's and James's work. It is a common literary ploy to postpone the reader's desired conclusion – the moment when the right woman finally gets the right man. In Wharton's and James's fiction, however, this deferred gratification typically leads to a non-event: hero and heroine must accept the social constraints that prevent their happiness and go their separate ways. Architecture, I argue, is instrumental to Wharton and James in bringing this impasse about. Through physical barriers – walls, doors, secluded chambers – literary architecture provides the tangible support needed to resist transgression; it reinforces manners and in that way leads to writing. Architecture, for Wharton and James, hence has the potential to be the space of writing – the buffer which keeps the storyless silence of possession safely at bay. Facing the barrier erected by moral convention, one invents rather than consumes.

My inclusion of James in this study confirms the degree to which Wharton's fascination with architecture was motivated not only by gender but also by class and by what both authors perceived as the literary excesses of sentimental fiction. The creed of noble restraint separated the true cultural elite from the vulgar rich as well as from the horde of financially successful (and mainly women) scribblers. In promoting restraint, Wharton and James reasserted the superiority of private over public life and, in so doing, reclaimed the cultural spotlight, to some degree, from the Vanderbilts and the marketplace; they returned standards of taste to the custody of the more established social elite and protected that custody through exclusive salons such as that over which Wharton herself presided. Through a concrete discussion of the literary effects of doors and floor plans, room arrangements and gardens, I hope to show that we can look at the architecture of Wharton and James as more than a 'metaphor' or analogy for their novels; rather, architecture created the very conditions without which those novels could not exist. In this sense, literary architecture provides an instructive case for American studies of a completely interdisciplinary phenomenon, one perceived as such even by its own creators. It is not a matter of the house being a 'text' or a helpful metaphor. The architecture of Wharton and James proves that a house does not have either to be a text or be in a text in order to be literary.

Architecture was necessary to Wharton's and James's literary authority because it was precisely the submission to restraint that established them as authors. Unbridled consumption, on the other hand, led, ironically, to the undoing of one's power. This paradox was illustrated for James by the ill-fated Biltmore. Biltmore expressed a fantasy of omnipotence encouraged by the hubris of Wall Street and its capitalist 'giants', of which George Vanderbilt's father Cornelius was a famous example. Rather than build a palace at Newport or a rustic cabin suited to the Smoky Mountains, the son flouted social custom and practical constraints. It is as though he counted upon the sheer force of his money to tame nature and to bring society to him. In its arrogance, the house echoes Cornelius Vanderbilt's purported remark: 'Law! What do I care for the Law? Hain't I got the power?' (Bailey and Kennedy, 1994, 2:

542). The novelist of manners, on the other hand, believes we can only gain power through our understanding of social laws. In his critique of Biltmore, James shows why such monarchical fantasies in post-Civil War America must fail by contrasting Vanderbilt's 'monument' to the 'niggery wilderness' that surrounds it. Rather than the apparent harmony of interior and exterior achieved by the French château or the Southern plantation with their cultivated grounds, Biltmore has no control over its environment: the Big House is too big, the slaves have been freed and the surroundings have reverted to anarchic wilderness. As though admitting defeat by the intransigent forces of society and nature, the Vanderbilts abandoned Biltmore some years later. Still the largest house in the country, it remains today a fossil of the Gilded Age, untaxed income and conspicuous consumption.

The failed architecture that looms so large in the writings of James and Wharton fails because of the social economy it expresses. The business of the Gilded Age, with its domineering vision so alien to the novelists' respect for the subtle architecture of society, obliterated interiority and made no conversation. In contrast to the perversity of Biltmore, Wharton and James made their business the delicate probing of those historic conventions and constraints that directed social intercourse. Novelists of manners establish their authority not through their fantastic control of their characters' fates but by the accuracy with which they represent the social and economic architecture through which we move and over which we have so little control. Wharton and James describe, prescribe and even build actual houses and evaluate them for the quality of the social discourse that they catalyse. In the following sections, I will discuss the concrete way in which James and Wharton synthesise architecture and manners, the business they conduct within that space, the power they achieve as a result and the price they pay for it.

The architecture of manners

The deterioration of an effective relation between public and private was evident to Wharton in the domestic architecture of the interior door, a feature whose 'fate', Wharton claims, architects and decorators had 'pursued with … relentless animosity': 'First, the door was slid into the wall; then even its concealed presence was resented and it was unhung and replaced by a portière; while of late it has actually ceased to form a part of house-building and many recently-built houses contain doorways without doors' (Wharton and Codman, [1897] 1978: 48). In *The Amer-*

ican Scene, James suggests why a novelist of manners would find a house *'without doors'* so preposterous:

> In such conditions there couldn't be any manners to speak of; … the basis of privacy was somehow wanting for them; … nothing, accordingly, no image, no presumption of constituted relations, possibilities, amenities, in the social, the domestic order was inwardly projected. It was as if the projection had been so completely outward that one could but find one's self almost uneasy about the mere perspective required for the common acts of the personal life, that minimum of vagueness as to what takes place in it for which the complete 'home' aspires to provide. (10)

Manners for James and Wharton functioned as doors. They were the architecture of human behaviour, through which one's inner feelings and longings might be concealed or revealed. Similarly, they signalled where one could and could not go. Houses without doors resulted in social relations unmediated by privacy, 'vagueness' or an 'inwardly projected' 'social, domestic order' – the 'conditions' established by doors.

Manners, according to social anthropologist Norbert Elias, are a set of conventions that confer social status by showing that the mind has brought one's physical urges under control. By cleaning one's nose with a handkerchief, for example, rather than one's finger, one advertises one's power of restraint. Immediate physical gratification is renounced for the higher reward of being deemed civilised and well bred (Elias, 1982: 300–12). In this established social system, Wharton and James saw the potential for a whole body of literature. It is a story of human sacrifice, of renouncing one's innermost desires (for example, love, revenge and illicit passion) for a potentially higher plane of life. The layers which manners add onto life, separating people from one another and from their desires and providing a screen for possible deception, become the very source of narrative. It is precisely this tension between one's inner desires and one's outward actions that Wharton and James find lacking in Gilded Age America. Manners have deteriorated from significant acts of restraint and sacrifice to empty observances of social convention – from substantial doors, to a porti're, to doorless doorways that have lost all meaning.

Henry Adams, friend to both Wharton and James, reports one scene from Newport's vapid social life that suggests modern young men will stop at nothing – will march straight into a woman's boudoir – in order to have their fun:

> [Mrs Stevens's] house [in Newport] is a sort of centre for the New York fast set. The young men stroll in and shout up stairs to know if the ladies are

> there and go up to their boudoirs. One rather clever game was extemporised at the house … Three young men are selected as judges. The young ladies are then brought out in turn and given marks on a certain scale, say 5, for their points; as for instance, Hair, 4; figure, 3; hands and feet, 2; complexion, 5; and so on. The one whose marks are highest in the aggregate, wins. (Levenson et al., 1982, 2: 204)

This, then, is a house without manners. Not only has the privacy of the principal floor been violated but also even the home's most important distinction – between upstairs and downstairs, between the bedrooms and the rooms of public reception. In *The Decoration of Houses*, Wharton warns against grand stairways or any stairway that is visible upon entering the house. To protect the sanctity of the home's private quarters, she recommends a staircase and by that she means a stair encased in its own room, protected by a door at the foot of the stairs and another one at the top (112–17). Such a structure occurs at the Mount, as we shall see, and increases the barrier between public and private, between her entrance hall and her boudoir. Mrs Stevens's house must lack such a barrier, since the 'fast set' can shout upstairs. Significantly, this structural accessibility leads to or permits the social transgressions. In his account, Adams associates the fact that the young men 'go up' to the boudoirs with the 'clever game' that has been 'extemporised at the house'. It is as if the beauty contest grew out of the easy-going house and the lifestyle it promotes. The women's features are broken down and assigned a comparative numerical value; the vague, portentous question of a woman's beauty – and hence social value – is reduced to cold figures of commodification.

For Wharton and James, consumption is linked to transgression and they utilise this thrill as their own characters tread closer to the inner secrets of another character's life. But this thrill is only made palpable against a literary architecture of deferral and restraint. By contrast, the modern transgressive impulse makes itself unnarratable because it knows no limits. There is no poetry, no question and no possible story. Private spaces and thoughts have been made conspicuous, brought out to view and consumed for most effective publication.

The rebelliousness of the modern generation was a predictable and, in some senses, justifiable protest against the exaggerated and senseless layering of Victorian life. Wharton herself rebukes the Victorian estrangement of interior from exterior in *The Decoration of Houses*. She points, for example, to the window treatment religiously adhered to in the sitting-rooms of her mother's era:

> The windows in this kind of room are invariably supplied with two sets of muslin curtains, one hanging against the panes, the other fulfilling the supererogatory duty of hanging against the former; then come the heavy stuff curtains, so draped as to cut off the upper light of the windows by day, while it is impossible to drop them at night. (20)

Wharton depicts the Victorian home as a Poe-like setting where one is buried alive. She describes the debilitating effect of such a setting in a frequently-quoted early short story:

> I have sometimes thought that a woman's nature is like a great house full of rooms: there is the hall, through which everyone passes in going in and out; the drawing room, where one receives formal visits; the sitting room, where the members of the family come and go as they list; but beyond that, far beyond, are other rooms, the handles of whose doors are perhaps never turned; no one knows the way to them, no one knows whither they lead; and in the innermost room, the holy of holies, the soul sits alone and waits for a footstep that never comes. ([1893] 1968, 1: 14)

Wharton's psychological floor plan depicts an increasingly alienated course from most public to most private space. The soul is hopelessly removed from the house's business of everyday life. Wharton and James sought to bring the interior and exterior spaces of life back into a tense narratable relation that led from the vestibule all the way to the climactic 'holiest of holies'. Their power to do so stemmed from their understanding of manners. Wharton and James achieve spaces that 'do' a great deal, spaces that are at once conventional and surprising, even magical. The most concrete example of such a space is The Mount.

The business of going in

The Mount is also, like the house in the short story quoted above, a 'great house full of rooms' that leads from the outer rooms of Wharton's social life to her 'holiest of holies' – her bedroom. This is where, lying in bed, she wrote her stories. The path from the front door to Wharton's bedroom, essentially the last room in the house (with the exception of the servants' rooms upstairs), takes one through a series of rooms. At The Mount there are no open or vaguely-defined spaces – hallways are treated as enclosed rooms or 'galleries' joined by doors. Even the gardens were planned by Wharton as square 'rooms' connected by corridors or 'walks'. What Fryer terms the 'rigid' layout of The Mount has suggested to R. W. B. Lewis that Wharton had an 'obsession with enclosed as against unbounded spaces' (1975: 121). But Wharton's home exhibits both the ceremony and containment of the old high society and the expansive circulation of the new bourgeoisie. Seven sets of doors lead to the drawing-room alone. The proliferation of doors draws one ever deeper into the house – there is always another door one can go through and a seemingly endless number of paths one can take.

The series of doors that led Wharton toward her inner life created precisely the 'inwardly projected' 'social ... domestic order' that James said manners required. The Mount serves as a gloss on James's curious phrase because the journey through the rooms of The Mount is indeed 'inwardly projected'. Its doors always open into a room, as Wharton says they must, in order to 'facilitat[e] entrance' and give 'the hospitable impression that everything is made easy to those who are coming in'. But at the same time Wharton positions her doors to 'screen that part of the room in which the occupants usually sit' (Wharton and Codman, 1897: 61). Wharton's doors offer an invitation to enter and yet protect privacy through their controlled revelation of the house's interior. Like manners, the doors heighten intimacy while they also make social relations more formal. The opening door, for example, restores the key dramatic moment of entrance to its full intensity: it creates a prolonged moment of suspense during which neither the intruder nor the occupants can see each other – a moment of simultaneous revelation and concealment, as the occupants have time to stop what they were doing and turn to meet the new guest. Thus, an inwardly projected domestic order seems as determined to probe the inner life as it is to defend its sanctity. So, too, characters in the novels of Wharton and James rarely blurt out their feelings, but proceed through a discursive path of indirection.

'While the main purpose of a door is to admit', Wharton writes in *The Decoration of Houses*, 'its secondary purpose is to exclude' (103). Key doors in the house serve to separate outsiders from insiders, servants from residents and day visitors from overnight guests. Wharton's architectural creed reveals the extent to which doors themselves become a pivotal means of establishing a social order; it is they that do the including and excluding, with the result that they establish an inner elite by determining who is allowed in – and, crucially, how far in. The Mount establishes its subtle social order in large part through movement. Insiders have the greatest number of paths available, outsiders the fewest. Servants have access to the entire house but only through certain doors. While Wharton used The Mount for more general social entertaining, it provided, first and foremost, a retreat for her inner circle of literary friends, which, in addition to Henry James, included, among others, her literary mentor Walter Berry, writers Percy Lubbock and Gaillard Lapsley and the playwright Clyde Fitch. Wharton referred to this group as 'the Happy Few' (Lewis, 1975: 425). Their elite status is registered by the fact that day visitors would have had a limited experience of the house while resident guests would have the privilege of knowing more of its inner mysteries.

One enters The Mount on the ground floor. The entrance hall is cave-like; Wharton conceived it as a grotto. At the south end of the hall is the door to the staircase which leads to the first floor and the principal rooms. At the top of the staircase one finds more doors (see figure 13). To the left is the first floor gallery, straight ahead lies the dining-room and, to the right, the door to the stairwell to the second floor. In the first floor gallery, one confronts more sets of doors. Two sets of double doors on the right lead to the drawing-room. At the far end of the gallery appears to be a set of double doors to Mr Wharton's den. And tucked in the corner, out of sight, lies the door to Edith Wharton's library. All of these principal rooms are also joined by doors between them – one can

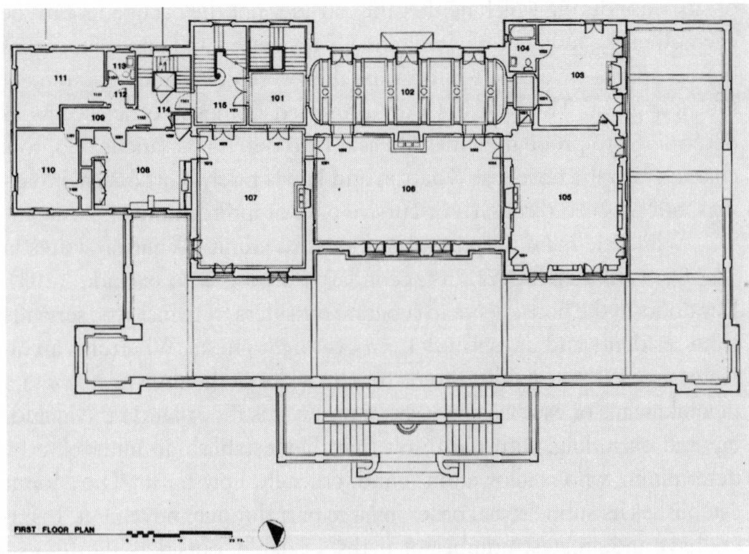

13 The Mount, First (Main) Floor Plan, John G. Waites Associates Architects, *The Mount: Home of Edith Wharton*. Key: 101 Main Floor Stair Hall; 102 Gallery; 103 Mr Wharton's Den; 105 Edith Wharton's Library; 106 Drawing-Room; 107 Dining-Room; 108–14 Service Wing; 115 Stair Hall to Second (Bedroom) Floor.

enter Mrs Wharton's library directly through a door from Mr Wharton's den or through the drawing-room, which in turn adjoins the dining-room. Each of these rooms also opens onto the terrace that wraps around the east elevation of the house, making for a second, outdoor hallway.

The way in which such a sequential floor plan might stimulate the production of fiction is demonstrated by a scene in James's *The Portrait of a Lady* (1881). At the start of the novel we find the main character, Isabel Archer, sitting, as is her habit, in the 'office' of her grandmother's house. The house is itself curious; once a double house, it has now been made into a single one. The office, which James describes as 'a mysterious apartment which lay beyond the library', must have been the foyer to the old second house, as James describes:

> The place owed much of its mysterious melancholy to the fact that it was properly entered from the second door of the house, the door that had been condemned, and that it was secured by bolts which a particularly slender little girl found it impossible to slide. She knew that this silent motionless portal opened into the street; if the sidelights had not been filled with green paper she might have looked out upon the little brown stoop and the well-worn brick pavement. But she had no wish to look out, for this would have interfered with her theory that there was a strange, unseen place on the other side – a place which became to the child's imagination, according to its different moods, a region of delight or of terror. ([1881] 1988: 78)

Once the foyer, the 'office' is now the last room on the first floor of the house. The old front door hence juxtaposes the public street with the most private room in the house. The bolted door leads not to the street but instead to Isabel's fantasies. This door that Isabel 'can't go into' again produces a richer environment than the drab brown stoop outside. The hope of ever actually possessing her vision – of getting up from the chair and walking through the door to the fulfilment of her innermost desires – is renounced for the ultimately more satisfying ability to wonder just what might be there.

In contrast with those of The Mount and Isabel's home, the floor plans of modern houses were aggressive models of consumption, where one could take in much in one glance or march straight upstairs and have one's fun. The literary counter-aesthetic of hindered pursuit and ultimate renunciation which I have been describing here is exhibited by what are essentially the last rooms in The Mount – the bedrooms on the second floor (see figure 14). These rooms are also, in an important sense, 'offices'. When shown to her guestroom, one of Wharton's guests

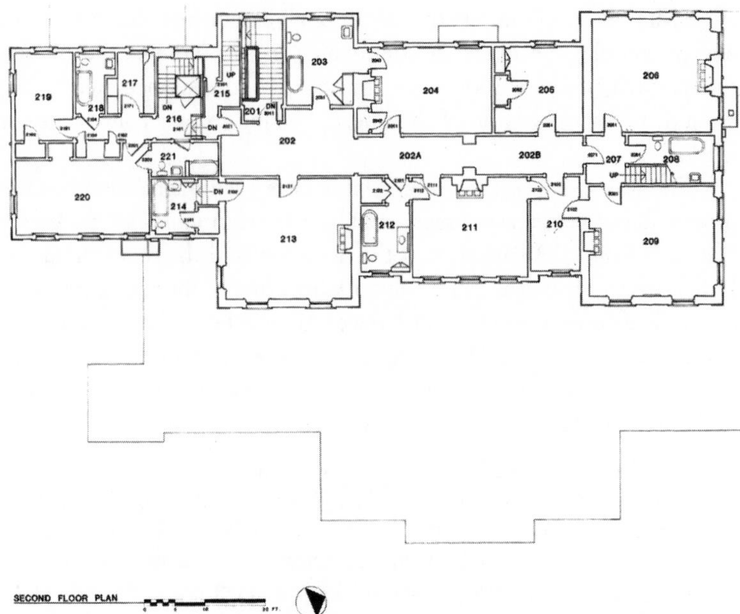

14 The Mount, Second (Bedroom) Floor Plan, John G. Waites Associates Architects, *The Mount: Home of Edith Wharton*. Key: 202–202B Second Floor Gallery; 203–5 West Guest Room Suite; 206 Edith Wharton's Boudoir; 207 Anteroom to Edith Wharton's Suite; 209 Edith Wharton's Bedroom; 210–12 Teddy Wharton's Suite; 213–14 East ('Henry James') Guest Room Suite; 215–21 Service Wing.

exclaimed, 'What a perfect desk – everything conceivably needed for writing is there' (Lubbock, 1947: 28). When we consider Wharton's description of her writing process, we see that the bedrooms are perhaps spaces where one sublimates, rather than consummates, one's inner desires. (Both authors appear to have led largely celibate lives.[6]) Wharton describes her writing in bed as a rather dream-like erotic state. She 'waits breathlessly' for her characters to 'possess' her. She 'labors' and gives 'birth' to her novels (Wharton, 1934: 198–204). Buried deep within her house, Wharton, like Isabel, embarks on endless paths of fiction.

In contrast to such seclusion, the business elite, according to James, enjoys the sweeping vistas through their cavernous rooms and yet feels vaguely conscious of having reached a dead-end. In *The American Scene*, James describes a lavish New York dinner-party where, despite all the impeccable surroundings (a 'palace') and the beautiful ladies ('glittering with gems', their gowns a 'semblance of court-trains'):

> It was impossible not to ask one's self with what, in the wide American frame, such great manners might be supposed to consort or to rhyme. The material pitch was so high that it carried with it really no social sequence, no application, and that, as a tribute to the ideal, to the exquisite, it wanted company, support, some sort of consecration. The difficulty, the irony, of the hour was that so many of the implications of completeness, that is, of a sustaining social order, were absent. There was nothing for us to do at eleven o'clock – or for the ladies at least – but to scatter and go to bed. There was nothing, as in London or in Paris, to go 'on' to; the going 'on' is, for the New York aspiration, always the stumbling block. (163)

Rather than lead to some climactic event, the 'consecration' of their magnificence, the evening trails off inconsequentially into another American example of 'this struggle in the void – a constituted image of the upper social organism floundering there all helplessly'. The evening and the environment lack an overall narrative that leads, ultimately, to the attainment of a superior, interior space of production. The 'palace' is perfect, but in outward form only. James implies that the 'pitch' from the start is too high. One starts at the top and has no place left to go. There is no hierarchy of space, 'no sequence'; the evening does not connect or 'rhyme' with anything outside of itself. Only a 'great court-function' would have sufficed to 'crown the hour' and this the American 'upper social organism' of course cannot provide (162–3).

The too high formality of the New York party missed not only the spatial but also the temporal development of a social evening. Where would a dinner-party at The Mount have 'gone on to' after eleven o'clock? The house's spaces provide a full range of scenarios for a productive evening. There is no need to go elsewhere, outside the estate, to an 'after-opera' party for instance, in order to achieve the evening's crowning moment. Depending upon how large or literary her company, Wharton would have led them to the drawing-room, the library or, if the evening and the company were fine, the terrace. Rather than a progression to increasing formality and ceremony, the rooms at The Mount suggest a course from formal relations to less formal, the intimacy increasing with the lateness of the hour. Whether enjoying the greater social mobility of the drawing-room, with its chance for a tête-à-tête, or the rare opportunity to hear Henry James read aloud in the library, as Wharton loved to do, one had perhaps the sense of moving closer to business. Wharton tells of one remarkable episode, late at night on the terrace, that led directly to a published story. James was prompted to tell the small gathering of intimates 'all about … his relations, the Emmets'. At this, Wharton claims, James proceeded to give one of the best performances of his career. Entering a trance-like state, through 'rectifications and restatements' James 'summon[ed] [the Emmets] to life': 'there they stood before us as they lived'. Wharton goes on to speculate, 'I wonder if it may not have been that very night, the place and his reawakened associations aiding, that they first came to him and constrained him to make them live for us again in the pages of "Small Boy" and "A Son and Brother?"' (Wharton, 1934: 193–4).

Wharton is careful not only to establish a climactic course between her rooms but also within each room itself. Each room at The Mount is preserved, in her words, as 'a small world by itself' (Wharton and Codman, [1897] 1978: 22). Each retains, as James called it, 'that room-suggestion which is so indispensable not only to occupation and concentration, but to conversation itself' (James, [1907] 1946: 167). The library functions as a stage set that not only accommodates but also nurtures serious literary study (see figure 15). A chaise longue offers a comfortable place to immerse oneself in a novel; a table for periodicals suggests a browse through the contemporary literary scene; a cluster of seats around the fireplace invites focused literary discussion; and a fancy

15 Library, The Mount, *c.*1905.

writing desk serves, since we know Wharton did not write fiction here, perhaps mainly as a symbol to remind the room's occupants of the final stage in the writer's absorption of great literature. Like the narrative structure of the rooms as a whole, the library furniture divides the preliminary work of writing fiction into several discrete tasks which together form the path described by Wharton in the artist's own development – from the study of 'the great literature of the past' and contemporary works, through reading and conversation, to the stage where the writer is ready to write her own work (Wharton, [1925] 1966: 18–22). We move, in James's words, between 'concentration', 'conversation' and 'occupation'. The careful arrangement of the room achieves and reunites both meanings of 'occupation'. The professional occupation which the library supports is one of spiritual fullness-of-being occupied by the deep and elusive meanings of human relations.

Viewed from this angle Wharton does not, as Kaplan suggests, '[pit] professional authorship against domesticity', nor does she entirely '[view] writing as work rather than leisure' (1988: 66). Instead, Wharton raises domesticity to an art without which the literary could not exist. To her guests' praise of their writing desk, Wharton replied, 'Oh, I am rather a housekeeperish person' (Lubbock, 1947: 28). Elsewhere, Wharton suggests that housekeeping might be the very best training for a would-be novelist. She praises the training she received from the generous hospitality modelled in her parents' home:

> I have lingered over these details because they formed a part – a most important and honourable part – of that ancient curriculum of house-keeping which, at least in Anglo-Saxon countries, was soon to be swept aside by the 'monstrous regiment' of the emancipated: young women taught by their elders to despise the kitchen and linen room and to substitute the acquiring of University degrees for the more complex art of civilised living. (Wharton and Codman, 1897: xlviii)

The Mount establishes a straight line between success as a housekeeper and success as a novelist. Each practice requires an acute sense of detail and arrangements. Wharton not only wrote in bed but also it was from there that she delivered the day's orders to her housekeeper. Still, Wharton insisted that her life was strictly divided between her 'inner' and her 'outer' worlds, between her hours in bed writing in the morning and the moment when she switched to her role as a leisure-class hostess, got dressed and 'went downstairs to meet her guests' (Lewis, 1975: 4). Yet there is much to suggest that, for Wharton, to be an author was to be a consummate hostess. As author, she strikes that ambiguous pose of the hostess, who controls her guests by serving them: 'The situating of my tale … I am conscious of conducting', Wharton writes; but once the preparations are done, she 'waits breathlessly' for the arrival of her characters, who 'are all of a sudden in possession of one'. 'I am merely a recording instrument and my hand never hesitates because my mind has not to choose, but only to set down what these … people say' (Wharton, 1934: 198–204). Wharton 'has not to choose' in part because, by her environmentalist creed, the scene she has set delimits the kinds of things that might be said.

The power of surrender

Power, to the extent that one can possess it, comes for Wharton and James only through submission to and identification with the greater laws of human behaviour. Again and again in their novels, characters must resist the intense urge to seize the object of their desires, to cross the line of 'civilised' behaviour; by resisting, they achieve a superior, noble status. Frequently, as with Isabel Archer, the scene involves the character accepting or preferring, rather than transgressing, some architectural barrier to their desires. In James's novel *The American*, Christopher Newman stands outside the 'pale, dead, discoloured wall' of the Carmelite convent where his beloved, a Parisian aristocrat, has confined herself. There, he gives up the chance to revenge himself upon her family, whose treachery deprived him of their daughter and drove her to become a nun: 'the barren stillness of the place seemed to be his own release from ineffectual longing' ([1877] 1978: 305). So too, in *The Wings of the Dove*, Milly Theale 'turn[s] her face to the wall' and gives up on life ([1902] 1986: 424). At the end of Wharton's novel *The Age of Innocence*, Newland Archer stands outside the Paris apartment where his beloved Ellen Olenska lives. He has spent a lifetime fantasising their life together. Now that the chance to consummate their secret love is (as he imagines) finally within reach, Archer decides nevertheless to resist: 'It is more real to me here than if I went up', he realises ([1920] 1987: 362). Renunciation of the body's inner longings and of love is a 'note', as James would say, repeatedly sounded by these sober examples of self-imprisonment that establish a character's magnificence. Placed hard up against the busy world outside, like Christopher Newman outside the Carmelite convent in the heart of Paris, the opposing wall creates an excruciating temptation and the assistance to overcome it.

In her 'Sketch of the Past' Virginia Woolf writes about the literary rewards that could be gained from this Victorian 'manner' of restraint. She and her sister, Vanessa:

> both learnt the rules of the game of Victorian society so thoroughly that we have never forgotten them ... We still play the game. It is useful. It has also its beauty, for it is founded upon restraint, sympathy, unselfishness – all civilized qualities. It is helpful in making something seemly out of raw odds and ends. ... But the Victorian manner is perhaps – I am not sure – a disadvantage in writing. When I read my old Literary Supplement articles, I lay the blame for their suavity, their politeness, their sidelong approach, to my tea-table training. I see myself, not reviewing a book, but handing plates of buns to shy young men and asking them: do they take cream and sugar? On the other hand, the surface manner allows one, as I have found, to slip in things that would be inaudible if one marched straight up and spoke out loud. (quoted in Schulkind, 1976: 129)

Here Woolf weighs the pros and cons of writing like a hostess. Her predictable, self-validating conclusion, that one can say more through restraint, makes her hesitancy that manners might be a 'disadvantage in writing' a perfect example of the 'surface manner'. She is sure that her hostess skills are an advantage, but she would not be so brash as to say so. The surface manner is an advantage, because it is an indirect form of power; one dominates one's guest in the act of serving him. Her power is measured according to her skill at administering concrete social forms – through the ritual of dispensing the tea, the cream and sugar, the plate of buns. Such decorum places the guest at ease and even off guard. He doesn't notice that he is being reviewed. Restraint becomes, in a sense, a form of deception, a 'game' by which the hostess acquires unusual, superior powers. Woolf understands that things 'slipped in' are more valuable than things spoken 'out loud'. In this she adheres to the paradoxical Romantic code voiced by Keats: 'Heard melodies are sweet, but those unheard / Are sweeter' ('Ode on a Grecian Urn', in Abrams et al., 1974: 2, 663). Only through artistic restraint can one come close to hearing what cannot be heard, speaking what cannot be said, and possessing what cannot be possessed.

Solid proof of Wharton's powers as a hostess/author lies within her house, which is not without a magical or, as Wharton would say, 'more real' quality of its own. The house achieves several quiet feats that might leave the visitor's head spinning. The entrance side of the house, when we finally reach it after a suspenseful, circuitous drive, looks more like the back of the house (see figure 16). The unexpectedly small front door seems more suitable to a town-house, while the rest of the façade resem-

16 The Mount today, courtyard side/west elevation.

17 The Mount today, terrace side/west elevation, service wing on right.

bles a French château. This same oscillating effect, whereby the house seems alternately to contract and expand in size, continues inside the house. The carefully separated chambers suggest a town-house, while their French doors leading to the terrace and gardens give the breezy sweep of a summer villa. Wharton's treatment of her service wing is similarly destabilising. We see the service wing and yet we do not see it. Wharton uses several tricks to screen it from our consciousness: she indents the wing's walls thus making it drop back from the dominant presence of the 'main' house; she surrounds her forecourt with walls that focus attention away from the wing; finally, she uses the terrace to define again the main part of the house and place the service wing in the margins (see figures 17 and 18). The result is a house that looks symmetrical, even though it so clearly is not.

The terrace side of the house, when we reach it, looks to be much more like a formal front of a summer villa, only there is no road leading to it. (Predictably, Wharton has saved the best side of her house for its inhabitants.) In fact, this side of the house looks almost like another

18 The Mount early 1980s, terrace side/east elevation, service wing on left.

house, since it is based upon a much-admired British estate, Belton House (Marshall, 1997: 19–20). The whole structure, however, is unified and Americanised by its traditional New England colour scheme: white with green shutters. Henry James caught the house's double nature when, in 1904, he called it 'a French château mirrored in a Massachusetts pond' (Edel, 1984, 4: 325–6). James's conflation of Wharton's Laurel pond with Thoreau's Walden Pond suggests that James found her house to be incongruous with its prosaic setting; The Mount was in its own way 'factitious', as Wharton had accused the Vanderbilt mansion of being. But James's comment also testified to Wharton's ability to draw from a combination of sources to make a house that hovers noncommittally between republican restraint and aristocratic munificence. The literary architecture of manners indeed seemed to promise that you could have it all. By making consumption look like restraint, control look like submission and work look like leisure, the novel of manners offered a stimulating profession that allowed one to criticise and yet fully enjoy a life of luxury.

Through their superior sense for the arrangement of 'situations', Wharton and James hoped to reform business into a graciously mannered pursuit and novel writing into a moral yet lucrative business. Several of James's heroes are cultured businessmen; the most endearing among them – Mr Touchett in *The Portrait of a Lady*– serves as proof of the curative power of architecture. The novel opens as Mr Touchett, a 'shrewd American banker', takes tea on the lawn of his English country-house, Gardencout. The house has reached a venerable age, testified to by the fact that it was 'a good deal bruised and defaced in Cromwell's wars'. Mr Touchett had bought the house 'originally because … it was offered at a great bargain: bought it with much grumbling at its ugliness, its antiquity, its incommodity'. Thirty years have passed and Mr Touchett, now retired:

> had become conscious of a real aesthetic passion for it, so that he knew all its points and would tell you just where to stand to see them in combination and just the hour when the shadows of its various protuberances–which fell so softly upon the warm, weary brickwork– were of the right measure. ([1881] 1988: 60)

Thirty years ago Mr Touchett thought of life mainly in terms of money. His attraction to the house as a 'bargain' and his 'grumbling' at the house's 'incommodity' suggest that he saw everything as a commodity. Under the spell of the house, however, Mr Touchett is reformed. He has stopped grasping or 'touching' and simply admires. The house is not an assertion of his individual greatness, but rather a sign of his identification with and appreciation for a larger human history and social order. But this does not mean that Mr Touchett has become an imitation British squire. Instead, he represents an organic and compelling merger between American business and European manners. After Mr Touchett makes a somewhat forward remark, his son Ralph chides him for his lack of British restraint. To this the father 'seren[ely]' replies, 'I say what I please' (66). In Mr Touchett, American directness earns justifiable 'serenity' through contact with Europe; in turn, he corrects the stifling boredom of European gentility, as Ralph's friend Lord Warburton, who has joined them for tea, confirms: 'I'm never bored when I come here … One gets such uncommonly good talk' (64). That, to James's mind, is high praise indeed. By relocating to England, an American businessman has not only acquired, but also improved upon, the art of conversation.

Of his own beloved home, Lamb House in southern England, James wrote, 'I have lived into my little old house and garden so thoroughly that they have become a kind of domiciliary skin, that can't be peeled off without pain' (Edel, 1985: 643). So, too, likening Wharton to a mollusc in her shell, James said, 'No one fully knows our Edith, who hasn't seen her creating a habitation for herself' (Berman, 1987: 314). In a notable way these two homes contain their own version of an outdoor room. At Lamb House, James often wrote in his Garden Room, a free-standing structure, which he reached in a few steps through his garden. As to Wharton's 'secret garden', I have endeavoured to show how The Mount achieved this magical space *indoors*, not the least in Wharton's prolific, sensuous bedroom overlooking the garden 'rooms' below. Such spaces helped to reassure Wharton and James that what we imagine is, in the end, all we really possess.

Notes

I wish to thank George Dekker, Jay Fliegelman, Thomas L. Schwarz, Priscilla Wald and Mary Corbin Sies for helpful comments and criticism.

1 Wharton also visited Biltmore, at Christmas 1905, ten months after James. Wharton warmly praises the estate's grounds (designed by Frederick Law Olmsted) in a letter to her friend Sara Norton, but makes no mention of the architecture of the house itself. Eleanor Dwight points out that Wharton 'who was used to enjoying the settings of the very rich, was not as oppressed as James by Biltmore' (1994: 134).

2 For a wonderful description of Wharton's floor plan of The Mount and how that plan resonates in some of her novels, see Fryer, 1986: 65–75. The wide-ranging associations Fryer covers in her discussion of Wharton's architecture has opened up numerous paths of enquiry. I draw upon some of these in my analysis of Wharton's architecture as a specific social and economic order.

3 See, for example, architectural historian R. G. Wilson's account of The Mount in 'Edith and Ogden: writing, decoration and architecture', in Metcalf, 1988: 133–84. For a more theoretical study of James's use of architecture, see Frank, 1979: 167–216.

4 Fryer argues that it was not until Wharton escaped Newport and New York and built The Mount that her full creative powers were at last unleashed (1986: 65–74). Kaplan (1988: 77–80) contends that Wharton managed to escape the tradition of domestic, sentimental women's literature by writing *The Decoration*. Wharton's concept of 'interior architecture', set forth in *The Decoration*, provided an enabling 'metaphor' by which Wharton was able to get control of the home and enter the male-dominated marketplace as a 'professional' author.

5 Fryer discusses the structure of Wharton's first novel, *The House of Mirth*, as analogous to the floor plan of The Mount (1986: 75). For 'apprenticeship', see Kaplan, 1988: 67.

6 On Wharton's sex life with her husband, see Lewis, 1975: 55. On James's celibacy, see Edel, 1985: 166–7.

Bibliography

Abrams, M. H. *et al.* (eds) (1974), *Norton Anthology of English Literature*, 2 vols, 3rd edn, New York, Norton.

Bailey, T. and Kennedy, D. (1994), *The American Pageant*, 2 vols., 10th edn, Lexington, MA, Heath.

Berman, A. (1987), 'Edith Wharton: on her 125th anniversary', *Architectural Digest*, 44:11.

Dwight, E. (1994), *Edith Wharton: An Extraordinary Life*, New York, Abrams.

Edel, L. (1984), *Henry James Letters*, 4 vols, Cambridge, MA, Harvard University Press.

Edel, L. (1985), *Henry James: A Life*, New York, Harper.

Elias, N. (1982), *Power and Civility*, New York, Pantheon.

Frank, E. E. (1979), *Literary Architecture: Essays Toward a Tradition*, Berkeley, University of California Press.

Fryer, J. (1986), *Felicitous Space: The Imaginative Structures of Edith Wharton and Willa Cather*, Chapel Hill, University of North Carolina Press.

James, H. [1877] (1978), *The American*, New York, Norton.

James, H. [1881] (1988), *The Portrait of a Lady*, New York, Penguin.

James, H. [1902] (1986), *The Wings of the Dove*, New York, Penguin.

James, H. [17 October 1904] (1984), 'To Howard Sturgis', in L. Edel (ed.), *Henry James Letters*, 4 vols, Cambridge, MA, Harvard University Press.

James, H. [1907] (1946), *The American Scene*, New York, Scribners.

Kaplan, A. (1988), *The Social Construction of American Realism*, Chicago, University of Chicago Press.

Levenson, J. C. *et al.* (eds) (1982), *The Letters of Henry Adams*, 6 vols, Cambridge, MA, Harvard University Press.

Lewis, R. W. B. (1975), *Edith Wharton: A Biography*, New York, Harper.

Lubbock, P. (1947), *Portrait of Edith Wharton*, New York, Appleton Century Crofts.

Malcolm, J. (1995), 'A house of one's own', *The New Yorker*, 5 June, 58–78 .

Marshall, S. (1997), *The Mount – A Historic Structure Report*, Edith Wharton Restoration, Albany, New York, Mount Ida Press.

Metcalf, P. C. (ed.) (1988), *Ogden Codman and The Decoration of Houses*, Boston, David P. Godine.

Schulkind, J. (ed.) (1976) *Moments of Being: Unpublished Autobiographical Writings*, London, Chatto and Windus.

Wharton, E. [1893] (1968), 'The fullness of life', in R. W. B. Lewis (ed.), *The Collected Short Stories of Edith Wharton*, 2 vols, New York, Scribners.

Wharton, E. [1920] (1987), *The Age of Innocence*, New York, Collier.

Wharton, E. [1925] (1966), *The Writing of Fiction*, New York, Octagon.

Wharton, E. (1934), *A Backward Glance*, New York, Scribners.

Wharton, E. and Codman, O. Jr [1897] (1978), *The Decoration of Houses*, New York, Norton.

Index

Note: 'n' after a page reference indicates a note number on that page.

Abbott, Edith 153
abolitionism 73
  and home decoration 65–6, 70–1, 80
  material culture of 58, 59, 60, 65–6, 71, 72, 76–7, 78, 79
Accum, Frederick, *Practical Treatise on Gas Light* 94
Adams, Henry 192–3
Agnew, J-C. 10
Alcott, Louisa May 8, 163–83
  Behind a Mask 168–71, 177
  Jo's Boys 178–9, 181–2
  Little Women 145, 149, 165
  'Marion Earle' 174–5
  'The Rival Prima Donnas' 175–7
Altick, Richard 97
antislavery
  objects and images of 59, 66–8, 70, 71, 73, 76–8
    Tomitude 60, 61, 79
    workbags 72, 76, 77
  women's involvement in campaigns 58, 65, 71–2, 73–6, 81
architecture 106–7, 186–91
  effect on social relations 9, 192–3
  effect on writing of literature 9–10, 187, 188
  gendered space and 142–3
  for privacy 147–8, 193
Asquith, Lady Cynthia 106, 117
Auden, W. H. 35–6
Auerbach, Nina 168
Austen, Jane 105, 110
  Mansfield Park 164–5
  Northanger Abbey 105–6
  Pride and Prejudice 110
autobiography 40–55

Bachelard, Gaston 19, 23–4, 25, 26, 27, 137
  Poetics of Reverie 52
Barbauld, Anna L., *Hymns in Prose for Children* 76–7
Barber, Mary 128
Barry, Thomas 173, 174
Bartman, Saartje 78
Bebel, August 115
Beecher, Catharine 61–2, 145

Bell, Thomas, *Out of this Furnace* 151–2
Benjamin, Walter 10
Berry, Walter 196
Biltmore 186–7, 190, 191
Birmingham Female Society for the Relief of Negro Slaves 75, 77
black people, representation of 78, 79
body, and space 11, 12, 41, 42, 43–5, 51, 53, 55n1
Booth, Edwin, interpretation of *Hamlet* 171–2
Boris, Eileen 156
Bosanquet, Charles 123
Bosanquet, Charlotte 62–4
Boston Antislavery Fair 79
Brighton Royal Pavilion, gas lighting in 96
Brown, Gillian 145
Browne, Hablot, K., 'The Visit to the Brickmaker's' (*Bleak House*) 127–8
Burnett, Frances Hodgson, *The One I Knew Best of All* 28–9
Burnett, John 24
business, manners and 189, 190, 191, 198–9
Butler, Elizabeth Beardsley 157
Byington, Margaret 154

Campbell, C. 7
candles 89–90
Carlyle, Jane 111–13
Cather, Willa 146
Chadwick, Edwin 126
childhood 27–8, 29–30
  returning to 52, 53, 54–5
Churchill, W., *The Dwelling–Place of Light* 143, 153
Clark, Anna 121
Clarke, Joseph, *The Labourer's Welcome* 46, 47
class, and the meaning of homes 143, 156–7
Colomina, B. 6
consumer boycotts 74, 80
consumption 7–8, 25–6
Corbin, Alain 12, 21–2, 23
  The Foul and the Fragrant 126
cotton industry 31, 32
Cowan, Ruth S. 7
Crowell, Ivan 34
Cullwick, Hannah 115–16
cult of domesticity 2, 121

Daiches, David 44
Davidoff, Leonore 63, 103, 104, 108–9
Davies, J. L. 124
Denier, Tony 162
desired interior 26–7, 28–9, 30
Dickens, Charles 20, 91, 94
  Bleak House 64–5, 126, 127–8, 133
  Dombey and Son 97
  gas lighting in works of 97
  Hard Times 99
  Our Mutual Friend 97
  Sketches by Boz 96
district visiting 12, 121–38
District Visitor's Manual 124
divorce 155–6
domestic *see* home
domestic architecture *see* architecture
domestic realism 163, 171, 173, 181–2

domestic service 104
  see also servants
domestic technology 7, 113, 150
domesticity 6, 103, 144–6, 150, 151
  cult of 2, 121
  working–class 121–2, 127–9
doors 9, 192
  and architecture of manners 191–2
  Wharton and 191, 195
  to working–class houses 127–8, 129, 130–1
doorstep etiquette 12, 130–1
drawing–room 62–4, 70–1
dream–work 11, 24, 26, 27, 28, 52

Eastlake, Charles 88
Edis, R. W., *Decoration and Furniture of Town Houses* 91
Egg, A. L., *Past and Present* 47
electricity 89
Elias, Norbert 192
Eliot, George, *The Mill on the Floss* 99
enclosed space 2, 23
Eyles, Leonora, *The Woman in the Little House* 21

Falk, P. 7
family, theatre and 164–5
Female Visitor to the Poor, The 124
female workforce 109–10
feminine space 2, 71, 81
Ferguson, Moira 70
Fetterley, Judith 170
Fitch, Clyde 196
floor plans 196–8
Forrest, Edwin 171–2, 180
Foucault, Michel 11
Franzoi, Barbara 104
Freud, Sigmund 11
Frost, Sarah A., *Mr John Smith* 166–7
Fryer, Judith 189, 194

Gallagher, Catherine 125
gas explosions 98
Gas, Light and Coke Company 96
gas lighting 84–93
  effect on decorations 89–90
  fictional representation of 96–7
  social and symbolic meanings of 93–100
gas meters 92
gaseliers 88, 92–3, 100n1
Gaskell, Elizabeth 34–5
  Mary Barton 18–19, 25–6, 27
  North and South 126
Gauldie, Enid 24
gendered space 108, 142–58
Gilded Age, lifestyles of 187, 188, 191
Gilman, Charlotte P. 148, 149, 150
gin shops 97
Girouard, Mark 72
Godey's Lady's Book 144–5
Goodnow, R. R. and Adams, R., *The Honest House* 148–9
Grier, Katherine 2

Hale, Sarah J., 'Empire of Woman' 144–5
Hall, Catherine 63, 103, 104, 108–9

Halttunen, Karen 9, 162, 181
Hamlet 171–2
Hardy, F. D., *Playing at Doctors* 47
Heidegger, Martin 10
Helly, Dorothy O. 3
Herne, James A., *Margaret Fleming* 163
Heyrick, Elizabeth, 'On the Reasons for Immediate not Gradual Emancipation' 74–5
Higonnet, M. 2
Hoggart, Richard, *Uses of Literacy* 19–20, 20–1
Holme, Thea 111, 112
home 2, 103
  decoration of 62, 63–4, 64–5, 66, 80
  earning money in 147, 151, 153–4, 156–7
  gas lighting in 85–93
  as sanctuary of middle class 103–19, 147–8
  as site of moral education 76–7
  as workplace 104, 109–18
  see also working–class homes
home history 59, 69, 70–3, 81
home ownership, in USA 152–3
Horn, Pamela 117
household organisation 6–7
household plants, effect of gas on 91
houses, division into rooms 148, 151–2
housewife 110–13
  invisibility of 118
housework 6, 7, 110–11, 118
  American women and 145, 150
Howard, Bronson 163
Howells, William D. 163
Hunt, Charles, *My 'Macbeth'* 47
Hunt, John 125

Ibsen, Henrik
  A Doll's House 182
  Ghosts 163
identity 2, 11, 50
images 47, 49–50
imagination 27
imperialism 79
industrial capitalism 6
industrialisation, gas lighting and 98–9
interior 9, 10
  architecture of 106–7
  fictional representation of 96–9
  as sphere of self-expression 10
interior decoration 9, 62, 63–4, 107
  lighting and 89–90, 91, 97–8
  in USA 144
interiority
  lack of 186–7
  models of 40–6

Jacobs, Harriet, *Incidents in the Life of a Slave Girl* 146
James, Henry 9, 192
  The American 202
  The American Scene 198–9
  and architecture 186–7, 188–9, 207
  and Biltmore 186–7, 191
  and The Mount 200, 206
  The Portrait of a Lady 197, 206–7
  The Wings of the Dove 202
James, John A. 109, 118

Kaplan, Amy 189, 201

Kelley, Florence 157
King, George, *Advice to Customers on Gas Economy* 92
Knight, Anne 80

Lacan, Jacques 51
lair 23, 126
Lancashire, cotton industry in 31, 32
Lapsley, Gaillard 196
Lasdun, S. 63
Lee, R. 157
Lefebvre, Henri, *The Production of Space* 137
legislation 156
  on home working 153, 158
Lemire, Beverly 33
Levi-Strauss, Claude 26
Lewis, R. W. B. 194
library (The Mount) 200–1
lighting, fashion for 89
  see also gas lighting
literary architecture 187, 188–9, 190–1
literature, privacy for production of 9, 10, 187, 188, 198
lodgers 147, 154
Loftie, Mrs 88
Logan, T. 7
London, gas in 90–1
Loudon, J. C., *An Encyclopaedia of Cottage, Farm and Villa Architecture and Furniture* 62–3, 64
Lubbock, Percy 196, 198
Luckock, James 108

Macbeth 180–1
McMillan, Margaret, *The Nursery School* 22
Manchester and Salford District Provident Society 134
Mandler, P. 122
manners 191–4, 195, 203
Martineau, Harriet, *Deerbrook* 127
mass-produced objects 7–8, 25–6
Mayhew, Henry 20, 21
melodrama 162–3, 174–5, 179, 181
memory 13, 26–8, 52, 55
men, in domestic workforce 113, 116–17
Merleau-Ponty, Maurice 51, 55n1
Meyer, S. 118
middle class 3, 4–5, 62–4
  in antislavery campaigns 74–5
  desire for goods 7–8
  home as sanctuary of 103–19, 147–8
  household organisation of 6–7
  and privacy 104–6, 147–9
  use of gas lighting 87–8, 100n2
middle–class women 80–1, 158
  definition of domestic space 144
  running a household 109–11, 149, 150
  surveillance of working–class homes 122, 157–8
  in USA 144
Midgley, C. 74, 79
miniaturisation 10, 26–7
mirrors 46–7, 48, 49
  text as 51–3, 54, 55
missionaries 125, 129, 132, 133–4, 136
Mohanty, Chandra T. 5

Moore, H. 3, 4
Mott, Lucretia 80
Mount, The (home of Edith Wharton) 188, 194–7, 199–201

National Consumers' League 157
nostalgia 13, 21, 52
novels
  American homes portrayed in 145–6, 149
  childhood portrayed in 29–30
  gas lighting portrayed in 93–4, 96–8, 99
  middle–class women in 110
  representation of the theatre in 163–6, 168–71, 174–83
  visiting the poor portrayed in 125–8
nursery 107

objects 60, 64, 72
  of abolitionism 65–8, 71, 72, 73, 76–8
    Tomitude 60, 61, 79
    workbags 72, 76, 77
  in the drawing-room 63–4, 71–2
  mass-produced 7–8, 25–6
  miniature 26–7
  status of 8
  in working–class homes 25–6
  see also rag rug
O'Brien, Patrick 132
Oldfield, J. R. 66, 73
oneiric deprivation 24
ornamentation 62, 144
otherness 13, 50, 51
overcrowding 24, 151–2, 155
Oxford Parochial District Visiting Society 125

'Paper Makers' Grievance' 36
paper manufacture 32
Pater, Walter 51–2, 53, 54
  experiences of childhood home 42–3, 49, 50
  The Renaissance 10
Paull, M. A., *The Romance of a Rag* 32–3, 34
Pease, Elizabeth 80
Perrot, Michelle 137, 162
philanthropy 5, 64–5, 76
  see also district visiting
Planché, J. R., *The Jacobite* 173
poetics of working–class life 20, 21–6
political activism 5, 80–1
political propaganda 70, 71, 77
Poovey, Mary 121, 126, 137
privacy 11–13, 146,
  architecture for 147–8, 193
  middle class and 104–6, 147–9
  working class and 122, 124, 133, 138n1, 154–6
private/public spheres 4–5, 80, 122
  theatre and 165, 166, 168–9, 178, 182
private theatricals 8, 162, 165, 168–9
productivity 144, 147, 189, 201
public space, in the home 130, 148–9

rag rug 19, 30, 33, 36, 37n7
  Hoggart and 20–1
  making of 30–3
Ranyard, Ellen 125, 130

Reach, Angus 127
Redmond, Sarah 78
Reed, C. 11
reflection 10, 48–9
Rennie, Jean, *Every Other Sunday* 116
restraint 188, 190, 192, 193, 202–3, 206
Reverby, Susan 3
Richardson, Henry H. 147
Roberts, Elizabeth 33
Robinson, Harriet H. 144
Romero, L. 2
rooms 23–4, 148, 151–2
Roorbach, O. A., *A Practical Guide to Amateur Theatricals* 164
Rubinstein, David 22
Ruskin, John 51, 53–4
  childhood homes of 40–2, 48–9, 50
  The Poetry of Architecture 49
  Praeterita 41, 51, 53
Rutter, J. O. N. 94, 98–9

Salvaggio, Ruth 4
Schivelbusch, Wolfgang, *Disenchanted Night* 84
Schlereth, Thomas J., *American Home Life, 1880–1930* 69
Schopenhauer, Arthur, 'On Woman' 168–9
Scott, Walter, *Guy Mannering* 13
second-hand clothing 33–4
secret garden 189
self-expression 10
servant-housewife relationship 6, 149–50
servants 109, 112, 113–16, 117–18
  living conditions 149–50
  privacy and 149
  in USA 149–50
Shattuck, C. 172
shops, gas lighting in 96
Simmel, G. 9
Sinclair, Upton, *The Jungle* 153
slave ship, print of 66–7
slavery 145, 146
Smith, Charlotte 143
social reform 153–4, 156, 157
social space 122, 125, 137, 142
social status
  home as indicator of 142, 143
  manners and 192
Society for the Abolition of the Slave Trade 73, 74
space *see* body, and space; gendered space; interior; public space; social space
spaces within houses 23–4
Spencer, Ethel 148, 149
staircases 193
Stevenson, R. L. 51, 52, 53, 54
  A Child's Garden of Verses 44–5, 49–50
  experiences of childhood home 43–6, 49–50
Stewart, Susan, *On Longing* 26
Stowe, Harriet Beecher 78–9, 145, 149
  house of 59–62
  Uncle Tom's Cabin 145–6
Streightoff, F. H. 151

Tafuri, Manfredo 14
taste 63–4, 88–9, 190
Tate, Claudia 146

Taylor, Ann M., *Practical Hints to Young Females on the Duties of a Wife, a Mother, and a Mistress of a Family* 110
Templeton, J. 2
text, as mirror 51–3, 54, 55
textile industry 31–2
theatre 8
  domestic space and 8–9, 163, 164, 166
  fictional representations of 164–83
  gas lighting in 96
  private sphere and 162–83
threshold, policing of 12, 129–33
topoanalysis 23–4
Tristram, Philippa 127
Trollope, A., *Barchester Towers* 97

United States of America
  abolitionism in 79
  housing and privacy in 142–58

Vanderbilt, Cornelius 190
Vanderbilt, George 186
Veblen, Thorstein 144
Vincent, David 122
visitors to the poor, guides for 123, 124, 134, 135
visual experience 41–2, 48, 49
voyeurism 13, 20, 59–60

water, consumption and carrying of 114–15
Wedgwood, Josiah 71
Welter, Barbara 144
Wharton, Edith 9, 147
  The Age of Innocence 202
  The Decoration of Houses 187, 193–4, 208n4
  and domestic architecture 188–9, 191
  The House of Mirth 143
  at The Mount 194–7, 200–1, 203–6
Wigley, M. 10
Wilberforce, William 76
Wilder, Laura Ingalls 146
Wilson, George 129
windows 44, 154, 193–4
Winsor, Frederick 94, 95
Wollstonecraft, Mary, *The Wrongs of Woman* 29–30
women 143
  in antislavery groups 58, 65, 71–2, 73–6, 81
  arrangement of interiors 63, 81
  different meanings of home for 143, 151, 156–7
  in public sphere 4, 5, 80–1
  in work 4, 109–10
  see also middle–class women; working–class women
Woolf, Virginia 9
  'Sketch of the Past' 202–3
work
  separated from home 103–4, 109
  within the home 6–7, 104, 109, 110–16, 117–18, 151
working class 19–21
  domestic visiting 122–38
  and home ownership 152–3
  poetics of 20, 21–6
  privacy and 122, 124, 133, 138n1, 154–6
  stories told by middle class 29–30
working–class homes 12–13, 121, 154–5

access to for visitors 129–33, 157–8
interiors of 19–20, 21, 22–3, 28–9
objects in 25–6
rooms in 154
surveillance of 122, 157–8
unvisitable 134–6
working–class women, in USA 150–1

Wright, G. 3
writing-table 187

Yezierska, Anzia, *Hungry Hearts* 143
Young, Arthur 31

Zola, Emile, *Au Bonheur des Dames* 96